LICENSE TO STEAL

LICENSE TO
STEAL

*How Fraud Bleeds
America's Health Care System*

UPDATED EDITION

Malcolm K. Sparrow

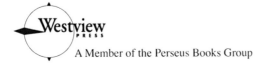
Westview
PRESS
A Member of the Perseus Books Group

Copyright © 2000 by Westview Press, A Member of the Perseus Books Group

Published in 2000 in the United States of America by Westview Press, 5500 Central Avenue, Boulder, Colorado 80301–2877, and in the United Kingdom by Westview Press, 12 Hid's Copse Road, Cumnor Hill, Oxford OX2 9JJ

Find us on the World Wide Web at www.westviewpress.com

Library of Congress Cataloging-in-Publication Data
Sparrow, Malcolm K.
    License to steal: how fraud bleeds America's health care system/Malcolm K. Sparrow.—Updated ed.
        p.   cm.
    Includes bibliographical references and index.
    ISBN 0-8133-6810-3
    1. Medical care—Corrupt practices—United States.   2. Medicare fraud.   3. Medicaid fraud.   I. Title.
RA395.A3 S764 2000
362.1'0973—dc21

                                                                                                    00-020812

Design by Jeff Williams

The paper used in this publication meets the requirements of the American National Standard for Permanence of Paper for Printed Library Materials Z39.48–1984.

10   9   8   7   6   5   4   3   2   1

CONTENTS

Part 4
Prescription for Progress

PREFACE

During calendar year 2000, national health spending for the United States will exceed 1.3 trillion dollars.[1] That's $1,300,000,000,000. This figure represents roughly 13.6 percent of the Gross Domestic Product (GDP), up from 5.7 percent in 1965, and from 8.9 percent in 1980.

Compared with other developed countries around the world, America spends heavily on health care, yet seems to get less for it. No other nation spends more than 10 percent of its Gross Domestic Product on health care. (Canada comes in second, at 9.1 percent.) Americans fare little better, if at all, for all their extra spending. Even Japan, the United Kingdom, and Denmark—which spend less than half as much on health care (as a percentage of GDP)—show better health outcomes.

When compared against other developed market economies, using a broad range of macro-level health-outcome indicators, Americans seem to be doing well below average.[2] According to the World Health Organization (WHO), out of twenty-two nations in that category for which comparative data is available, Americans rank only 17th for life expectancy at birth, and 19th in terms of infant mortality rates. For some other indicators, America comes very close to the bottom: Only one country (Belgium) has a lower percentage of pregnant women attended by trained personnel during pregnancy; and in only two countries (Greece and Portugal) do infants have a higher probability of dying before their fifth birthdays. In addition, 44 million Americans still have no health insurance coverage at all.

No doubt a great many factors—demographic, genetic, technological, lifestyle, climate, dietary, as well as variation in the structure of health care delivery systems—can help to explain these comparative health outcomes. In trying to understand why Americans manage to spend so much more on health care, with zero or negative comparative health advantage, this book considers one simple truth that is usually shuffled to the bottom of the pack by the health care industry, by health care economists, and by policy makers.

That simple truth is that vast sums of money are stolen from the health care system every year. A significant proportion of each health care dollar goes not for the provision of health care, but to criminal enterprise.

How much gets stolen? The magnitude of this problem is measured in terms of hundreds of billions of dollars each year. How many hundreds of billions of dollars? For the time being, nobody knows for sure. If we were lucky, perhaps just *one* hundred billion. More likely, two or three. Quite possibly four, and conceivably five. (That would be $500,000,000,000.)

My examination of this subject began seven years ago with two research grants from the National Institute of Justice (NIJ). The task was to examine the state-of-the-art of fraud controls used within the health care industry. That task, and my continued involvement with the issue since, has taken me to countless major national conferences over the last nine years. Even when attendance at such conferences runs close to a thousand, I am invariably the only "academic" present, and I am often asked by other attendees why I am there. The reason I have been there seems all too plain: I believe this is an important public policy problem, a potentially massive drain on the nation's health care resources. Health care fraud not only bleeds the system but also represents a colossal injustice as crooks enrich themselves at taxpayers' expense. Surely the question should be, "Why are there not more serious researchers paying attention to this problem?"

One possible answer, I suppose, is that because fraud control does not fit neatly under the rubric of criminal justice, health care policy, medicine, public administration, economics, political science, or other well-established academic disciplines, no one has ever really studied it before. None of the officials responsible for controlling fraud within the Medicare or Medicaid programs, nor anyone within the commercial insurance industry, ever took "Fraud Control 101" in college, because no one ever taught it. Within the industry, one can find training on fraud investigation, but very little attention to fraud control. Investigation focuses on the cases that come to light (i.e., the visible slice of the pie), whereas control focuses on the invisible mass. With health care fraud, as with many other forms of white-collar crime, *what you see is not the problem.* The problem, by its very nature, is largely invisible, and we make a grave mistake if we inform ourselves about the problem only by paying attention to what comes to light. Fraud control, as a science, is little studied; as an art, it is scarcely appreciated. It is hardly yet even a subject, though—as we shall see—it presents an extraordinary array of complicated intellectual challenges.

Another possible answer, slightly less academic and a little more sinister, is that serious research on this issue is not much appreciated. Scores of professionals are heavily invested in the status quo, will profit greatly if the health care fraud problem remains invisible, and have powerful incentives to reject or ignore research findings that elevate the visibility of the issue. "A lot of fuss over nothing," they will say. "Find a more serious problem."

Within the academic community, and even among health policy specialists, I have found that the issue of fraud, waste, and abuse—if mentioned at all—is more often presented as a question of political rhetoric than as a serious intellectual or practical challenge. And, on the few occasions when fraud earned a second mention, the context usually included some phrase like "not such an issue under managed care," the implication being that fraud in the system is no longer a matter for serious concern.

I am puzzled that health care economists, in trying to account for medical costs inflation, pay scant attention to the subject of fraud and abuse; when I ask them why directly, they tell me that "there is no data on that." Without aggregate data on fraud loss rates (they are correct; it does not exist), their econometric models simply cannot accommodate the issue so the economists leave it out. Their models fail to explain the inflation of medical costs, year after year after year. When I first presented the findings of the NIJ study in 1996, in the form of the first edition of this book, Judith Randall's review in the *Washington Post* pointed out the tendency of policy makers (and economists in particular) to ignore this issue:

> There are some economists who dismiss health fraud as relatively trivial and irremediable in any case. . . . Sparrow's account will not only shatter their complacency, but will also show them that . . . reform is possible.[3]

Four years after the publication of the first edition of *License to Steal*, there are a number of compelling reasons to bring this subject to the fore once again. First, Congress and the Clinton administration have paid unprecedented attention to the issue over the last six years, and consequently we have learned much about the nature of the beast and the difficulties of controlling it. Those lessons need to be drawn together and shared.

More important, with the Clinton administration drawing to a close, we face a major decision point with respect to health care fraud-control efforts. Whatever new administration follows, its senior officials will need to decide rather soon how much emphasis to place on the control of health care fraud, or whether to emphasize it at all. And as they contemplate that

choice, they will confront three quite irreconcilable perspectives on the issue. Without reliable data upon which to base their decision, they will have
to choose which of these three perspectives has the greatest credibility.

The Industry Perspective

A few years ago, the health care industry, and particularly the major
provider associations, greeted each new fraud scandal with the "few bad
apples" defense: They implored government not to saddle the honest majority with inconveniences (like additional audits), or to besmirch their
profession, because of the actions of a corrupt few.

As we have learned more about who is cheating, and how, and as the
government's "war" on fraud, waste, and abuse has heated up—particularly as the Department of Justice has made more frequent use of the False
Claims Act, so the industry's position seems to have shifted from "a *few*
bad apples" to "*no* bad apples." If there are bad apples anywhere, industry
groups would have us believe they operate within the government—auditors, investigators, and enforcement thugs, with no appreciation of the
complexities and niceties of medicine, running amok and damaging patient care. Scarcely ever do we hear the provider associations condemn
even the most egregious acts of their members.

I have listened on many occasions and at considerable length to industry representatives framing their response to the government's control efforts. What I have heard could be summed up in the following five statements. It seems they would have the American public believe

- that overly aggressive government investigators are mercilessly
  hounding honest providers, without cause, and that ALL providers
  now face intolerable risks from random acts of investigation and
  prosecution;
- that providers settle (e.g., when receiving a demand under the
  False Claims Act) only because they are powerless to defend themselves against the formidable weaponry now being used by the
  government;
- that government investigators are incapable of distinguishing, or
  make no effort to distinguish, honest billing errors from deliberate
  fraud;
- that billing errors do, of course, occur, but they result from a combination of extremely complex rules, coupled with overburdened

and unqualified billing clerks (which providers can afford to pay only $10 an hour);

- that provider organizations pleading guilty to criminal fraud and paying hundreds of millions of dollars in settlements do so out of expediency, the cheapest and quickest way to get the government off their backs so they can get back to their mission of delivering medical care; and that—at the end of the day—they really did nothing wrong.

The vast majority of physicians with whom I have discussed these issues (and whom I believe to be quite honest) are horrified when they learn of the cynical manipulation of the system for gain by members of their own profession; they are disgusted with the thieves who masquerade as health care providers—not least because of the damage they do to public trust in the medical profession.

These medical professionals also seem somewhat surprised and alarmed by the strident positions their own professional associations adopt. The most strident, of late, have been the American Medical Association (AMA), the American Hospital Association (AHA), and the home health care lobby. Practitioners fear that these associations' aggressive responses will give the public the impression that the entire health care industry opposes the government's efforts. While the associations say they have "zero tolerance for fraud," what they do often suggests they have "zero tolerance for fraud control"; that appearance, for the industry and the medical associations, is a public relations disaster in the making. After all, the Department of Justice's focus on health care fraud is not based on a whim, but driven by public concern and anger.

The Administration's Perspective

The second perspective—put forth by the outgoing Clinton administration—is that administration officials recognized the seriousness of the problem early on, during the first term; engaged the problem through a broad array of sustained legislative, administrative, and law enforcement initiatives; and, by the end of the second term, they have largely succeeded in bringing it under control. The beast is tamed. No longer a need for alarm. Time to back away from the harsh rhetoric of a "war against fraud"; time to adopt a more conciliatory posture and work with industry to iron out the few residual difficulties and misunderstandings.

It is certainly true that the Clinton administration recognized the seriousness of this problem early on, and that they have engaged it energetically with a range of initiatives. (Chapter 2 describes the administration's war on health care fraud, waste, and abuse, and the reactions it has provoked.) And one can understand the administration's desire, having staked out their position on the issue, to declare success before they leave office.

Their claims of success warrant careful scrutiny. The particular device they have chosen as the basis for declaring success is a study of Medicare overpayments, instituted in 1997 and repeated in 1998 and 1999. The study, conducted each year by the Office of Inspector General (OIG) at the Department of Health and Human Services (HHS), draws a statistically valid random sample of Medicare claims paid during the previous year, and audits them to determine an "overpayment rate." That overpayment rate is then extrapolated to the entire Medicare fee-for-service budget, providing an estimate of "improper payments."

The first study, reported in July 1997 and based on claims paid during 1996, shocked the nation. It produced an overpayment estimate of $23.2 billion, or 14 percent of Medicare payments. That loss rate exceeded the conventional wisdom of the time, enshrined in a 1992 General Accounting Office (GAO) report, which held that fraud and abuse might account for as much as, but certainly no more than, 10 percent of health care costs. Lawmakers were stunned by the $23 billion projection. *USA Today* captured the public sense of frustration with an editorial titled "Medicare Wastes Billions as Inept Management Rules."

A year later, the study was repeated. The overpayment estimates came down to $20.3 billion, or 11 percent. Another year later, the OIG announced that the overpayment rate had been reduced further, to $12.6 billion (7.1 percent of payments).* This is how the Inspector General's Office reported the change:

> In a recent audit of the Health Care Financing Administration's (HCFA) financial statements, OIG found that improper Medicare payments to health care providers dropped dramatically last year. The error rate in Fiscal Year (FY) 1998 was 7.1 percent; that amounts to a remarkable 45 percent reduction on overpayments in just 2 years. [4]

---

*In March 2000, while this book was in production, the OIG released findings from the fourth payment error study, based on claims paid during 1999, estimating the overpayment rate at 7.97 percent of Medicare fee-for-service claims, or $13.5 billion.

Based on this series of studies, senior administration officials have repeatedly asserted their success in "cutting the Medicare improper payments rate by 45 percent in just two years." Almost every time they mention the subject of health care fraud and abuse, they note this achievement. In March 1999, when Vice President Gore announced the administration's next round of proposals for fighting health care fraud and abuse, he prefaced his remarks with this observation:

> Although improper payments have decreased by almost half since 1996—the lowest error rate since the government initiated comprehensive audits three years [ago]—there is still more that needs to be done.[5]

Anyone hearing the administration's claim could be forgiven for imagining that things were looking up, at least within the Medicare program, and that fraud was well on the way to being brought under control. They could be forgiven for assuming that the term "improper payments" included all improper payments—whether fraudulent, abusive, or merely erroneous. They could be forgiven for assuming that the losses due to fraud were some *subset* of the 7.1 percent overpayment rate. They would be wrong on all counts.

Other government agencies seem to have swallowed the Inspector General's favorable interpretation of these results and promulgated the administration's upbeat spin; the GAO and the Department of Justice, as well as HCFA, have all quoted these findings in their own reports, using the 45 percent reduction as a demonstration of real progress in the battle against fraud and abuse in Medicare. HHS Secretary Donna Shalala and Inspector General June Gibbs Brown have cited it repeatedly, treating it as a central metric of their efforts to combat fraud and abuse.

Unfortunately, the measurement study that acts as the source for the administration's claims of success was designed with such a weak audit protocol (basically a desk audit, with no verification of the services provided) that any scam artist worth a dime knows how to pass through it undetected. This audit protocol essentially replicates a standard "utilization review" desk audit. The auditor first checks that the claim, as presented, was processed correctly (which they are, more than 99 percent of the time) and then requests a medical record from the provider by mail; the auditor then compares any forthcoming documentation with the original claim. If they match up, fine. If they don't, that payment, after further review, may be deemed "incorrect."

The scam artists have long since learned that they are perfectly safe, provided they lie twice; that is, they fabricate the claims in the first place, and then fabricate the medical records to match. As one fraud perpetrator testified in a Senate Committee hearing in 1997, beating this kind of audit is easy. John Watts, Jr., opened a home health agency and submitted several million dollars worth of fictitious claims to Medicare, many of them involving patients who were long since dead. *Whenever Medicare sought medical documentation, Watts says he simply paid nurses to create fraudulent medical records.* Because the OIG's desk audits do not involve contacting the patients, and therefore never verify that the services were delivered, the majority of fraudulent claims that fell within the sample would not be discovered.

Since the first Medicare overpayment-rate study was reported, there has been much debate as to the nature of the overpayments revealed. Government officials at first were tempted to call the overpayments "fraud and abuse," but the medical industry objected vociferously and insisted that the vast majority of them were simple billing errors. The question on the minds of the public and the media as they have sought to understand these studies' implications has been, "What proportion of these overpayments are actually fraud?" That's the wrong question, however. The point is that most fraud is not included in these overpayment rates. The audit protocol selected was so weak that the studies would only detect one narrow and particular category of overpayments—where someone billed for services and then, for whatever reason, failed to construct matching medical documents.

The original declaration that so alarmed the nation—that Medicare had lost $23 billion in 1996—was therefore a substantial understatement of the problem. This measurement study would not have caught the bulk of "false claims," nor claims involving falsified diagnoses, nor fabricated medical episodes, nor claims involving illegal kickbacks, nor computer generated fictitious billings . . . in fact, it would not have caught most of the major types of fraud schemes that we see proliferating within the industry.

Since 1996, the government has deliberately sought to involve Medicare beneficiaries and other members of the public in the control of fraud. Through various networks, the administration has urged and trained Medicare beneficiaries to examine their statements of medical benefits and report anything that strikes them as suspicious. The OIG itself runs a hotline to take reports of fraud (1–800-HHS-TIPS). Most of the calls to that hotline relate to "services not provided," which is the most obvious and basic form of fraud known to the health system. Apparently, judging by their investments in these programs, the administration knows well the value of talking to the patients: The patients, it turns out, often have an important and different story to tell.

It seems odd, in retrospect, that in designing the Medicare overpayment study, the administration would have overlooked the importance of talking to the patients; they omitted that essential step for the majority of claims they examined. Perhaps officials understood that they had chosen only to measure a particular and narrow sliver of the problem. Perhaps they thought that doing more than that would be too expensive, or too embarrassing. Possibly, being new to the measurement business, they genuinely did not understand the importance of using rigorous audit protocols. They certainly know it now, though, because the merits and limitations of measurement methodologies have been discussed at some length over the past three years. Yet administration officials continue to make the same claims of success, apparently in the hope that their audience (especially Congress) will not understand these nuances.

It is imperative, at this stage in the game, that we be clear about what has been achieved and what has not. Success in reducing the narrow category of Medicare overpayments that the Inspector General chose to measure, from $23 billion to $10 billion, does represent progress of a sort. (This reduction has a number of explanations, including the possibility that the industry learned the OIG was not going to dig deeper, and so their willingness to fabricate the supporting medical documentation increased. These issues are considered in detail in Chapter 3.)

The idea (implied or inferred) that the fraud and abuse problem has been uncovered, successfully addressed, and cut almost in half in just two years is dangerous and misleading. It is misleading because no basis exists for such a claim; one has only to examine the dynamics of the business and measure the recent investments in control against the size of the problem (see Chapter 2) for optimism to evaporate. The idea is dangerous because, if not publicly debunked, it will inevitably bring a false sense of security, even complacency; and it surely feeds into the industry's own campaign to undercut the fledgling enforcement programs before they gather too much steam.

The Consumer's Perspective

The public believe neither the industry's propaganda nor the administration's claims of success.

The general public do not buy the industry's story about innocent billing errors. Seven in ten consumers understand health care fraud to be intentional, not merely the result of mistakes and inefficiency;[6] nor are they fooled for a minute by the story about health care providers drowning in a bureaucratic morass and suffering persecution at the hands of government. The public see the high-priced lawyers and the political connections the industry uses to battle the government's low-priced lawyers. They've heard about the billing optimizers and billing consultants paid a commission for every extra dollar they can squeeze out of the system— whether honestly or dishonestly. They believe that complex rules result from the industry's own cynical commitment to gaming the system. They've heard plenty of stories about billing operations that are both technically sophisticated and dishonest, and that employ creative strategies for testing and then circumnavigating existing controls.

The American Association of Retired Persons (AARP) generally concentrates its attention on the Medicare program, the cost of which reached $213 billion in calendar year 1998,[7] and is projected to reach $244 billion for the year 2000.[8] The AARP, however, has recently commissioned broader surveys of public opinion on the issue of health care fraud and abuse, drawing in consumers of all ages. In their latest survey (conducted in December 1998 and reported in 1999), they interviewed 2,000 consumers, 500 in each of four distinct age brackets: Generation X (18–29); Baby Boomers (30–49); Mid-Life Americans (50–64); and Seniors (65+). According to their survey results,[9]

- 83 percent of consumers believe fraud is either extremely widespread or somewhat widespread;
- 72 percent of consumers believe the Medicare Trust Fund would be in no danger of going broke if fraud and abuse were eliminated;
- 76 percent of consumers believe their own health care would improve if more was done to reduce health care fraud.

As the survey report put it, "The idea that fraud is rampant and little is being done about it is very much alive in the public's mind." Examining an itemized hospital or other medical bill and finding that half of it never happened is common experience. Equally commonplace, to complain about it and discover that either people don't care or they lack the resources or will to do anything about it. When asked to identify the most important reasons for the rising cost of health care, more survey respondents pointed to fraud and abuse in the system than to any other cause.

These surveys reveal a public unimpressed by public or private insurers' efforts, to date, to control the problem. The 1998 study reports that

- 76 percent of consumers are unaware of efforts to reduce health care fraud;
- 85 percent of consumers believe that health care fraud is increasing or staying the same;
- more than half (53 percent) believe health care fraud is increasing;
- 61 percent of respondents agreed with the statement that "insurance companies have no incentive to detect health care fraud because they can always raise your premium."

Respondents were not even confident of government's ability to respond when fraud was reported to them directly. When asked the question, "If you register a complaint about suspected health care fraud, do you think that the government or insurance company will do anything on your behalf?" half the respondents said "Yes" and half said "No."

The public are informed about this issue through their own experiences, and through the never-ending stream of horror stories served up by the media—fraudulent quackery of the most flagrant kind; psychiatric hospitals using bounty hunters to fill their beds; Medicare beneficiaries' homes containing floor-to-ceiling stacks of unwanted and unnecessary medical supplies; laboratories "sink-testing" blood samples (i.e., just pouring the specimen away); and entire urban communities making a substantial living off various forms of Medicaid fraud. The American public remains angry with the industry for its greed and with the government for its historic inability to eliminate the problem.

Decision Point

Health care fraud remains uncontrolled, and mostly invisible. For Americans, this problem represents one of the most massive and persistent fiscal control failures in their history. Many who work the system, or feed off it, like it so. For those who profit from it, health care fraud is not seen as a problem, but as an enormously lucrative enterprise, worth defending vigorously.

I hope that the new administration, whatever political stripe it carries, listens to the consumers on this issue. They have it right. As President Clinton commented in his State of the Union address in January 1994 (speaking of the need to reform the health system), "this is another issue where the people are way ahead of the politicians. That may not be popular with either party, but it happens to be the truth."[10] With regard to health care fraud and abuse, in the year 2000, it is still the truth.

I would urge providers who care about the integrity of the health care system to press their professional associations to adopt more credible positions. At some point soon, industry groups have to decide, and should be pushed to answer these questions: Are they in favor of fraud control? Or are they opposed? Will they support the government's attempts to root out corruption in the health care system? Or will they continue to thwart those efforts at every turn?

Malcolm K. Sparrow

ACKNOWLEDGMENTS

I have many people to thank for their roles in the creation of this book; too many to name them all. Let me at least name them by category, and just a few by name.

The most important contributors to this work have been the people who work within the system—investigators, analysts, claims reviewers, auditors, lawyers, and managers—hundreds of them, who have helped me understand the realities of fraud control and the constraints under which it is performed in the field. They generously shared their own views and convictions, even when those convictions were at odds with their organizations' official positions. Their views and convictions largely shaped my own. My contribution is to present and frame their collective experience.

Within the Department of Justice, I must thank Attorney General Janet Reno for inviting me to look into the issue of health care fraud and for the role she has played in keeping the Department of Justice focused on the issue, despite its complexity. Amongst her staff at various times, I thank Gerald Stern, Debra Cohn, Joshua Hochberg, Jeff Menkin, Jim Sheehan, and Dan Anderson for trusting me, including me, and educating me. The National Institute of Justice funded the original fieldwork that informs my analysis of control systems. Thanks to Lois Mock, program manager at the institute, for her skillful handling of that project.

At the Federal Bureau of Investigation (FBI), particular thanks to Joe Ford and Bill Esposito, who did so much in the early stages to build the bureau's understanding of, and commitment to, health fraud. More recently, Joe Ford has played a major role in the continuing investigations of Columbia HCA.

At the Health Care Financing Administration, I am indebted to Nancy-Ann Min Deparle, Mike Hash, Penny Thompson, Timothy Hill, Rose Crum-Johnson, Paul Miner, and Rhonda Hall for the trust they have placed in me, the access they have provided, and their candidness in sharing with me the obstacles they face.

Thanks also to George Grob and his staff at HHS OIG's Office of Evaluations and Investigations for their systematic and thoughtful evaluations of many of the more troublesome industry segments and practices over the years.

Closer to home, thanks to Corey Copeland, Chari Anhouse, and (more recently) Alison Hughes for absolutely first-class research assistance; and to my Kennedy School colleagues with deep knowledge of the health care system who have urged me over the years not to let go of this issue: particularly Mary Jo Bane, Hale Champion, David Ellwood, Jerry Mechling, Miles Shore, and Julie Wilson.

Thanks also to my technical collaborators on fraud detection methods at Deloitte Consulting and HOPS International. Particularly John DiMaggio, Ed Ruzinsky, Larry Friedman, Greg Viola, Simeon Kohl, Gene D'Angelo, George Rogers, and Phil Philpot. Seldom has the science of pattern recognition had a more worthy target, nor a more urgent cause.

Thanks to Leo Wiegman and the editorial staff at Westview Press. It has been a pleasure working with them.

Finally, particular thanks to two other groups to whom I am indebted. First, my growing collection of anonymous informants throughout the health care system—whom I never invited but seem to have attracted. They keep my feet firmly on the ground by telling me how the system really works, and what agendas are really being served. These are brave souls, usually quite isolated within their organizations, and I admire them enormously. Second, the growing army of investigative journalists who focus upon health care issues. So often these folk draw attention to major problems long before the relevant authorities cotton on.

Fieldwork for this research has involved series of interviews within a wide range of agencies and insurers. Interviewees were promised anonymity to encourage a frank and productive exchange. All unattributed quotes in this text are from interviewees to whom the promise of anonymity was extended. In those sections of the book that describe defenses against fraud, specific sites are not identified by name even though they may be identified by type. Some deliberate vagueness about which vulnerabilities appear where seems prudent to avoid advertising specific vulnerabilities in a way that might invite assault.

M.K.S.

Introduction:
Who Steals, and How?

In 1992, a New York deputy attorney general and special prosecutor for Medicaid fraud control, Edward J. Kuriansky, testified to Congress regarding what he described as

> A feeding frenzy on the Medicaid Program, a period of unprecedented white-collar wilding in which wave after wave of multimillion-dollar fraud has swept through nursing homes and hospitals, to clinics and pharmacies, podiatry and durable medical equipment, radiology and labs, and more recently, home health care. Each surge has brought its own special brand of profiteer in search of the next great loophole in the Medicaid system.[1]

The feeding frenzy continues. As targets for fraud, major health care programs are just too attractive. Stealing a million dollars or more is remarkably easy, and carries with it little chance of getting caught. You don't even need to know much about health care. It seems no previous qualifications are required.

The general public, and most members of the medical profession, may not be aware of the extraordinary range of characters queuing up to defraud the system, nor of the unlimited creativity of men and women determined to steal from the health care complex.

The following compilation of stories—just a small sample of what goes on, and focusing mostly on folk who stole a million dollars or more—is designed to illustrate the myriad types of assault that the health system suffers, and to show the complete lack of concern perpetrators have for the damage they do to patients' health and to the health care system.

As you read these stories, please bear in mind that all these scams have been detected, and it is tempting to take comfort in that. These are the scams we know about—and we know about them mostly because the perpetrators were brazen, stupid, or excessively greedy. Mostly the less sophisticated ones get caught. Many of the cases that do come to light result from whistle-blower suits where an employee, or competitor, or even a jilted lover turns the perpetrator in. More than half the settlements awarded the Department of Justice in health care cases now arise from whistle-blower (or *qui tam*) suits; and more than half the *qui tam* suits filed within the United States—even though the Federal False Claims Act applies to all false claims against federal funds—now relate to health care.[2]

Bear in mind, as you review these stories, the first important rule of fraud control: What you see is not the problem. It's what we don't see that really does the damage, and the efficacy of control systems depends upon how well they uncover, and then suppress, the invisible bulk of the problem.

Nevertheless, the cases described here, all of which came to light one way or another, serve to reveal the rich texture of who steals and how.

Fictitious Companies

Occasionally it becomes transparently obvious that existing control systems do not work the way we imagine they should. The *Miami Herald,* on August 14, 1994, blasted Medicare for paying thousands of dollars in claims to "Whope of America," a phantom corporation whose corporate address seemed to be a sand trap at the Fontainebleau Golf Club. An investigator from the Office of Inspector General, Department of Health and Human Services (OIG, HHS), quoted in the article, made this statement:

> What we have seen is a series of health care providers come into existence solely on paper. A company is incorporated using a fictitious name. The company submits a series of claims, usually between $200,000 and $1 million. By the time Health and Human Services becomes aware of the scam, the company and John Doe have vanished.[3]

- Another phantom company, Bass Orthopedic, comprising nothing more than two rented mailboxes and a phone number, was paid $2.1 million between November 1993 and April 1994. The phony billings listed the names of physicians and hundreds of patients, none of whom had ever heard of the company. When a federal judge ordered Bass's bank account frozen it was too late. Most of the money had disappeared along with the owner. No services were ever rendered.[4]

- Another company, Med EO Diagnostic, used the names of dozens of dead patients and a rented West Dade, Florida, mailbox to collect $332,939 from Medicare in May and June 1994. The owner—an unemployed tow truck operator—got caught only because he withdrew $200,000 in cash from the lab's bank account. A bank official became suspicious and called the police.[5]

The *Miami Herald* article quoted Senator William Cohen (R—Maine) as saying, "The solution doesn't take more legislation, it takes common sense. We have got to persuade the government to do what it is supposed to do." A similar point about the use of common sense was made by Bruce Vladeck (who later served as administrator of Health Care Financing Administration [HCFA]) as far back as 1980. "We might be better served if government policy was made and implemented not by Ph.D.'s in economics but by grandmothers employing the skills they practice at the butcher's."[6]

Generalists

One thing our grandmothers knew for sure: They'd prefer the butcher to know the butcher's business, not to have just walked in from a building site or some other line of work.

- When the FBI investigated a network of durable medical equipment (DME) companies in Florida between 1996 and 1999, they came across one Barry Douglas Haught, forty-five years old, of Tampa. Haught was listed as an officer of four different DME companies, as well as a Medicare billing service called Trans-Capital Investments. His professional experience spanned a number of different fields. He had been charged with racketeering in 1993 following an investigation into pornography in Polk County, and placed on three years probation after pleading no contest. Also, he had been involved in civil fraud in West Virginia, in 1993, involving phony oil-gauge tickets used to siphon $100,000 worth of oil from a supplier. Next stop for him: Medicare.[7]
- In Culver City, California, John Watts, Jr., (mentioned in the preface) opened a home health care agency and received certification from Medicare, even though thirteen months earlier he had been in prison, and his prior business experience was as the owner of a nightclub. All he needed to submit claims to Medicare was the pa-

tient's name, a Medicare number, and the necessary diagnosis and procedure codes. Over seventeen months, he billed Medicare $5.6 million for more than 80,000 home health visits, of which almost half were completely fraudulent.[8]

Physicians

The Medical Associations often protest that fraud is not committed by physicians, but rather confined to the range of ancillary services—equipment supply, transportation, home health care—peripheral to professional medical practice.

I wish it were true. Sadly, it is not.

- In June 1998, a Beverly Hills doctor pleaded guilty to defrauding Medicare of more than $216,000 between 1992 and 1996 by billing for treatments for patients who were either dead, in prison, or lived too far away for the doctor to have seen them on the days in question. A related civil action under the False Claims Act recovered a $1.5 million settlement.[9]

- In December 1997, an ophthalmologist in California agreed to pay $375,000 to settle a *qui tam* suit brought by a former office manager. The suit alleged he routinely billed Medicare for endothelial microscopy for every cataract patient he treated, even though it is a rarely used pre-cataract procedure and he never did it.[10]

- In Massachusetts, a dermatologist named Richard F. Finkel falsely billed Medicare for ostensibly removing cancerous skin lesions with liquid nitrogen. He used weight-loss patients, who had no need for such treatment, spraying them with liquid nitrogen without their consent and from such a distance as to be ineffective. In June 1999, the Department of Justice announced a default judgment of over $2 million against him for failing to answer the government's complaint of Medicare fraud.[11]

- In July 1999, Sami I. Michael, a provider of psychotherapy services at his "Diagnostic and Behavioral Health Clinic" in Steubenville, Ohio, was convicted in U.S. District Court for operating a scheme to defraud public and private insurance programs. Between January 1995 and June 1998 he billed health insurance programs for psychotherapy sessions, when patients were merely entertained by watching movies such as *Lethal Weapon, Tootsie, Ghostbusters,* and *Batman*.[12]

Dentists

- In September 1998, Thomas Anderson, a dentist, pleaded guilty in Michigan to submitting false claims to Medicaid. He was charged with abusing patients by pulling perfectly healthy teeth to create Medicaid eligibility for partial lower dentures.[13]

- In Independence, Missouri, Frank William Meyer, a dentist, sedated indigent children with morphine and another narcotic without their parents' consent, and then performed unnecessary and unusual procedures on them, such as root canals on baby teeth. He pleaded guilty to Medicaid fraud. During the sentencing hearings, the defense lawyer objected to the prosecutor's raising the issue of sedation on the grounds that it was irrelevant to the fraud case: "For the government to raise this issue before this court is merely to inflame the passions of the court."[14]

- In July 1999, Charles Phillip Akin, a sixty-four-year-old dentist from Driftwood, Texas, was convicted of conspiracy, fraud, making false claims, and money laundering. Akin and his associates defrauded Medicare by selling wheelchair cushions to nursing home patients. Instead of billing for the cushions, they billed Medicare for custom-fitted body jackets—orthotic devices that carry much higher reimbursement rates. For each cushion, they billed $1,289 and were reimbursed $858 (80 percent). Medicare paid over $1 million.[15]

Largest Corporations

So far, most of these examples have involved individual entrepreneurs, many of whom steal millions, acting alone. The prospect of institutionalized fraud is somewhat more alarming, especially given the magnitude of the sums involved. Let's jump to the opposite end of the spectrum and consider the largest health care providers in America. One should bear in mind that none of these corporations ever admits to wrongdoing, and they would all balk at mention of the word "stealing." Instead, they describe themselves as trapped by bureaucratic regulatory complexities and then trampled on for making innocent billing errors.

- In January 2000, Fresenius Medical Care North America, headquartered in Lexington, Massachusetts, pleaded guilty to charges
  of conspiracy and fraud and paid a record $486 million in fines
  and settlements. The company is the largest provider of kidney
  dialysis products and services *in the world*, operating more than
  800 dialysis facilities in the United States. The criminal conduct,
  involving payment of kickbacks to doctors for referrals and submission of thousands of false claims, took place at three units of
  the firm National Medical Care, which was taken over by the German health care giant Fresenius AG in October 1996. Prosecutors
  concede the German company put an end to these illegal schemes
  shortly after the takeover. The settlement comprised $101 million
  in criminal fines and $385 million for civil violations of the False
  Claims Act (false billings were submitted to Medicare, the Department of Defense, and the Veterans Administration health
  care system). Many of the false claims related to needless tests
  conducted on dialysis patients; some involved misrepresentation
  of the patient's weight loss to justify nutritional therapy, even
  when the weight loss was unrelated to the kidney disease. In one
  case, the weight loss was attributable to the amputation of a leg.
  Two former executives pled guilty and three others have been indicted.[16]

- The largest ambulance services provider in the United States, based
  in New York, paid $9.5 million to resolve allegations of Medicare
  fraud. Between 1990 and 1995 they submitted Medicare claims using false diagnoses in order to induce Medicare to pay for services
  that were otherwise nonreimburseable.[17]

- The largest privately held home health provider in the country,
  First American Health Care of Georgia, Inc., formerly known as
  ABD Home Health, was investigated for shifting unallowable costs
  to Medicare. The only costs permitted for inclusion on Medicare
  cost reports are supposed to be reasonable and necessary general
  and administrative expenses related to the care of Medicare patients. The owners, Jack and Margie Mills, had included in their list
  of Medicare-related expenses golf course memberships, green fees,
  a family vacation, and a BMW for a son in college. Ultimately, the
  owners and company were convicted of criminal offenses related
  to Medicare fraud, and $255 million was returned to the United
  States.[18]

Columbia/HCA

The single largest health care provider in the United States is Columbia/HCA—now the subject of a multiplicity of whistle-blower lawsuits, and federal and state investigations. Here is a sample of the suits and allegations swirling around Columbia, its subsidiaries, and its business affiliates.

- In 1991, James Alderson, CFO at North Valley Hospital in Montana, was fired for refusing to participate in improper billing procedures. Alderson filed a wrongful termination suit against Quorum in 1991, which was settled in 1993. In 1993, he filed a civil suit under seal, alleging improper billing practices and Medicare fraud at North Valley Hospital. This suit led to federal investigations.

- In January 1996, two Texas home health care agencies sued Columbia in U.S. District Court in El Paso, accusing them of funneling hospital patients to Columbia's own home-care services, even when patients voiced a preference for another provider; and paying for patient referrals.[19]

- In November 1996, *The Nation* published an article that included extensive interviews with nurses in the Good Samaritan Health System, which Columbia purchased in January 1996. Nurses claimed that extensive cutbacks and Columbia's focus on profit left the hospital dangerously understaffed and dirty. Some examples: patients not assisted in walking after surgery (which is important to their recovery); no regular monitoring of vital signs or checking on those with physical restraints; management telling nurses to administer cancer drugs, an area of expertise reserved for oncology nurses; dust balls in the surgical recovery room; sparse supplies, declining quality of surgical gloves, prostheses, etc.; and emergency care cut-backs or elimination at hospitals after Columbia takeovers. [20]

- In March 1997, government enforcement agents raided Columbia facilities in El Paso, Texas, and seized physicians' evaluations, physicians' referral patterns, details on the agency's incentive plan for its medical board, and a file titled "Educating Physicians of Monetary and Other Rewards."[21]

- In April 1997, in the wake of the government raid in El Paso, two separate class action lawsuits were filed against Columbia/HCA.

The first claims that the company schemed to defraud the federal government and inflate its earnings; the second claims that Columbia concealed important information regarding its business practices.[22]

- In June 1997, four Columbia executives were indicted in Florida on criminal charges of conspiring to defraud the government of $2.8 million by disguising Medicare, Medicaid, and CHAMPUS claims to obtain higher reimbursements at a hospital in Port Charlotte, Florida.[23]

- In July 1997, a shareholder lawsuit was filed against Columbia, accusing the board and management of injuring shareholders by breaching their fiduciary duties and grossly mismanaging the company. This suit also alleged that Columbia executives and directors engaged in insider trading by dumping stock in the company before the full extent of the government's investigations became public knowledge, with six executives and directors engaging in thirteen such stock sales that netted them $26.5 million.[24] That same month, Rick Scott, chairman and CEO of Columbia/HCA was ousted and replaced by Thomas Frist, who moved to change Columbia's image and negate Scott's aggressive marketing, acquisition, and incentive projects.[25]

- In November 1997, Valinda Rutledge, CEO of Columbia's Brandon Regional Medical Center, filed suit against Columbia alleging that she was fired after refusing to carry out directives from upper management that she thought were illegal and would jeopardize patient care. Those directives, she said, included pressure to hire an underling whose job would be to increase referrals to Columbia's home care services regardless of medical necessity or the legality of the referrals; instructions to cut 150 staff positions at the hospital despite Rutledge's objections that the layoffs would jeopardize patient care; and pressure to threaten physicians with canceling contracts for services if they did not shorten the lengths of stay for neonatal patients.[26]

- In February 1998, former Columbia employees revealed that the hospital chain had set performance targets for its hospitals that included the Medicare complication rate as one of the performance indicators. For many conditions, *complications* increase Medicare reimbursements substantially. According to employees, the chain had exerted pressure for hospitals to get the complication rate as close to 100 percent as possible.[27]

- In July 1998, Robert Bauer (former CEO of Indian Path Medical Center in Tennessee) filed a lawsuit against Columbia after being fired and blamed for unethical billing practices at the hospital. His suit claimed that these charges were false and that Columbia publicly put the blame on him to portray a good image and to deflect media and federal attention away from the company. The suit charges defamation, invasion of privacy, and wrongful termination.[28]

- In October 1998, the Department of Justice announced that it had joined the Alderson lawsuit and announced the charges. Defendant hospitals include over 200 owned by Columbia, 17 owned by Quorum, and 235 hospitals managed by Quorum. The lawsuit alleges that Columbia[29]

  - Disguised claims to receive reimbursement for expenses not related to patient care, including physician recruitment, membership dues, telephone and television costs for patients, and advertising and marketing costs.

  - Misrepresented operating expenses (which are reimbursed at a low rate) as capital costs (which are more highly compensated).

  - Misidentified capital costs for projects begun before 1990 as having been incurred after that date (the newer costs are reimbursed at a higher rate than the older ones).

  - Marked some work papers relating to its Medicare cost reports, "Not to be shown to Medicare auditors."

  - Kept reserve funds to repay the government in case the overcharges were discovered.

  - Forbade employees and consultants from disclosing to auditors the existence of a second set of cost reports (called "reserve accounts") and the reserve funds. (According to one FBI affidavit, managers gave instructions that if a particular Medicare auditor persisted in asking questions about certain costs, he should be offered a job at Columbia.)

  - Employed an accounting trick (known as "recapture") to induce Medicare to pay for hospital acquisitions, although Columbia pays no cash for the purchase. For example, Columbia's purchase of a Miami Beach hospital was structured so that the company paid no cash yet received $24.7 million from Medicare.[30]

- In December 1998, the government announced that it had joined a second civil suit, this one involving similar allegations to the Alderson suit. The suit alleges that Columbia and Basic American Medical, Inc. (which Columbia acquired in 1992) as far back as 1986 filed false reports that allowed them to collect reimbursements on costs they knew were not permitted. The complaint was limited to hospitals owned by Columbia before its merger with HCA in 1994.[31] Whistle-blower John Schilling, former financial supervisor at Columbia's West Florida Division, left Columbia after secretly making copies of 11,000 documents supporting his fraud allegations against the company and became an informant for the FBI. Schilling had complained to two sets of supervisors about suspicious billing practices, but no action had been taken.[32]

- In April 1999, the Department of Justice joined another whistle-blower lawsuit against Columbia/HCA and Curative Health Services. The suit alleges that they filed false claims to Medicare by shifting costs from Procuren (a wound care treatment for which Medicare no longer pays) to management fees, which *are* reimbursable. Whistle-blower Joseph Parlow, CFO of Columbia-Southwest Florida Regional Medical Center, claims that he went all the way up the chain of command with his complaints about the corrupt management fees paid to Curative, but nothing was ever done to redress them.[33]

- In May 1999, the Department of Justice joined a whistle-blower suit filed in June 1995 by Sara Ortega, a former employee of Columbia/HCA in El Paso. The suit alleges that Columbia Medical Center West in El Paso improperly shifted costs to its back care center to increase Medicare funding and paid kickbacks to physicians for patient referrals to the hospital.[34]

- In July 1999, the Department of Justice joined a whistle-blower suit filed by former Olsten vice president, Donald McLendon, alleging that Olsten and Columbia/HCA acted together to disguise costs associated with Columbia's purchase of home health agencies (which are not reimbursable by Medicare) as management fees (which *are* reimbursable). The suit also alleges that Columbia illegally billed Medicare for sales and marketing activities, particularly the employment of *community educators,* who arranged referrals from physicians, and *home health coordinators,* who identified patients about to leave the hospital and channeled them to Columbia-owned home health agencies. The suit also alleges that Columbia improperly billed Medicare for home care visits for patients residing in Assisted Living Facilities—services that were already covered by Medicare or Medicaid payments to the facilities.[35]

- Also in July 1999, of the four Columbia executives who stood trial on criminal charges, Jay Jarrell and Robert Whiteside were convicted, Michael Neeb was acquitted, and the jury was unable to reach a verdict for Carl Dick. Jarrell and Whiteside were found guilty of six counts of fraud, face up to five years in prison, and could pay $250,000 for each count of fraud.[36]

- In August 1999, Columbia settled a lawsuit concerning Medicaid billing practices by paying a fine of $1.25 million; but denied all allegations. Among a range of alleged violations, the complaint accuses executives of failing "to create an adequate and reasonable compliance or auditing program to prevent illegal activities, or to detect them after they occurred and stop them." Whistle-blower Kathy Aldrich, a former night charge nurse, alleged that Columbia submitted false claims to a Medicaid managed care program that provides mental health and substance abuse treatment. According to Aldrich, the claims were false in a variety of ways: Patient medical records were falsified; bills were submitted for services that were medically unnecessary, not ordered by treating physicians, and/or not provided; the hospital double-billed for some therapies; and the hospital billed for services as if they were provided by qualified mental health professionals, when they were actually provided by unqualified or underqualified employees.[37]

- Also in August 1999, the Justice Department asked the Judicial Panel on Multi-District Litigation (for the second time) to combine all the *qui tam* cases pending against Columbia/HCA Corporation, whether sealed or unsealed. At the time, there were eight cases fully unsealed and several more cases still sealed from the public, possibly as many as ten.[38]

- In December 1999, former Columbia executive Robert Whiteside, convicted in July, was sentenced to two years in prison. His attorney, Gabe Imperato, said, "I don't care whether you get two years or two decades in prison, it's a devastating thing for an individual

to, at one point, be a successful professional in the health care industry and then face jail time. These people didn't view themselves
as criminals."[39]

If and when Columbia eventually settles with the government, industry
speculation puts the potential price tag at or above $1 billion, which
would be the largest settlement of its kind in history. (Such speculation
has been around for more than two years.)[40] For now that's mere speculation. Even if Columbia did pay a billion dollars to settle these suits—
which have rumbled along for seven years already—some in the industry
might regard that as a necessary "cost of doing business." After all, Columbia receives revenues of roughly $18 billion each year. What really
would hurt them, of course, is exclusion from participating in government programs, a sanction referred to within the industry as "the kiss of
death." But Columbia owns and operates such a large chunk of the health
care delivery system that they will surely argue—as other major providers
have argued before them—that patients' access to services would be seriously diminished. Such an argument may have merit (especially in rural
areas, where a Columbia hospital might be the only provider of acute
care) and presents a genuine dilemma for the government when it considers excluding any major corporation.

Whenever government resolves its differences with major corporate
providers, exclusion is usually bargained away within the terms of financial settlements. That guarantees continuity of care for the patients, but
leaves the providers in business (maybe under some kind of compliance
agreement) at least until the government discovers what else they are up
to. Major corporations, in presuming government's attention to have
shifted elsewhere, have been known to persist in the *same* dishonest practices even after reaching settlements with the government.

By 1998, enforcement efforts turned towards a number of other major
players in the industry, signaling a growing recognition by auditors and
investigators that fraud and abuse problems were not just concentrated at
the bottom of the food chain, amongst low-life hoods.[41]

Laboratories

For those who would steal, one of the most valuable commodities in the
business is blood. There is almost no limit to the number of tests you can
perform with one vial of blood. And who knows whether you actually

performed them or whether you "sink-tested" the samples (i.e., just poured them away)?

During the 1980s, in one quite famous New York scam, Surinder Singh Panshi, a physician, earned the media nickname "Dracula, Inc.: Bloodsucker of the Decade."[42] On August 4, 1988, Panshi was convicted of stealing over $3.6 million from the Medicaid program between January 1986 and July 1988. His scam involved purchasing blood from addicts and Medicaid mills and then falsely charging the state for thousands of blood tests that had never been ordered, referred, or authorized by physicians and were in no way medically necessary. Panshi had previously been prosecuted in 1986 for false billings and lost his license to practice medicine. He went into the lab business instead and purchased two labs in Queens and one on Long Island.[43]

In 1986, the Panshi labs billed Medicaid a combined total of $1 million; in 1987, more than $12 million; and in 1988, over $31 million. By then Panshi employed a dozen or more "blood collectors"; they set up blood-drawing centers in small apartments and prowled the streets in search of donors, paying them—mostly drug addicts—$10 per vial.

How far could such a scheme go before being closed down? As of February 1988, the three Panshi labs accounted for more than 20 percent of all Medicaid billings by the state's laboratories, even though there are nearly 450 labs in the state. The scam was finally discovered when emergency room physicians in New York hospitals began to see a rash of patients who were anemic as a result of having sold up to a quart of blood two or three times per week. Some emergency room patients received extensive transfusions, only to go out and immediately sell their blood again. The problem became so serious that three doctors from Columbia-Presbyterian Hospital published an article in the *New England Journal of Medicine* titled "Lab-Fraud Anemia." [44]

The media also began receiving anonymous tip-offs, which they passed on to the Medicaid fraud-control unit. Despite the extent and rapid acceleration of the scam, it was not detected by an audit, or by a detection system, or by a claims-processing edit or audit, or by a pre- or postpayment review. The payment system had no systematic method—no instrumentation—capable of revealing even such flagrant abuse.

During the decade of the 1990s, lab fraud has continued apace and become somewhat more sophisticated, and major clinical laboratories have become an important focus for investigators. The first major lab to come under the microscope was National Health Labs (NHL), one of the nation's largest providers of clinical diagnostic testing. In 1992, NHL plead guilty to two criminal charges of submitting false claims to government health insurance programs and agreed to pay $111 million to settle with the government.[45]

When the pattern of false billings by National Health Laboratories came to light, it was not through systematic detection apparatus. NHL had found an *institutional* way to defraud the government; they altered the order forms physicians use to order blood tests. A standard item on such forms is a SMAC test (sequential multiple analysis computer), an automated battery of tests conducted from one blood sample. NHL amended the form so that two additional tests, one for cholesterol and one for serum ferritin (iron in the blood), were added into the SMAC test and were inseparable from it. Physicians believed that the two extra tests, which they would rarely have ordered separately, had been included in the SMAC test at no extra cost. NHL billed the Medicare and Medicaid programs the standard $18 for the SMAC test, plus an additional $18 each for the additional cholesterol and ferritin tests.[46]

How long could such practice go undetected, and what was the mechanism of its discovery? In 1988, before the practice began, the Medicare program paid less than $500,000 to NHL for ferritin tests. In 1990, Medicare paid more than $31 million.[47] Even then it was not a routine audit, nor was it a prepayment review of medical necessity, nor a postpayment utilization review that brought the scheme to light. A salesman who worked for one of NHL's competitors became curious about NHL's unaccountably high profits and growth of revenues. He did a little research, figured out what NHL was doing, and filed a *qui tam* suit under the False Claims Act.[48] [The *qui tam* provisions provide a financial incentive for private individuals to initiate action against fraud involving public funds. A private person, known as the *qui tam* "relator," can bring a civil claim for a violation of the False Claims Act on behalf of the government. The government has the option of taking over the suit or leaving the individual to pursue it alone. The relator is entitled to share in monetary recovery if the government joins in the suit, and can take all of it if the government does not.]

To the general public, the medical profession's response to NHL's $111 million settlement may be somewhat puzzling. Shortly after the settlement was reached, an article titled "Medicare Case Underlines Importance of Physician Compliance with All Rules When Claims Are Filed" appeared in *JAMA* (Journal of the American Medical Association).[49] Although the president and CEO of NHL, Robert E. Draper, pleaded guilty to two counts of fraud and resigned from the company, the article nevertheless interpreted the action of the government in going after NHL as an extension of the definition of fraud applied to the health care industry. A former attorney for HHS, Thomas S. Crane, was quoted by *JAMA*:

> Up to now, most health care attorneys believed that the only thing that made a *criminal* case was services not rendered or clear fraud. Otherwise it would be a civil case. This means that for physicians there should be a new sense of caution. What the government is saying is that when a physician signs a Medicare or Medicaid claim form, there is an implied representation that all of the rules are complied with. Of course, minor mischaracterizations are not going to be prosecuted as criminal cases, but the government is clearly in mind to press the view that physicians are obligated to see that all of the rules are complied with when they file a claim. I think this is a big cautionary sign.

In view of what NHL had done, the idea that the definition of fraud was being stretched seems surprising. NHL systematically, and as a matter of company policy, tripled its billings to the government for SMAC tests by including two additional tests that doctors would not normally prescribe. They redesigned their order forms to mislead physicians as to the cost of these tests.

NHL, in its postsettlement statements, preferred to characterize the entire issue as a question of conflicting expert medical opinions by saying "the tests were done believing they are necessary for a full diagnostic evaluation, are medically sound, and supported by the medical and scientific communities." In other words, NHL claims to have acted perfectly responsibly. Even if the medical necessity of the two tests were debatable (which it is not), NHL still made an unannounced, unilateral judgment on the question, without consultation with payers, which happened to triple NHL's revenues with almost no impact on their costs. Of course, we should expect NHL to present this unfortunate truth in the best possible light.

Even in 1999, the industry still seems to view NHL's actions as perfectly fine. Many regard the NHL investigation as symbolizing the government's adoption of an overly aggressive posture, and a stretching of the definition of fraud beyond all reasonable limits. In a published discussion of corporate compliance, one industry expert—C. Kim McCarty of Quest Diagnostics—recalled the NHL settlement thus:

Six years ago on Black Friday, as we call it, the resolution of the National Health Labs (NHL) fraud and abuse case was announced. The clinical lab industry was a little surprised with the government's aggressiveness in this case and somewhat surprised about the theories of liability used. In announcing the settlement, the U.S. Attorney noted that there wasn't a health lawyer in the country who would have advised clients against the very practices that NHL had to pay $111 million to resolve. So that was a real wake-up call for our industry.[50]

In retrospect, it seems the U.S. Attorney that McCarty referred to was correct: Health lawyers all around the country must have been advising other labs to behave in similar ways, because many of them evidently were. Since the NHL settlement, continuing multiagency investigations under the title "Operation Labscam" (involving U.S. Attorneys' Offices, the Department of Justice, the Medicaid Fraud-Control Units [MFCUs], the FBI, the Defense Criminal Investigation Service, the OIG [HHS], and the Medicare program) have found such practices to be somewhat pervasive:

- In October 1996, Damon Clinical Laboratories, Inc., headquartered in Needham, Massachusetts, pleaded guilty to conspiracy and paid $119 million to the government. Of that sum, $35 million was a criminal fine and the remainder resolved their civil liabilities. Damon's practices were remarkably reminiscent of NHL's. Damon labs had manipulated the ways physicians order blood tests so that Medicare was billed for thousands of unnecessary tests. In particular, they bundled serum ferritin tests and serum iron tests (which are seldom necessary) into their basic blood chemistry panel, called a "LabScan." Also, thousands of Medicare program beneficiaries underwent unnecessary monthly blood draws, simply to enable Damon to bill for tests. Subsequently, in January 1998, four of Damon's former executives—the former president, two senior vice presidents of operations, and a corporate controller—were indicted for conspiring to defraud Medicare of over $25 million. The indictment of the four executives represented an attempt to hold high-level executives accountable for corporate behaviors.[51]
- Also in 1996, the San Diego regional laboratory of Allied Clinical Laboratories pleaded guilty to a similar scheme. Laboratory Corporation of America (successor-by-merger to Allied) paid $187

million in criminal and civil fines to settle allegations against Allied and other laboratories they owned.

- In February 1997, SmithKline Beecham Clinical Laboratories, Inc. agreed to pay $325 million in settlement of a civil false claims action brought jointly by the Department of Justice, the OIG, the FBI, the Postal Inspection Board, the Defense Criminal Investigative Service, and the Railroad Retirement Board. SmithKline's laboratories had engaged in unbundling laboratory tests, billing for tests not performed, inserting false diagnosis codes to obtain reimbursement, paying kickbacks to physicians for patient referrals, double billing, and billing for calculations that nobody had ordered and that were medically unnecessary.[52]

- In April 1998, Corning Life Sciences, now known as Quest Diagnostics, paid $6.8 million to resolve allegations that it had billed Medicare for lab tests not ordered by a physician. Corning was already subject to a "Compliance Agreement" with the OIG in connection with a prior false claims settlement.[53]

- In August 1999, sales representatives at a Brooklyn laboratory, Liberty Testing Laboratory, were indicted for taking blood samples from elderly and disabled patients. Many of the samples ended up in representatives' home refrigerators, each sample apparently earning them a commission of $150. The lab submitted $5.3 million in Medicare claims in just one year, and allegedly netted $1.7 million in fees for blood tests that weren't even performed.[54]

Teaching Hospitals

Among the most respected institutions within the health system are the teaching hospitals, the majority of which are affiliated with major universities. One of the continuing probes by the Justice Department focuses on Medicare and other billings from these institutions.

The most common problems uncovered to date relate to treatment provided by residents and interns under the supervision of qualified physicians. Teaching hospitals are only permitted to bill Medicare or Medicaid for the services of the supervising physician if he or she was present at the time, personally examined the patient, and assumed the same responsibilities as for other paying patients. If the "attending physician" is not present, then the services of the residents and interns at the teaching hospitals are already covered by government grants designed to cover the costs of training. Apparently, many of these hospitals have been systematically breaching the billing rules in situations where the attending physician was not in attendance, and the government's continuing "PATH" audits (Physicians at Teaching Hospitals) focus on these issues. In 1995, the University of Pennsylvania settled their case for $30 million. The University of Virginia settled for $8.6 million. More recently,

- In March 1998, eighteen physician clinical practice plans associated with the University of Pittsburgh agreed to pay $14 million for false or improper billings to the Pennsylvania Medicaid Program; these related to billings for services provided by residents or interns under the supervision of a physician.

- In March 1999, the Justice Department joined a whistle-blower lawsuit, originally filed in 1996, against the University of Chicago.[55] The suit alleges the university had knowingly engaged in a "pattern and practice" of fraud and overbilling in the hospital's Medicare and Medicaid claims; the suit estimates that 40 percent of claims submitted between 1991 and 1997 had been fraudulently upcoded to inflate reimbursements by millions of dollars.

The "PATH" audits continue.

Billing Specialists

If health care providers have trouble with their billings, they can always ask for help from billing consultants. Then, however, they have to choose whether they want a consultant who will help them bill it *correctly* (that is, the way it happened), or one who will help them squeeze every available last dollar out of the system, by fair means or foul.

Many billing consultancies—the industry remains almost completely unregulated—have traditionally been paid on a commission basis, and many of them have reconfigured claims, unbundled laboratory tests, manipulated clinical diagnoses to obtain higher reimbursements, and even added on services that were not provided.

In the first major case of its kind, Metzinger Associates, billing consultants, settled a false claims action in May 1997 with a rather unusual deal. As well as paying $60,000 in fines and being excluded from Medicare for three years, they agreed to give the U.S. Attorney's office in Philadelphia 250 hours of consulting time to help them understand some of the more artful ways in which Medicare billings were being inflated.[56]

Another opportunity to steal, which brings with it the opportunity to exploit the accounts of large numbers of other providers, falls to billing companies that handle claims submissions for many different clients. In July 1999, a Florida-based emergency physician billing company, called "Gottlieb's Financial Services, Inc.," and its corporate parent agreed to pay $15 million to settle allegations of submitting false health care claims to a range of insurance programs. Allegations involved upcoding claims and billing for more extensive services than those actually rendered.[57] Where such billing services also act as financial intermediaries (collecting the money from the insurers and distributing it to their clients), they are in a position to steal by using the accounts of multiple providers, and often without the providers' knowledge.

Organized Crime

In 1992, Louis J. Freeh, director of the FBI, announced the entry of some new players into the game. FBI intelligence revealed that cocaine traffickers in Florida and California were switching from drug dealing to health care fraud.[58] Why? Because health care fraud is safer and more lucrative, and the risk of being caught is smaller. Moreover, if they are unlucky enough to get caught, these criminals know the punishments for health care fraud are likely to be much less severe than those for drug dealing.

More recently, in February 1997, the *New York Times* reported that New York City and New Jersey's Mafia families were shifting their focus from their traditional extortion and bid-rigging rackets to three new lines of white-collar crime business: health insurance, prepaid telephone cards, and small brokerage houses. The *Times'* information was based on reports from the FBI and from experts on organized crime.[59] The attorney general of New Jersey, Peter G. Verniero, described infiltration of the health care industry as "our most serious organized crime problem."[60] The pattern of recent arrests and indictments suggest these organizations are attracted to the managed care (rather than the traditional fee-for-service) marketplace. They perceive opportunities to broker entire health care networks, linking health care providers, physicians, hospitals, and dentists with group plans for large corporations and unions. Having constructed the networks, they then find methods of siphoning funds out of the network through a variety of excessive fees, using intimidation if necessary to get their way.

Meat, for Money

Thousands of patients encounter unscrupulous providers everyday. Sometimes they are responding to the offer of a free eye-exam, or free supplies, or free testing; sometimes they are offered cash to take part in some "experimental treatment program at the local clinic." Sometimes they've been told they actually have a disease that they don't have. In most cases, the patients probably imagine, during the encounter, that the provider has their interests and health in mind.

To those who would steal, patients are a mere commodity. A device. Profit centers. The language some of the providers use to describe them filters out eventually: "Get the head in the bed, and keep it there." Round 'em up. Meat in the chair, for money.

That leaves open the question of how best to guarantee a healthy supply of patients, a matter to which a considerable amount of criminal creativity has been applied. Scam artists have used all the following methods:

- *Old-fashioned kickbacks:* In 1997, a medical center in the Midwest agreed to pay $17.5 million to settle allegations that it paid two doctors $1 million for patient referrals. The referrals generated around $42 million in Medicare business for the hospital. The kickbacks were paid through sham consulting agreements with the physicians.[61]

- *"Recruiters":* A Florida man, who owned two DME companies and a medical diagnostic company, paid patient recruiters to bring Medicare beneficiaries to selected physicians; he then paid the physicians to order DME and diagnostic testing. Through his companies, he submitted Medicare claims for these services, all medically unnecessary. When he was finally caught and convicted, he was ordered to pay over $1 million in restitution.[62]

- *Cull the neighborhoods for kids:* In July 1998, a dentist, an optometrist, and a chiropractor who worked in the same clinic in Louisiana were arrested and charged with using drivers to cull neighborhoods for children covered by Medicaid. The practice, called "circuits," had a going rate of $10 for every patient brought to the doctors' offices. [63]

- *"Runners":* Jesus N. Castillo, a physician in Miami, was convicted in July 1996 of fraud and money laundering. From 1991 to 1994, he operated three clinics in a strip mall. Castillo hired runners to find elderly and homeless people covered by insurance and bring them to his clinics; he paid the runners between $200 and $300 for each "patient." (Note the higher prices paid for patients in Florida; they suggest that one can bill higher amounts per patient there than elsewhere without triggering scrutiny.) Of Castillo's fifteen to twenty runners, some earned as much as $20,000 per year from these fees. Castillo ran the patients through batteries of tests, nearly all of which were unnecessary, and billed Medicare and Medicaid more than $10 million.[64] What's more, he had fabricated his medical qualifications.

- *Use your own family:* Idaho Blue Cross Blue Shield recently found one chiropractor in the state who had billed for services for all the members of his own family, keeping the total per patient just below the maximum permissible ($800) each year, for two years running. The plan does not permit providers to bill for services to their own family members.[65]

- *Make it a condition of employment:* A Texas woman with no experience in health care set up a home health agency in the pantry of her husband's restaurant. She hired home health aides on the condition that they first recruit a patient, regardless of whether or not a physician had ordered care or whether they were eligible for Medicare. (Medicare was billed anyway.)[66]

- *Try the motor vehicle office:* The president of "Major Health Services, Inc.," a DME supplier in Ohio, pleaded guilty to 2 counts of mail fraud in October 1998. He paid approximately $140,000 to settle false claims made to TRICARE (the armed forces health insurance program, previously called CHAMPUS) and some private insurers. He had obtained a list of people using license plates for the handicapped; he then directed his Colorado-based telemarketing operation to offer them, at no charge, scooters and adjustable beds. His company then billed insurers for more sophisticated and expensive equipment such as motorized wheelchairs and hospital beds.[67]

- *Or the police station:* A New Jersey chiropractor, Gina Garcen-Ciallella, paid police department employees to provide her with auto accident reports; she used the reports to recruit patients.[68]

- *Go to Disneyland:* In 1998, Florida charged fourteen individuals with racketeering, organized fraud, and conspiracy. The defendants had lured Disney workers to fake diagnostic clinics where patients were paid between $100 and $200 for their insurance information. False claims totaling more than $850,000 were then submitted to Disney's insurance carrier.[69] United Airlines and Albertson's Grocers were also targeted in the scheme.[70]

- *Take them skating:* In September 1998, an Atlanta businessman, owner of "The Human Resources Inc. Concept" pleaded guilty to defrauding the Medicaid program of $7.3 million. The defendant and his employees recruited inner-city school children eligible for Medicaid to enter after-school and summer school programs at a community center and roller rink. The defendant sent employees door-to-door in poor areas to recruit children to what was promoted as a set of academic, cultural enrichment, and recreational opportunities. The parents never knew Medicaid was being billed for individual and group psychotherapy sessions. Former employees of the company testified that no counseling services were provided, and the children did not need such services. The defendant was sentenced to three years and ten months in federal prison, and ordered to pay $7.3 million in restitution.[71]

- *Offer them candy:* On November 6, 1998, ABC's *20/20* documentary program showed healthy children in Indiana being given rides to chiropractors' offices. At the offices, the children received manipulations, plus candy and fast food, and were then driven home again. Medicaid was charged more than $100 for each child each visit. Robert Guzek, a physician from Michigan City, was interviewed on camera. When asked why he would perform seventy-four manipulations on a perfectly healthy seven-year-old girl, Guzek said the therapy was to maximize her good health. When one of the drivers who worked for the clinics was interviewed, she said she was paid $10 to $15 for each *new* child, with pressure to bring lots of them in every day. Parents let their kids go, apparently, because the kids liked the candy and parents didn't think it harmful. The *20/20* segment showed two children who were picked up from home, "serviced," and dropped off again, all within nine minutes. A civil suit by the State of Indiana charges Guzek with $4 million in improper billings over a two-and-a-half-year period.[72]

- *Give them bicycles or television sets:* One of the Indiana chiropractors, Robert Guzek, admitted to giving away bicycles and television sets as inducements when recruiting children for his clinic. In December 1999, he was fined $1 million and had his license suspended for one hundred years.[73]

- *Buy accident victims from "cappers":* In California, a "capper" is one who buys the names of (genuine) accident victims and then sells them to attorneys. Referrals are then made to clinics, which provide some services and bill for many more.[74]

- *Gifts for the elderly:* In August 1999, George Gorodetsky, owner of two DME supply companies in Seattle, was arrested for defrauding Medicare and Medicaid. According to the U.S. Attorney, elderly Russian immigrants were lured to stores or to doctors' offices with promises of gifts. Their Medicare or Medicaid numbers were taken and used in subsequent billings for back braces and elbow supports—to the tune of $1.9 million. The patients did not receive the equipment, nor did they need it.[75] (This example illustrates a much broader trend, where providers within an immigrant or ethnic group target their own population, exploiting the trust within such communities, and minimizing the chance of complaints to American authorities.)

- *Offer free foot exams:* In September 1999, thirteen podiatrists and five assistants were charged with Medicare fraud in New York City. Patients were lured with offers of free foot exams to "Citywide Footcare," which then billed Medicare around $30 million between 1996 and 1998, mostly for fraudulent services. According to U.S. Attorney David Finn, the scheme targeted elderly and minority residents of low-income neighborhoods. Michael Brumer and Lawrence Klein, physicians, who oversaw the operation spanning clinics across New York City, had been suspended from Medicare in 1989 for fraud and for "gross negligence and incompetence." Three of the other doctors had previous suspensions, and two had previous convictions for Medicare fraud. For one particularly busy day—January 12, 1998—one of the physicians (Albert Kalajian) billed fifty claims to Medicare covering 150 procedures on twenty-eight patients, for $8.6 million.[76]

- *Borrow someone else's captive population:* One cost-efficient method for recruiting patients is to do it "by the boatload": Use populations already organized and housed by someone else. An obvious target is nursing home populations—a problem recognized by the General Accounting Office (GAO) in 1996.[77] Here are some recent examples:

‣ *Target patients suffering from Alzheimer's disease or dementia:*
   In April 1999, Forest Health Systems, Inc. of Illinois and Forest Hospital agreed to pay $4 million to settle a *qui tam* suit.
   The hospital had targeted patients suffering from Alzheimer's
   disease and dementia for its partial hospitalization program,
   even though patients with such conditions do not benefit
   from the treatment provided in such programs. Some elderly
   patients, who spoke no English, were bused from nursing
   homes and assisted-living facilities to a Forest-affiliated facility, where virtually no psychiatric care was provided. The
   whistle-blower suit was originally filed in 1996 by a registered
   nurse and a certified nursing assistant.[78]

‣ *Offer free eye exams for everyone:* One group optometry practice sent salespeople to the director of nursing or social
   worker at different nursing facilities to offer routine eye examinations for all the patients, at no cost. Such examinations
   are not covered by Medicare; the nursing staff provided access
   to the patients' records, enabling the optometry practice to
   use them as the basis for billings to Medicare. The nursing
   home residents did receive their free eye examinations, but
   Medicare was billed for all kinds of other services that were
   never provided.[79]

‣ *Diapers for everyone:* William Harris, of Toledo, Ohio, owned
   a firm that between 1993 and 1996 sold incontinence kits to
   nursing homes. His firm purchased adult diapers for between
   $.25 to $.45, which he then billed to Medicare as more complex devices (such as "female urinary collection devices") at
   between $8.35 and $22.57. After his firm was suspended from
   Medicare for billing fraud, he set up three more companies
   and kept on billing. He eventually pleaded guilty to a count of
   conspiring to submit $42 million in false claims to Medicare,
   and of laundering $9 million. He also consented to seizure of
   his real estate assets, which included more than 1,000 rental
   units in Toledo and eleven properties in the Cayman Is-
   lands.[80]

‣ *Long-distance diapers:* In July 1999, Michael Paul Bielaus was
   indicted in New Orleans for conspiring to defraud Medicare
   of over $7 million. Bielaus and his sales force used the
   promise of free adult diapers to sign up nursing homes for his

company's "special program." He then billed Medicare for a range of urological supplies, for which few of the patients even qualified under Medicare rules. Bielaus, who was involved with a number of different health care companies, pleaded guilty in Pensacola earlier in the same month to similar charges and admitted to having submitted more than $8 million in fraudulent claims from two companies in Destin. He had also set up a mail drop in Buffalo, New York, so that he could pretend to conduct business in New York State and submit claims through Upstate Blue Cross, a New York insurer, which pays for some supplies that other regions do not.[81]

- *Lock them up:* In 1994, National Medical Enterprises (NME), owners of one of the nation's largest psychiatric hospital chains, pleaded guilty to paying kickbacks and bribes for patient referrals. Many of the allegations involved the recruitment of community workers and church workers to refer patients for psychiatric care, and many patients complained of being held against their will. NME agreed to pay $362.7 million in what was, at the time, the largest settlement between the government and a health care provider.[82] In addition, NME paid over $230 million in settlement of suits brought by sixteen private insurers and more than 130 patients.[83]

There is little reason to believe that the NME settlement eliminated abuses by inpatient psychiatric facilities. In May 1997, the *Boston Sunday Globe* questioned the business trends of many of the major psychiatric and general hospitals throughout Massachusetts. The *Globe* cited the case of one twenty-four-year-old woman who was receiving treatment at Westwood Lodge Psychiatric Hospital, paid for by Medicare, for an eating disorder. On Christmas Eve, she was abruptly transferred to a locked ward, together with a number of other patients who had admitted themselves voluntarily, and confined for a week. When she asked why, a member of staff told her "the census is down." [84]

The *Globe* investigation placed such individual experiences in a broader context. Reporters observed that the Westwood Hospital had been acquired in March 1995 by "Charter Behavioral Health Systems" in Atlanta, Georgia; the company had previously paid $2 million to the government to settle charges of improperly paying providers in Virginia for referring Medicaid and Medicare patients. The report also pointed out the shifting market base for this and other hospitals in the state: [85]

> Just a few years ago, Westwood Lodge psychiatric hospital was up against it: ownership in flux, patient stays declining, insurers drying up. But in a move that mirrors the changing landscape of mental health care in Massachusetts, it is now turning a handsome profit with a new clientele—poor, elderly or disabled people who are committed against their will and whose treatment is paid for with taxpayer money.

Cutbacks in mental health coverage by private insurers may have driven psychiatric hospitals back to Medicare and Medicaid patients. In 1997, these two programs paid for roughly 72 percent of psychiatric admissions to private hospitals in Massachusetts, up from 40 percent in 1990. Between 1990 and 1997, locked wards had proliferated, the number of patients being admitted to them against their will (and, according to the *Globe*'s research, on some pretty flimsy pretexts) rising by more than 50 percent. One psychiatric nurse told the *Globe* that her hospital "had strict admission standards in the beginning. Now it takes anyone who shows up." [86]

Commenting on the dozens of Massachusetts general hospitals that have added locked psychiatric wards since 1988, despite the squeeze on mental health reimbursements by private insurers, Daniel Fisher, a psychiatrist and advocate for the mentally ill, explained, "They spend a lot of time converting medical beds to psych beds because it is so lucrative. . . . They have to make sure they keep them filled so they don't lose money."

For their part, hospital officials argued that they commit patients for the patients' safety and for the safety of those around them, not because of their insurance. They say economics has nothing to do with the growing public reimbursements, nor the escalating number of involuntary commitments, nor the hiring of for-profit consultants to run the wards. They say they have added locked wards and are paid more because of the increasing severity of illnesses.

Cooperating Patients

Life is easier for the fraud perpetrators if the patients cooperate. *Paying* them to do so is easier than imprisoning them, and safer than sedating them.

- New York psychologist, Viola Wiegand, was convicted in April 1997 for sending Medicare 10,000 false claims, reaping $2.5 million for services she did not provide. In exchange for 25 percent of whatever insurers paid her, she persuaded individuals to feign automobile and workplace accidents. She would then diagnose posttraumatic stress disorder and bill for therapy over protracted periods. According to her billing patterns, she claimed for as many as thirty-five sessions per day, at sixty or ninety minutes each session.[87]

- In October 1997, three men in Minnesota pleaded guilty to money laundering charges that arose from the staging of phony car accidents. They had cheated insurance companies out of $500,000 for treatment of accident-related injuries at bogus medical clinics, set up in vacant offices.[88] (Organized criminal rings, linking clinics, attorneys, and auto repair shops have grown up all around the country.)

One veteran investigator, who makes a habit of calling Medicaid patients to ask them what services they have or haven't received, told me that, the first time they were asked, significant numbers of patients denied knowledge of services billed in their names. After a week or so, however, they would suddenly recall the illness and the treatment. Noticing that these apparently forgetful patients were concentrated in specific neighborhoods, the investigator wondered what had happened *between* times. Presumably, the "patients" were alarmed when first contacted by Medicaid officials, and followed their natural instincts to deny knowledge. Then, after consultation with their friendly neighborhood provider, they realized it would be better to go along with the story *as billed*—at which point they suddenly remembered the illness and treatment in question.

Communities and Networks

The idea that entire communities can make a living out of health care fraud is not new. In 1992, the FBI, in one of their earliest forays into health care fraud, launched "Operation Goldpill." In synchronized raids across the country, they arrested one hundred pharmacists, other health care professionals, and prescription drug distributors, who were then charged with carrying out widespread fraud through excessive billings and the illegal diversion, repackaging, and distribution of prescription medicine.[89] Operation Goldpill targeted a particular type of pharmacy fraud involving illegal recycling of prescription medicines.

Pharmaceutical recycling schemes typically work as follows: Physicians set up clinics in a large city. They employ "runners" to recruit poor, or homeless, or drug-addicted, or otherwise indigent people, most of them covered by the government's Medicaid program, who would willingly spare half an hour to earn some ready cash. Each recruit is led to the clinic where the doctor (in a few minutes) diagnoses a fictitious ailment and then issues a prescription for expensive medication. The doctor subsequently claims an hour's consultation for each patient from Medicaid.

The "patient" is then taken (or sent) to a local pharmacy to have the prescription filled—again at government expense. Upon leaving the pharmacy, the patient finds someone just outside, car trunk open, waiting to buy the drugs back from the patient for $10 or $15. The recruited patients are pleased to accept the cash, and probably return the next day for a repeat performance. The buyers are known as "non-men," because they deal in noncontrolled drugs. Through the non-men, the drugs are repackaged and fed back into the pharmacy supply chain; the recyclers reap enormous profits, once again at the insurer's expense. Such schemes have particularly plagued the Medicaid program, especially in the nation's major cities. Operation Goldpill was the first coordinated, nationwide attack on this type of scam.

Pharmaceutical fraud—the focus of Operation Goldpill—does not seem to have abated since 1992, either. Investigators in major U.S. cities describe "whole communities living off Medicaid fraud." For many recipients, they say, Medicaid fraud is a full-time job. Anyone can make $150 to $300 per day if they "hustle": getting prescriptions, selling them to pharmacies, or getting the drugs and reselling them. The cost to the government is more like $2000 per day per person, with the providers and middlemen taking the rest. As one investigator told me, "They take that Medicaid card like you take a cash card—they just have to make a couple of stops at a physician [to get a prescription] and pharmacy [to sell the prescription, or the drugs] to get the cash."

Health care fraud is often committed by networks of individuals, often bound together by ethnic ties, sometimes by simply living in the same neighborhood, or—as was the case with Operation Goldpill—all members of the same graduating class at pharmacy school.[90]

- *Pay everybody:* According to indictments handed down in November 1998, Nelson DeLaCerda of Florida (operating as Flamingo

Medical Supply, Inc.) submitted fraudulent claims for home oxygen therapy to Palmetto Government Benefits Administrators, a Medicare carrier located in Columbia, South Carolina. DeLaCerda allegedly had an extensive payroll: He used an oxygen testing service that provided phony test results; he paid a physician $100 cash for each signature on fraudulent or blank prescription forms; he paid cash to Medicare beneficiaries in exchange for being able to use their numbers to bill Medicare; and then he paid a Florida billing service to inflate the fraudulent claims yet further.[91]

No Meat, Faster Money

Eventually, every self-respecting scam artist confronts the most fundamental dilemma of the health care fraud business: Is it really worth bothering with the patients?

Patients are a nuisance. They take up your time. Sometimes they are actually sick. Sometimes they are uncooperative. Sometimes they tell on you if you don't smooth-talk them or pay them enough. Why not just *bill*? After all, you could bill a lot more, and a lot faster, and take much more care to bill *correctly* if you didn't waste so much time with patients, pretending to provide medical care. If you decide not to see patients, the only constraint on how much you can make is how fast you can bill and how widely you can spread the billings (across multiple patients, provider numbers, and insurance companies) so that nobody notices. With those pesky details, computers help a lot.

The real mystery is why so many scam artists actually do bother with the patients. If they understood how easily they could hide their billings within the 900 million claims Medicare processes each year, they might change their ways. Of course, those who want to stay in the same place and do business under the same name for a long time would prefer, should they happen by some misfortune to get caught, that their cases hinged on complicated questions of medical necessity (then they can hire expert witnesses to defend them) rather than on relatively unambiguous questions, which juries can fathom, such as *were the services provided.*

Many industry officials recognize the ease with which automated billing schemes can rip millions out of the system. During the course of my fieldwork, I interviewed the director of monitoring and analysis at one of the four DME regional processing sites for Medicare:

If I wanted to do fraud I'd call South Carolina [National DME Suppliers' Clearing House] and get a [supplier] number, pay a $75 fee, set up in some office across the street and start billing. I'd bill $5 million in thirty days and walk away. It's mine to keep. Period.

Coming from an official directly responsible for monitoring such abuses and as knowledgeable about the defenses as anyone, this statement certainly leads one to question the adequacy of existing control systems.

Officials have had plenty of warning concerning these threats. Some significant cases of computerized billing fraud came to light more than ten years ago. For example, in 1988, a Bronx shoe store owner was sentenced to between one and three years in prison for bilking $1.1 million from the state Medicaid program. His computerized billing system, automatically preprogrammed according to a recipient's sex and age, added such extra items as heels, lifts, arches, and supports to thousands of orders for women's and children's prescription footwear, and billed for scores of men's shoes the store did not even stock. The owner of the store also set up a second billing company on Long Island so that state auditors would not detect the jump in his Bronx store's claims from $103,114 to over $1 million in a few months.[92]

Also in 1988, a New York court convicted Sheldon Weinberg, a physician, and his two sons of stealing $16 million from Medicaid between 1980 and 1987. The Weinbergs falsely billed Medicaid for close to 400,000 phantom patient visits by programming their medical center's computer to generate phony claims and backup medical charts for as many as 12,000 fictitious visits per month.[93]

In order to operate any sizeable billing scheme, one has first to obtain a collection of patient names and insurance numbers—another little problem that has generated some interesting ideas. One obvious method (to borrow a term from the world of credit card fraud) is to engage in "dumpster diving"— sorting through the trash of a hospital or clinic; or you can buy *lists* of patients, which circulate on the black market; or recruit a co-conspirator within a claims processing operation; or bribe someone who works in a hospital billing office to bring home a floppy disk full of patient names and numbers. Here are some other ideas:

- *Break in:* In December 1997, burglars broke into two clinic buildings in southeast Florida, in one case smashing through a wall. Nothing appeared to have been taken, except patient records.[94]

- *Collaborate with an insider:* Daniel Perez was paid $8 per hour as a clerk, and in March 1997 he was charged with embezzling $1.3 million from Medicaid. He was employed by Unisys Corporation, the contractor used by Florida's Medicaid program to process claims. Apparently part of a much larger conspiracy, Perez had identified within the claims processing system more than twenty providers who hadn't billed Medicaid since 1994. He changed their addresses within the provider databases, and unauthorized claims in their names then began to flow. According to the Florida Department of Law Enforcement, conspirators cashed checks ranging from $3,000 to $28,000 at banks throughout Florida, New York, Connecticut, the Bahamas, Puerto Rico, and Columbia. State officials estimate they may have lost over $20 million to this scheme.[95]

- *Use your own voter lists:* Florida State Senator Alberto Gutman, chair of the Florida Senate Health Care Committee, pleaded guilty to using voter lists from his district to concoct a fraudulent Medicare scheme. The indictment against Gutman states that he helped create ghost patients and phony documents, and had a secret interest in two home health care firms, receiving nearly $2 million in improper claims. He was also accused of paying off corrupt doctors and encouraging grand jury witnesses to lie about the scheme. His fifteen years as a state senator ended in October 1999, when he resigned after pleading guilty to conspiracy. He faces two years in prison. His wife, also charged in the scheme, previously entered a plea agreement.[96]

Widespread, well-orchestrated computerized billing schemes represent one of the most serious modern threats to the financial integrity of health systems. In February 1998, the *New York Times* reported that government investigators were trying to unravel one such scheme, which they estimated had already resulted in more than $1 billion in fake claims. This particular scheme, they believed, was aimed at commercial insurance companies rather than public programs. The bills submitted used the names of scores of patients and doctors, none of whom appeared to have knowledge of the scheme. Entire medical episodes, complete with diagnoses, had been fabricated (resulting, among other harms, in patients being listed with illnesses they had never had). According to the *Times'* sources within law enforcement, only a few (mostly low-level) operatives had been arrested, and the scheme was organized so that none of these knew the identities of those above them in the conspiratorial hierarchy.

Investigators discovered that some of the lower-level participants, whose job it was to cash the checks, didn't even know which crime business they were in. They knew they were laundering money, but thought it was *drug* money.

Investigators could not tell for sure whether this was one big scheme or a proliferation of smaller, similar ones. One clue pointing to a mega-conspiracy was the fact that the same patient and doctors' names popped up all over the country. But that could equally well be explained by the fact that lists for such purposes circulate freely on the black market. The scheme, however, revealed the deliberate and artful construction of thousands of fake claims, each of which used real patients and doctors' names and numbers, the diagnoses and procedure codes matching up perfectly. The dollar amounts were designed to stay below thresholds likely to trigger scrutiny. Many of the clinics or businesses from which the fake claims originated would appear for a while, bill fast and furious, and then vanish without a trace before authorities could catch up with them. A spokesman for the Florida Department of Insurance told the *Times*, "In terms of health-care fraud, this is the biggest thing on our plate. It's out of control; it's draining our resources."[97]

Two southern Florida men were indicted in January 1998 for their part in a similar scheme. According to the indictment, they had defrauded twenty-seven private companies out of more than $10 million. Both men had prior criminal convictions for fraud or drug trafficking. The perpetrators allegedly set up thirteen fictitious companies that posed as medical service providers, submitted over $50 million in fraudulent claims, and received more than $10 million, which they deposited in bank accounts they controlled under aliases.[98]

In October 1999, the GAO published a review of recent cases involving career criminals and organized crime. Commissioned by Senators Susan Collins (R-Maine) and Dick Durbin (D-Illinois), the study reviewed seven criminal health care fraud investigations, each concluded between 1992 and 1998. These scams fraudulently claimed amounts ranging from $795,000 to more than $120 million, and involved (between them) more than 160 sham medical entities: "For the most part, these entities existed only on paper." These broad-based billing scams made extensive use of patient brokering, rent-a-patient schemes, recruiters and runners, drop boxes, bogus corporations, and phony corporate bank accounts. "These activities sometimes continued even after subjects were indicted, arrested, or jailed." In one case, a perpetrator set up companies in the names of other criminals he had met in jail. Each of the seven cases exploited between 35 and 2,500 beneficiary accounts. In some cases, the conspirators obtained physicians' details and UPINs (unique physician identification numbers) from available registers (e.g., "The Little Blue Book") or from the Internet; in other cases, they paid cooperating physicians $50 or $100 to falsify medical records, creating purely fictitious medical diagnoses and courses of treatment. In four of the seven cases, the subjects of the investigation had criminal records for crimes unrelated to health care. Two of them were on probation for other crimes when they committed health care fraud. The groups' leaders had little or no known medical or health care education, training, or experience. The investigations revealed criminal groups teaching health fraud techniques to others.[99]

Fifteen Million in a Day

During my field research—as I toured Medicare contractors, Medicaid programs, and private insurers—I became so concerned about the possibility of such schemes running undetected for long periods, or forever, that I addressed the threat with staff at each institution. To make the discussion more concrete, I constructed a hypothetical fraud scam in which a perpetrator might steal $15 million in just one billing cycle. Here's the scam:

Suppose a perpetrator, operating from a small clinic or physician's office, electronically submits a modest $1,500 claim for treating one patient. Imagine the treatment is for some trauma or accident-related injury—the kind of injury that does not depend upon gender or age or the presence of an underlying medical condition, and thus could befall anybody. A week later, the perpetrator receives a check for $1,500 from the insurer. The provider may or may not have seen the patient; it doesn't matter. The important thing is the provider has established that this claim went through the system, electronically, to payment (called "auto-adjudication") without tripping any kind of review. In other words, the diagnosis, the treatment, the coverage, and the pricing all fell within normal parameters.

Now the perpetrator takes his computerized file of eligible patients, which he purchased on the black market, downloaded from a hospital database, or obtained from a corrupt employee within the insurance company. He programs his office computer to generate 10,000 claims, all identical to the original, but using 10,000 different patients' identities. He submits all 10,000 claims on the same day, using free software provided by the insurer.

Question: Will the perpetrator receive a check or checks amounting to $15 million (10,000 x $1,500) at the conclusion of the next processing cycle? One would certainly hope not.

At each site, I discussed this scenario with the management of the various functional units. Postutilization review would probably not pick up on this scheme until at least three months later; by this time, the perpetrator would have long since vanished. Prepayment edits generally serve only to ensure that each claim is presented and processed correctly and that no one patient has had too much of something lately. What else, if anything, would flag such a scheme and prevent the loss?

A number of prepayment controls, had they been adopted, would have eliminated this risk entirely. For example:

1. An automatic suspension of high-dollar-value checks (above some arbitrary threshold), pending human review of the contributing claims.
2. Provider-level monitoring, where a provider's payments in each cycle are aggregated and reasonable thresholds are set for each specialty. To be of use against this hypothetical scam, the provider's aggregate behavior would have to be monitored *pre*payment, not postpayment.
3. Acceleration-rate checks, which compare a provider's aggregate activity in one cycle with previous billing patterns as a way of watching for sudden accelerations. Again, it would have to happen *pre*payment.
4. Random review of some modest percentage of claims (so that at least *some* of the 10,000 would come up for routine verification). The verification would have to include some external validation methods such as calling the patients.
5. Any kind of cluster-detection software, operated prepayment, which could spot unnatural similarity in the provider's claims even though they each referred to a different patient.

Any of these five prepayment controls would easily detect the scheme. Unfortunately, even in the year 2000 (more than a decade since we began seeing such computerized billing schemes), not one of these defenses is yet standard in the industry. The majority of claims processors, including most of the largest Medicare contractors, do not employ these controls. Random review, with external validation, is extremely rare. Provider-level profiling and acceleration-rate monitoring are increasingly common, but only occur several months after payment, under postutilization review.

Cluster-detection methods are almost unheard of within the industry; they are applied only postpayment, if at all.

That leaves only the first item: Review of the big checks. Managers at three of the top five Medicare contractors in the country and also at one of the largest private payers in the country, when presented with this scenario, all expressed a vague hope that somebody, somewhere within their organizations, reviewed big checks before they were sent out. In each organization, no one could identify who it would be, which department would be responsible, or what the dollar threshold was that would trigger such a review. The managers eventually conceded it probably did not get done at all. At least for the processors I visited (which were selected because they were reputedly the best in the business), the scam would work, and the perpetrator would most likely get his or her $15 million check at the end of the week.

During my exit interview with senior management at one of Medicare's four DME regional contractors, I discussed this extraordinary vulnerability with the vice president for finance, who had overall responsibility for Medicare payment integrity at the firm. We considered the possibility of $100 million scams, each of which might only take a day or two to perpetrate, and I asked him and his assembled managers how many times they thought their company would need to fall victim to such schemes before being put out of business. His answer, as obviously true as it is alarming, was, "Oh, [company name] probably wouldn't even notice—it's not our money." He explained that the Medicare claims payments were "just government money passing through." What was *their* money? Answer: As claims processors, their money is the difference between what they get paid by HCFA to process claims and what it costs them to process them.

A senior Medicare official filled me in on the rest of the story. He said, "You know the *cheapest* way to process a claim? Pay it without question."

At another insurance company, which seemed somewhat more cognizant of the risks, staff told me they thought the industry would never realize "what a monster they had created with [electronic claims processing]" until some company somewhere took a $20-million hit in one weekend. Only then would the industry wake up to the threat. That assumes, of course, that someone would notice the $20-million hit. If anyone happened to be in the air-conditioned computer room at the time, probably the only thing that person would notice would be the hum of the cooling fans. Perhaps, later, utilization review might notice the pattern if they happened to examine the right segment of the industry. Or perhaps not. If they did, one has to wonder whether we would ever hear about it. Many companies, anxious to maintain their shareholders' confidence and afraid of appearing incompetent, would never tell. Such multimillion-dollar losses could conceivably occur with some regularity throughout the industry without the ultimate losers—the taxpaying public and premium-paying policyholders—ever hearing of it.

A senior Medicaid fraud investigator, who said he had been trying to tell everyone about the dangers of electronic claims submission for more than ten years, warned, "With EDI (Electronic Data Interchange), thieves get to steal megabucks at the speed of light and we get to chase after them in a horse-and-buggy. No rational businessman would ever invent a system like this."

PART ONE

The State of the Art

1

Control Failures

What makes the health care system in general, and claims-payment systems in particular, such attractive targets for fraud? Why (if public opinion on the subject turns out to be correct) does fraud continue to run rampant, attracting such an extraordinary array of characters? Why has health care become America's favorite get-rich-quick playground?

The fundamental reason is that the industry's standard detection and control systems are not aimed at criminal fraud at all. The software "edits" and "audits" built into modern, highly automated claims processing systems have all been designed with honest providers in mind and serve the purpose of catching errors, verifying eligibility, making sure procedure codes match up with the diagnoses, and checking that the price charged is within bounds. When claims fail these standard tests, the system automatically returns them to the submitter, with a computer-generated explanatory message detailing exactly what they did wrong.

Criminals, intent on stealing millions of dollars as fast as possible, have an easy time. All they need to do is to aim their claims smack in the center of medical orthodoxy and policy coverage—like finding the sweet spot on a tennis racket—and they can rest assured the automated systems will process their claims at the speed of light and with no human involvement at all (a process called "auto-adjudication"). In other words, to beat all the industry's prepayment defenses, all they need to do is bill correctly. Provided they bill correctly, they are free to lie. They can fabricate or alter diagnoses. They can bill for additional services that were never performed. In many cases, they can fabricate entire medical episodes, and even bill for courses of treatment for patients they have never ever seen. The rule, for the thieves in the system, is simple: *Bill your lies correctly.* Provided they do that, they can rely on the payment systems to *process their lies correctly,* and pay them.

Investigators and analysts all across the country have witnessed the growth, during the 1990s, of what they call "perfect paper schemes" (a term of art carried over from the time when most claims were submitted on paper). Others call them "canned records." Perpetrators explore the claims-payment system with what could be termed the shotgun-and-rifle approach. First, to see what happens, they blast a broad range of claims at the system. Some fly back with auto-rejection notices. Some may prompt a human review, which generates mail. Some will be paid, probably electronically, without a hiccup. Having found the "holes" with the shotgun blast, perpetrators then train their rifles on those holes, firing over and over again. The essential tools of the trade, at that point, are a computer and an extensive list of patients' identities. For some types of claim, they also need a list of physicians' identification numbers so that they can plug into each claim the identity of a referring or authorizing physician.

When they have found combinations that work, perpetrators ratchet up the volume, spreading the fraudulent activity across hundreds or thousands of patients to avoid detection. Nothing within the routine operations of the payment systems checks that the patient was sick; or that the patient received the treatment; or that the patient has ever heard of the provider in question. Most patients never know that their identities were used. A subset of patients, who receive "explanations of medical benefits" or other notifications from their insurers, and review them, find providers, illnesses, and treatments of which they knew nothing. Many report it. And most often the resulting "dispute" is handled—if it is handled at all—as a simple "billing error." (More of that later, in Chapter 3.)

Insurers, public and private, pay on trust, which—given the presence of so many thieves in the system—is sorely misplaced. The principal vulnerability of large, automated payment systems isn't to unauthorized intrusion, or "hacking," as is popularly believed. Instead, the major worry is that these systems will work perfectly, quickly, and efficiently, time after time—but with incoming claims that are themselves false. The surprising motto for the modern, hi-tech version of health care fraud is that *fraud works best when processing systems work perfectly.*

A distressingly high proportion of officials within major claims processing environments seem curiously unaware of these fundamental flaws in their payment safeguards. When you question the vulnerability of their systems to fraud, they respond quite often by talking about "quality controls" and the high rates of "payment accuracy" achieved. Do they call the patients and ask whether it happened? In many claims processing environments, never.

Two Distinct Sciences:
Fraud Detection and Utilization Review

This book focuses on criminal fraud, rather than on the grayer areas of abuse and overutilization. The reason for drawing the distinction is that fraud controls play to a distinctively different audience. Control systems may work very well in pointing out billing errors to well-intentioned physicians and may even automatically correct errors, adjust claims, and limit code manipulation. But those same systems might offer no defense at all against determined, sophisticated thieves, who treat the need to bill "correctly" as the most minor of inconveniences. Most competent fraud perpetrators study the rule book carefully—probably more carefully than most honest providers—because they want to avoid scrutiny at any cost; they therefore "test" claims carefully before increasing the volume.

The industry's standard controls are designed with only one audience in mind: honest providers. These providers are sometimes error prone; perhaps not up-to-date on administrative requirements and regulations; on occasions sloppy and disorganized; often confused by complex or indecipherable rules. For this audience, control systems serve the purpose of correcting errors, testing eligibility, matching diagnoses to procedure codes, checking pricing, and, if necessary, sending claims back for correction.

But effective fraud-control systems must deal with a second, quite different, audience: sophisticated, well-educated criminals; some of them medically qualified; some technologically sophisticated; all determined to steal just as much as they can just as fast as possible. They read manuals, attend seminars, take the free software provided by the insurers, and really appreciate all the help and training they can get in how to bill correctly, how to avoid prepayment medical review, and how not to "stick out" under postpayment utilization review. They attend the conferences organized by their segment of the industry. In closed-door sessions—where they check first that no law enforcement or government officials are in the room—they put their heads together and work out which areas of billing are being scrutinized by the Office of Inspector General (OIG) or other authorities, and which are free and clear. (We know this, because law enforcement agents have managed to infiltrate such sessions.)

One of the most basic failures of control is the industry's historical failure to distinguish *processing accuracy* from *claim verification;* to distinguish the utilization pattern revealed by a provider's claims from the truthfulness of those claims; to distinguish the detection of unusual or inappropriate patterns of medical treatment from the detection of deception; to distinguish the science of utilization review from the science of fraud detection.

These two sciences overlap where criminal behavior, through the claims it produces, leaves behind it a pattern of medical unorthodoxy; to a limited degree, then, exercise of traditional utilization-review procedures (such as "provider-profiling" techniques) turns up fraud cases from time to time. The cases such methods turn up usually involve the less sophisticated and excessively greedy perpetrators who have billed so much, and in such a concentrated fashion, that they've made it into the "top 2 percent tail" of one of the industry's standard utilization distributions. The smart ones leave behind them no such trail; they fashion their lies on orthodox medical treatments and don't charge any more for *not* providing a service than honest doctors charge for providing it.

As long as fraud schemes do not produce anomalous billing patterns (bear in mind that the range of patterns monitored remains extremely limited—see Chapter 10), they will remain invisible, not only at the time of payment, but most likely forever. Most of what these systems lose to fraud nobody but the perpetrator ever knows about.

Find a Weakness and Exploit It Mercilessly

The cases that do come to light reveal the basic billing philosophy underlying many major schemes: Find a weakness and exploit it mercilessly. Time and time again, little pimples grow quickly into monstrous sores. Consider the following examples, all of which involve the actions of a single provider who has identified and then exploited a particular weakness:

- Surinder Singh Panshi, physician, "Bloodsucker of the 1980s," discovered the value of blood and dispatched his blood collectors all across New York City. In 1986, the Panshi labs only billed Medicaid a total of $1 million. The following year their billings jumped to $12 million. In 1988, to more than $31 million, accounting for more than 20 percent of Medicaid lab billings for the state of New York.

- National Health Labs' billings for ferritin tests, once they'd figured out how to incorporate them into their billing scheme, grew from less than $500,000 in 1988 to more than $31 million in 1990. Nobody noticed, until the whistle-blower suit came in from one of NHL's competitors.

- A 1997 Government Accounting Office (GAO) report disclosed that, in the fourth quarter of 1992, Medicare paid one supplier $211,900 for surgical dressing claims. A year later, for the same quarter, the tab exceeded $6 million. The Medicare claims processing contractor never became suspicious, despite the 2,800 percent increase. [1]

- Another Medicare supplier, who provided body jackets (custom-fitted spinal braces) billed roughly $2,300, quite steadily, for five successive quarters. Then, having established a track record without scrutiny, the supplier increased their quarterly payments first to $32,000, then $95,000, then $235,000, and then $889,000, all in successive quarters.[2] These escalating payments did not trigger a review by the Medicare contractor.

- William Harris, of Toledo, Ohio (mentioned in the introduction) discovered that he could buy diapers for less than $.50 and resell them to Medicare for upwards of $8. He billed $42 million, based on this one simple idea.

What Is "Control"?

Faced with these kinds of assaults, what would it mean to run an effective fraud-control operation? Does it mean making lots of arrests? Or maximizing the rate of financial penalties and recoveries? Not quite. Of course, law enforcement is an indispensable tool—a fraud-control tactic. But investigation is not the same as control, even though investigations may serve the purposes of a control strategy. Authorities make a grave mistake when they focus too heavily on the outputs of enforcement operations, because the simplest way to maximize the outputs of an enforcement operation is to permit law breaking to run rampant, and then skim off the easy cases by the bucketful.

Given the dynamic and constantly shifting nature of the game—which is characteristic of white-collar crime—we need a more meaningful idea of what constitutes effective control. And whatever conception we adopt has to take into account the essentially invisible nature of the problem—that you see only the parts of the problem that you detect; and hence if you employ lousy detection systems, you may not *see* much of a problem at all.

"Whack-a-mole," a familiar children's arcade game, presents an almost perfect model for fraud control. The game consists of a horizontal wooden deck with a set of little moles (in America) or mushrooms (the European version) embedded in it, just flush with the surface. From time to time these moles, or mushrooms, pop up in a completely unpredictable pattern. The child stands over the game with a rubber mallet in his or her hand and whacks them back down as fast as possible. The game tests the child's ability to react, fast and accurately, whenever new movement appears. To be good at this game, the child needs three simple skills: first, to be able to see clearly what is happening; second, to react quickly when something new pops up; third, to have effective *implements* in hand at the time, adequate for suppression.

Fraud control demands the same three things. We have to design control apparatus that emulates the children who play this game: alert, poised, full of keen anticipation, constantly scanning the board for new movement, and proud of the speed with which they react.

For effective fraud control, the following are necessary: first, the employment of instruments and systems that enable one to spot early, and to see clearly, emerging patterns of fraud; second, the ability to react quickly enough to eliminate vulnerabilities before too much damage can occur; third, the possession of effective tools that are available for deployment whenever and wherever new threats are spotted.

This kind of control-orientation suggests three important evaluative questions that we can use to identify what control systems in place within the health systems do well, and what they do badly:

1. What instruments or systems exist that enable insurers to see clearly the scope and nature of fraud threats and to spot new threats as they emerge?
2. How quickly does the control system react to new threats? When a new type of fraud scheme is identified, how long does it take to curtail the associated losses—days, months, or years?
3. Once something new does come to light, how effective are the tools in hand? Are they effective in eliminating the vulnerabilities, once recognized?

Within the health care industry, it is striking how much officials focus on the third of these three questions instead of the first two. Legislative initiatives, at the federal and state levels, provide more offenses that can be charged, stiffer penalties, additional grounds for exclusion, and increased resources for investigation and prosecution. They generally fail to address the ability to see the problems in the first place, create proactive intelligence systems designed to discover emerging threats, mandate a broader range of approaches to fraud detection systems, measure the fraud problem systematically, or incorporate a random component into the claims review operation (which would include external verification of the claims, e.g., interviewing the patients). However much we enhance control systems' ability to deal with fraud when it comes to light, the impact of such measures is limited by the fact that most fraud still remains invisible. In most fraud-control environments (not just health care), control inadequacies are much less a function of inadequate statutory powers than they are of inadequate instrumentation and sluggish response.

Rotten Segments, Sluggish Response

The sluggish response of control systems is revealed not only by the volume of payments that individual perpetrators can generate in short order, but also by the propensity for entire industry segments to grow up around questionable or fraudulent billing practices. In assessing the effectiveness of controls, it is always interesting to watch what happens to billings within a certain problem area when someone finally pays attention, does some focused audits, or makes a criminal case or two. Often the billings for an entire segment plummet precipitously, even without a change in regulations or policy. In some cases, the drops have amounted to more than 90 percent of the historical billings for the segment.

A reduction of 90 percent suggests a previous fraud prevalence of at least 90 percent (assuming that not everyone who was cheating is deterred and that honest providers have no reason to change their habits when cheats are caught). Some might argue with this interpretation by suggesting that legitimate billings could also be affected by the focused attention of law enforcement. Perhaps so—if that attention brings with it a change in policy or clarification of previously unclear regulations. But when a provider or providers are convicted of fraud in a criminal court (which suggests no ambiguity about the illegality of their actions), and that is all that happens, it is hard to understand why honest providers or legitimate billings should be affected. Previous literature on white-collar crime has often used information about such changes in behavior to draw inferences about previous levels of noncompliance.[3]

In recent years, the cycle of rapid escalation in particular industry segments, and sometimes in particular geographic areas, followed by precipitous declines when the control system eventually responds, has appeared over and over again. When Ed Kuriansky, former head of New York State's

Medicaid Fraud Control Unit, testified of "wave after wave of multimillion-dollar-fraud sweeping through the industry," he was describing precisely this phenomenon.

The following segments represent just a sample of those that have generated significant concern, at some time in the past and in a particular location, and then appear to have been substantially controlled. In many cases, they were controlled quite quickly and easily once the problem was actually spotted. These examples are presented roughly in the chronological order in which they first came to attention:

- *Orthopedic shoes (New York State Medicaid Program):* In November 1985, increased audit attention to the excessive fraud associated with orthopedic shoes in the state's Medicaid program achieved an 85 percent reduction in the billing for corrective footwear, which crashed down from highs estimated at $47.2 million annually.[4]

- *Lab billings (New York State Medicaid Program):* New York's statewide clinical lab billings dropped from a high of nearly $170 million in 1988 to just over $20 million in 1992—an 88 percent reduction—as a result of a small number of criminal prosecutions.[5]

- *Transcutaneous electrical nerve stimulation units, or "TENS" (Florida Medicare):* During the early 1990s, the yearly disbursements by Medicare for TENS units in Florida climbed to over $10 million. Then one DME (durable medical equipment) company called Osmomedic (of Tampa) was prosecuted. Osmomedic had enjoyed a highly profitable trade during the early 1990s, specializing in TENS units. These units use pulsating electrical currents to ease the suffering of chronic pain such as that caused by arthritis. Osmomedic would buy the units wholesale at $65 apiece and then bill Medicare $685 for each one sold. Medicare "reimbursed" Osmomedic $484 per item. Osmomedic sent doctors on the road to visit scores of Medicare beneficiaries in their homes with the express purpose of diagnosing arthritis so that a TENS unit could be prescribed. In six months, Medicare paid Osmomedic and the doctors (who also charged Medicare for their visits) over $500,000. Immediately after the prosecution of Osmomedic, the annual billings for TENS units (from all companies serving Florida) plummeted from $10 million to approximately $500,000 (i.e., a reduction of 95 percent).[6]

- *Podiatric services (New York State Medicaid):* In the early 1990s, Medicaid expenditures for podiatric services in the New York region dropped from nearly $35 million per year to $13.4 million—a reduction of 62 percent —following enforcement attention to this provider group and with no change in policy.[7]

More recently, the Medicare program has witnessed phenomenal growth in certain industry segments—all across the country—only to discover, several years later, that a huge proportion of the billings associated with the new growth industry were fraudulent or abusive. Again, roughly in the order in which they have come to light:

- *Incontinence supplies:* In 1994, the OIG reported on trends in Medicare billings for incontinence supplies. In three years, total payments for these supplies increased by 160 percent, from $88 million in 1990 to $230 million in 1993. Oddly enough, during the same period, the number of Medicare beneficiaries receiving these supplies fell from 312,000 to 293,000; the average annual payments, per patient, had jumped from $282 to $786. Patients needing these supplies suddenly seemed to need an awful lot more of them. When the OIG examined a sample of the billings from 1993, they discovered that "questionable billing practices may account for almost half of incontinence allowances in 1993." The OIG's report on the matter also noted that $88 million, out of the $230 million paid in 1993, had been paid for incontinence accessories that were not used in conjunction with a prosthetic device—which is the underlying qualification for Medicare reimbursement.[8]

  (For those not versed in the terminology of the OIG, I should explain that "questionable" in this context means that they are pretty sure the claims were fraudulent. They know they probably could not prove criminal intent in many instances even though all the circumstances point to it. They dare not actually call these claims "fraudulent" because they'd get pounced on immediately by the industry lobbyists and their political allies. Instead, they call them "questionable.")

- *Durable medical equipment:* In 1996, the OIG conducted a study of DME billings in five states. They concluded, after examining the claims and their contexts, that 40 percent of the claims were inappropriate (i.e., would not have been paid had Medicare known the circumstances). Not 40 percent of those submitted, but 40 percent of those *paid.*

- *Wound care supplies:* In October 1995, the OIG reported their investigation into Medicare payments for wound care supplies. Since October 1993, these claims, falling under the general category of DME, have been processed by specialist contractors called DMERCs (DME regional contractors). The DMERCs were established to concentrate all the DME claims within a few claims-processing contractors to facilitate the detection of regional and national billing patterns and anomalies. As part of *Operation Restore Trust,* the OIG examined claims from a 1 percent sample of Medicare beneficiaries who had received wound care supplies between June 1994 and February 1995. They concluded, after reviewing the claims, that as much as two thirds of the $98 million in Medicare payments during that period were "questionable." [9]

Also in October 1995, the OIG conducted another inquiry into "wound care suppliers" that concentrated on the marketing techniques suppliers used. These suppliers had targeted nursing home populations; in 23 percent of the nursing homes in which they operated, the supplier representative—not the nursing home's staff—decided the number of supplies to be delivered each month. 13 percent of the nursing homes had been offered inducements to allow the supplier to provide wound care supplies. There was no guarantee that the supplies Medicare paid for were being used for Medicare patients; many of them went into a general supplies closet, available to all staff and all patients.[10]

Following these discoveries in 1995, increased attention was paid to the issue of wound care supplies. Reexamining the issue in 1998 (to see if the problem had been fixed), the OIG found that Medicare Part B payments for wound care supplies had decreased by half in just one year, from $143 million in 1995 to $74 million in 1996. Also, they reported, "allowances that exceeded Medicare's guideline parameters dropped by 90 percent, from $65 million to only $7 million." [11]

As fraud threats wax and wane, one of the ironies of the control business is that allowing problems to grow out of control, and then suddenly yanking them back under control, actually makes a control operation look good. By allowing problems to fester (I'm not suggesting that anyone does this deliberately), intervening *late,* and then extrapolating the savings subsequently achieved (measured from the very peak of the billing rates, and extended over several years), officials can claim to have achieved very sub-

stantial savings indeed through their interventions. Occasionally, those at
the OIG, like many others, are tempted to quantify their achievements this
way to represent their work in the best possible light. For example, the
1998 OIG report on wound care supplies notes this accomplishment:

> The allowances for wound care supplies have decreased dramatically. . . .
> Concerted efforts by HCFA, the DMERCs and the OIG in the form of pol-
> icy changes, utilization review, and reports have contributed to the declines
> in Medicare allowances documented in this report. . . . As a result, $58 mil-
> lion in excessive allowances was saved between 1995 and 1996. If these al-
> lowances continue to be held in check, 5-year savings of nearly $300 million
> could be achieved.[12]

If anyone is wondering how to interpret administrators' claims of having
saved many billions of dollars through fraud-control efforts, this is usually what they mean. They project, over several years, the reduction
achieved after suppressing a problem, having allowed it to escalate in the
first place to ridiculously high levels—where fraudulent or "questionable"
claims make up 50 percent, or even 90 percent, of the total billings. From
a taxpayer's perspective, we'd all prefer these problems to be identified
and dealt with much earlier, before fraudulent or abusive billing practices
come to dominate entire industry segments. In terms of whack-a-mole
performance, existing fraud-control systems have a long way to go yet.

Three other industry segments have recently embarked on their own
wild ride, at the expense of Medicare:

Community mental health centers (CMHCs): These centers provide treatment and services to mentally ill individuals in the community. Payments
to them for Partial Hospitalization Program (PHP) services were authorized under Medicare in 1990. In 1997, the Health Care Financing Administration (HCFA) and the OIG reviewed payments for partial hospitalization services to CMHCs in five states: Florida, Texas, Colorado,
Pennsylvania and Alabama. As a result of the review, the OIG estimated
that in the twelve-month period ending September 30, 1997, 91 percent of
the Medicare payments had been made for unallowable or highly questionable claims. [13] Extrapolating to the PHP budget in those five states,
that meant that $229 million, out of a total of $252 million, ought not to
have been paid.

On a national scale, the growth rate for this segment has been stunning.
Between 1993 and 1997, Medicare payments to CMHCs exploded from

$60 million in 1993 to $349 million in 1997. Average annual costs per patient grew from $1,642 to $10,352. And the number of CMHCs in the country grew from 296 to 769, despite an 8 percent reduction in the number of patients being served.[14] Summarizing their findings, the inspector general reported that

> In a program designed to pay for intensive outpatient psychiatric services provided to acutely ill individuals in order to prevent their hospitalization, Medicare was paying for PHP services to beneficiaries who had no history of mental illness or who suffered from mental conditions that would preclude them from benefiting from the program. In addition, Medicare was paying for therapy sessions that involved only recreational and diversionary activities such as drawing, arts and crafts, watching television, and playing bingo and other games.[15]

Home health care: Changes in Medicare law in the 1980s led to increasing use of home health services under the program. But no one really anticipated the phenomenal growth that would follow. Between 1989 and 1997, the number of certified home health agencies (HHAs) increased from 5,700 to almost 10,000; and the number of home visits shot from 70 million to 250 million. In the same period, Medicare payments jumped from $2.7 billion to about $18 billion.[16] Eventually, with thousands of additional agencies queuing up to serve Medicare, HCFA imposed a moratorium on new entrants in an attempt to buy the time needed to impose better controls (including better initial screening and precertification surveys). (Chapter 2 describes the fierce resistance to these changes put up by the home health care lobby.)

In 1997, the GAO evaluated the controls in place at the time, particularly Medicare certification requirements for new Home Health Agencies:

> In summary, we are finding that Medicare's survey and certification process imposes few requirements on HHAs seeking to serve Medicare patients and bill the Medicare program. The certification of an HHA as a Medicare provider is based on an initial survey that takes place so soon after the agency begins operating that there is little assurance that the HHA is providing or is capable of providing quality care. Moreover, once certified, HHAs are unlikely to be terminated from the program or otherwise penalized, even when they have been repeatedly cited for not meeting Medicare's conditions of participation and for providing substandard care.[17]

For those who would steal, this has the makings of a great business opportunity. What proportion of the $18 billion paid to these agencies each year ought not to have been paid? The GAO researchers selected eighty high-dollar-value home health claims that had been processed and paid automatically by Medicare contractors. Review of these claims and their context resulted in denial of 43 percent of the total charges.[18] Does this mean that the improper payment rate across the industry was as high as 43 percent? Because the GAO deliberately selected higher-value claims, we cannot be sure they reflect the make-up of the entire population of claims. If you bear in mind, however, that most large fraud schemes are deliberately constructed around large numbers of *smaller* claims (to avoid arousing suspicion), generally that makes the biggest claims relatively clean; in this case, the overall improper payment rate would be higher than 43 percent.

The GAO report also noted that the claim review rate within Medicare for home health claims had been around 60 percent in Fiscal Years (FYs) 1986 and 1987, but had plummeted to only 2 percent in FY 1996. They attributed the decline to reductions in funding for Medicare payment safeguards during the period 1989–1996.[19]

The GAO also observed, with respect to home health, what several of the examples in the introduction observed more broadly: that you don't seem to need much health care experience to sign on as a provider and start billing the government. GAO found one owner of a home health agency whose most recent job experience was driving a taxicab; another ran a pawn shop as well as the agency. Previous criminal convictions were no bar to participation unless they happened to relate to health care fraud.[20] Medicare welcomed criminals provided they were new to this area of criminal enterprise. Nothing in the certification process related to the honesty of participants, only to their ability to deliver medical services.

In June 1997, the OIG conducted a more extensive review of Home Health Care services in four states: California, Illinois, New York, and Texas. They drew a sample of claims approved and paid by fiscal intermediaries during the fifteen-month period ending March 31, 1996. They found that 40 percent of the services reviewed did not meet Medicare reimbursement requirements. A substantial number of the claims (18.4 percent) related to beneficiaries who were not even homebound! They estimated that in those four states for that period, out of $6.7 billion paid for home health services, $2.6 billion would have been disallowed had the services been reviewed.[21]

Two years later, the OIG followed up with a repeat analysis of the same four states to see whether the legislative provisions' kicking in and the increased enforcement attention had reduced the chronic concentration of improper claims. Based on a sample of home health claims submitted and paid in FY 1998, the proportion of improper claims appeared to have dropped from 40 percent to 19 percent of the claims submitted.[22]

Home oxygen therapy: In August 1999, the OIG reported on the use of home oxygen therapy.[23] Nearly one quarter of all the Certificates of Medical Necessity (CMNs) they examined were inaccurate or incomplete, and the OIG estimates Medicare paid $263 million in 1996 for oxygen equipment covered by inadequate documentation. Thirteen percent of the beneficiaries who had received such supplies never used any of them.

The Nature of the Response

For whatever reason, the health insurance industry's standard control operations seem incapable of spotting problems early and cutting them off before enormous amounts of damage have been done. They seem not to be able to emulate the child playing whack-a-mole—alert, poised, ready to respond at a moment's notice to new signs of trouble, hovering in keen anticipation of new developments. Rather, they seem to wait until they are drowning in moles; at this point, law enforcement moves in to dip its bucket into the vast accumulated reservoir of fraud.

The state of the art in fraud control, as currently developed, falls short. Neither government nor the commercial insurance sector knows how to run a fee-for-service system and keep thieves out.

Even when policymakers eventually discover that yet another segment has gone hog-wild, they tend to avoid fixing the fee-for-service system. They are tempted instead to transform the structure of the reimbursement systems in ways that they believe will "eliminate the incentive for overutilization." Thus the trend, in troublesome segment after troublesome segment, is to replace fee-per-service structures with some kind of standardized fee structure—Diagnosis Related Groups, Prospective Payment Systems, or even fully capitated managed care—where the payments are made on a per-patient per-month, or per-patient per-diagnosis basis.

Hence we see structural changes in the basis for reimbursing Medicare providers for wound care supplies. These supplies will not be paid for separately as Part B services but will in the future be bundled into the per diem payments at each facility for as long as the patient's stay at the facility is covered by Medicare (Part A).[24] This change follows the recommendation of the OIG when the problem was first studied in 1995: "A long-term solution would require HCFA to bundle services in their Medicare or Medicaid payments to nursing homes."[25]

For the troubled home health care segment, a major part of the long-term solution is to move that, too, over to a prospective payment system. The same goes for PHP services at Community Mental Health Clinics and for Rural Health Center (RHC) services, given a history of abuses in that segment.

Now why exactly do policymakers jump to this particular answer as the cure-all for fraud trouble spots? One former director of program integrity for Medicare succinctly captured the argument, in congressional testimony, in 1997:

> A prospective payment system would remove the incentives for providers to inflate their charges and would work to ensure that Medicare was only paying appropriate costs.[26]

Normally, we would applaud policymakers for searching out systemic, structural, or permanent solutions to problems, rather than merely intensifying oversight for a brief period and running the risk that the problem would later re-emerge.

But the virtually automatic adoption of this approach, as the preferred solution for fee-for-service fraud, presents a number of drawbacks.

First, it suggests there is no hope of ever managing a fee-for-service system properly; the only "fix" available is to scrap it and replace it with something else.

Second, the fix is indiscriminate. Honest and dishonest providers are all treated alike. No distinctions are made, and the system does not improve at distinguishing them. They all have to switch over to the new system, at considerable cost and inconvenience, no matter whether they have cheated in the past or not.

Third, whenever a fixed-fee system is introduced within a segment that, under fee-for-service structure, had been riddled with fraud, the capitation or prospective payment rates are set way too high, based on past fee-for-service levels that reflect the historical plundering. This structurally guarantees all providers an income that has a substantial fraud premium built in.

Fourth, the introduction of capitated or prospective payment systems carries with it an entirely new set of problems and new fraud types; these are considerably more dangerous to human health than the traditional fee-for-service frauds. Yes, such structures do indeed remove the incentive for overutilization, but they immediately replace it with an incentive for underutilization. Unscrupulous providers, still in the system, quickly switch from one method of cheating to another. Rather than billing for lots of services, many of which were not provided, now they take the fixed fees and run; they leave behind a trail of patients who did not get the wound care supplies, or the home health visits, or the therapy, or the medical care that they needed. Some patients suffer, even die, as a result. (Chapter 4 examines more closely the nature of fraud and the challenge of fraud control within a capitated managed care environment.)

If anyone doubts the ability of unscrupulous providers to respond instantly to a change of structural incentives and to reconstitute their own practices to their own financial advantage (and to the detriment of their patients), witness the account given by the director of a Medicaid Fraud-Control Unit(MFCU). During a recent fraud-control workshop, he described what happened at one physician's office that happened to be under surveillance by a team of investigators at the time the transition to managed care took effect. Before the change (i.e., under fee-for-service), investigators reported that the physician was always at his office, that his parking lot was always full, and that he worked extremely long hours every day. From the day his reimbursement shifted to capitation, he was hardly ever at his office—and paid much more attention to his real estate holdings. Now patients were seen by nurse assistants; if they were really sick, they were referred to the county clinic. This physician's behavior changed immediately and substantially in response to altered incentives, and would appear, therefore, not to be much governed by notions of medical professionalism.[27]

The MFCU director explained that many legislators and policymakers within his state did not seem to think the shift in financial structure (from fee-for-service to capitation) could significantly alter medical practice. He expressed the wish that high-level policymakers could better appreciate the street-level realities of the business.

America's love affair with capitated systems—as a structural fix for all the ills of the fee-for-service system—is already in trouble. The rate of transition from one system to the other has not been as rapid as many predicted, and it appears to be slowing. In some parts of the industry, the transition is in reverse. As we learn more about the new problems introduced by the inversion of the financial incentives, it becomes all the more imperative to learn how to run a fee-for-service system well without being knocked down repeatedly by wave after wave of fraud.

We should not have to wait until hundreds of millions of dollars have been stolen before control systems respond. We should not have to rely so heavily on whistle-blowers—who might or might not step forward—to reveal major problem areas. We should not jump to structural solutions that make no distinction between thieves and honest providers.

We should be able to design and put in place a system of controls that would routinely check that services paid for were actually provided; that they were medically necessary; and that they were not simply part of someone's get-rich-quick scheme. But before we can do that, we must be perfectly clear about the reasons existing control systems break down.

2

How Goes the War?

When it came to regulating health care fraud and abuse, the Clinton Administration put aside its customary conciliatory language of "customer service" and "partnerships with industry." They declared *war*. They pulled in the FBI and a range of other investigative and law enforcement resources. In 1993, Attorney General Janet Reno announced that she was making health care fraud the Department of Justice's number two priority, second only to violent crime. Since 1993, President Clinton and his senior officials have announced repeated "crackdowns" of various kinds.

At the outset, control of fraud and abuse was to be part of the administration's plans for comprehensive health care reform, with structural alterations designed to remove incentives for gaming the system. Following the demise of the centralized reform agenda, the administration pursued fraud and abuse control through a number of other avenues.

In 1995, the administration launched "Operation Restore Trust" as a demonstration project in five states—California, Florida, Illinois, New York, and Texas. The program was designed to demonstrate the value of partnerships in combating fraud and abuse (particularly partnerships between federal and state agencies), and to develop new approaches in identifying and controlling Medicaid and Medicare fraud. Program activities revolved around establishing interagency coordinating mechanisms within each of the five states to share intelligence, select cases, allocate resources, and coordinate investigations. "O.R.T.," as it is now known, focused on three particularly fraud-prone industry segments: home health care, durable medical equipment, and nursing homes. The administration claims that the program expended $7.9 million in the pilot phase (the first two years), and identified $188 million in payments due back to the government for a return on investment rate of 23 to 1. Because of that initial success, the administration expanded the program into twelve more states.

The years 1996 and 1997 saw the enactment of two significant pieces of fraud and abuse legislation at the national level that granted a wide range of additional powers to regulators. The first was the Health Insurance Portability and Accountability Act (HIPPA)—also known as the Kennedy-Kassebaum bill—enacted in August of 1996.[1] Like Clinton's reform proposals, the bill focused centrally on insurance market reforms, but incorporated a range of provisions designed to beef up the antifraud campaign. In its major provisions relating to fraud and abuse, the (HIPAA) act

- required the Attorney General and Secretary of the Department of Health and Human Services (HHS) to establish a Health Care Fraud and Abuse Control Program (HCFAC) to provide a coordinating national framework for federal, state, and local enforcement agencies and enlist private sector insurers and members of the public—notably Medicare beneficiaries—to fight fraud;
- created the Fraud and Abuse Control Fund, designed to provide a dedicated and more reliable funding stream for program integrity and fraud-control efforts (i.e., one less liable to fluctuate wildly depending on other components of the administrative budget);
- increased the civil monetary penalties under the False Claims Act (from twice the amount of the false claim, plus $2,000 per claim, to three times the amount of the claim, plus $5,000 to $10,000 per claim);
- created a set of health care fraud-related crimes: fraud, theft, or embezzlement in connection with a health care offense, false statements relating to health care offenses, and obstruction of criminal investigations of health care offenses;
- extended injunctive relief relating to health care offenses (including freezing of assets) and established criminal forfeitures for federal health care offenses;
- strengthened exclusion provisions relating to health care convictions;
- authorized HCFA (Health Care Financing Administration) to establish a Medicare Integrity Program (MIP) to create a separate and stable long-term funding mechanism for program-integrity activities; permitted HCFA to split off various program-integrity and fraud-related functions from its existing Medicare contractors and contract separately with other (or new) entities not bound by

the traditional claims-processing culture (these new "MIP" contractors have been referred to by President Clinton as "Medicare fraud hunters");[2]

- mandated expansion of the Beneficiary Notification Program to require HCFA to send an explanation of medical benefits (EOMBs) to every beneficiary for all services; traditionally, EOMBs were used under Medicare only when a service was denied, or when it involved a copayment from the patient (if a service was fully covered and paid by Medicare, then no EOMB was sent);
- authorized HCFA to provide limited financial incentives (up to $1000) for beneficiaries who identify and report fraudulent or abusive billing practices;
- mandated the introduction of National Provider Identifiers (NPIs), whereby each provider or supplier has just one unique identification number (this number is designed to prevent providers and suppliers from spreading improper billings across a range of different identification numbers to make them harder to spot);
- required the secretary of HHS to exclude from the Medicare and Medicaid programs providers with felony convictions relating to health care fraud or controlled substances;
- required the secretary of HHS to establish the Adverse Actions Database of providers, suppliers, and practitioners against whom "final adverse actions" have been taken (this database will include civil judgments or criminal convictions related to health care fraud, actions by federal or state licensing or certification bodies, and exclusions for cause from Medicare or Medicaid);
- made knowing and willful transfer of assets to gain eligibility for Medicaid a criminal offense (this provision was later amended by the Balanced Budget Act of 1997 to clarify that the penalties apply to the financial advisor, not to the beneficiary).

Several further fraud and abuse provisions were attached to the Balanced Budget Act (BBA), enacted in 1997.[3] The BBA provisions

- authorized HCFA to require durable medical equipment (DME) suppliers, home health agencies, outpatient rehabilitation facilities, and rehabilitation agencies to post $50,000 surety bonds before receiving certification for Medicare or Medicaid;

- authorized the secretary of HHS to bar convicted health care felons from receiving Medicare and Medicaid payments for up to ten years if they had one prior conviction and permanently if convicted on two or more previous occasions; also extended exclusion authority to include family members (this would prevent barred felons from using relatives as proxies to get back in);

- authorized the secretary of HHS to refuse, or terminate, provider agreements based on a felony, even if unrelated to health care; also authorized HCFA to require providers applying to participate to submit their social security numbers and employer identification numbers so that HCFA can check their histories for past fraudulent activity;

- authorized HCFA to establish a Prospective Payment System (PPS) for home health care, setting October 1, 1999, as the date for it to begin operation (since postponed, at least until October 1, 2000);

- established civil monetary penalties of up to $50,000 for each kickback violation relating to health care services;

- established penalties for services billed by a provider who had already been excluded by Medicare and Medicaid;

- established penalties for hospitals that contract with excluded providers;

- required that home health and hospice billings be based on the location of services provided, rather than on the location of the agency, to cut out the practice of providers' establishing a token office or headquarters in another part of the country where reimbursement rates are higher.

The administration has a list of further initiatives, not yet passed into law, which it intends to pursue. They propose further legislative changes to

- enable federal health care programs to stop the payment stream while providers and their business arrangements (particularly relating to kickbacks) are under investigation;

- prevent providers from escaping their obligations (fines or returning overpayments) by declaring bankruptcy;

- extend the tools that already exist for Medicare and Medicaid to other federal programs, such as the Federal Employees Health Benefits Program;
- enforce the primary-payer obligations of private insurers more effectively by requiring all private insurers to report the identities of Medicare beneficiaries they insure (otherwise Medicare can remain unaware of other insurance coverages that ought to pay first).

The administration also proposes to eliminate excessive Medicare reimbursements for drugs (this is a *sensible purchasing* issue, not generally a fraud issue); to impose stricter controls on partial hospitalization benefits; and to ask the U.S. Sentencing Commission to examine current sentencing guidelines for health care fraud to see if penalties are serious enough. HCFA, announcing a new "Comprehensive Plan for Program Integrity" in February 1999,[4] declared its intention to improve five key management areas and to focus attention on five key benefit areas "with greatest potential for improved program integrity," namely, inpatient hospital care, congregate care (i.e., groups of beneficiaries gathered together under one roof who present attractive targets), managed care, community mental health centers, and nursing homes. HCFA has also begun to mobilize the Peer Review Organizations to help spot improper billing practices and report them.

Counterattack

The industry in general, and the provider associations in particular, were not of a mind to take all this lying down. They deeply resented the harsh rhetoric used by administration officials, the repeated "crackdowns on fraud and abuse," and the growing perception of criminality within the industry, to be expunged through stepped-up enforcement. Not a single provider group expressed support for the government's campaign. Two in particular—the home health lobby, and the American Hospital Association (AHA)—launched vigorous counterattacks.

In June 1997, the Office of Inspector General (OIG) reported the results of their review of home health claims paid in four states. More than 40 percent of the payments, they said, should have been disallowed, and a substantial portion had been paid for patients who did not even fit the definition of "homebound." Meanwhile, thousands of new home health agencies were queuing up for Medicare certification. In September 1997, realizing that this entire segment of Medicare was essentially out of control, the Clinton administration announced a moratorium on admission of home health agencies to the Medicare program to stop the flood of new entrants (at least until certification and survey requirements, including criminal background checks on aides hired, could be beefed up).

Under intense pressure from the National Association for Home Care and their political allies, the administration lifted the moratorium in January 1998. But by then, HCFA had instituted some of the new controls authorized by the Balanced Budget Act of 1997. They imposed the new requirement that home health agencies post a $50,000 surety bond before being allowed to participate. (The purpose of the bond is to ensure the financial viability of the enterprise, or to ensure that a pot of money will be there should fraudulent billings be discovered and the company vanishes. The object is to cut down on the plague of fly-by-night businesses jumping into, then out of, the home health business.) And, from October 1997, pending the eventual design and implementation of the new prospective payment system envisioned under the act, HCFA had instituted a new, temporary payment system designed to cut down on excessive payments. HCFA also doubled the number of home health audits and increased the rate of claims review.

By the fall of 1998, the National Association for Home Care complained that 1,240, or 8 percent of Medicare's 10,027 certified home health agencies, had either closed or withdrawn from the program as a result of the changes. Medicare's policy changes, they said, were driving their members out of business, leaving beneficiaries without home services. (GAO [General Accounting Office] and the OIG reported that they could not find a shortage of access to home health services as a result of these withdrawals.)[5] The home health associations mounted an all-out industry lobbying blitz, including a September 10, 1998, march on the Capitol. They appealed to the population of Medicare beneficiaries for support: The administration, they claimed, was deliberately destroying Medicare's home health benefits. Administration officials presumably thought they were trying to save them.

The Hospitals and the Battle over the False Claims Act

The home health industry's resistance pales in comparison to the formidable counterattack mounted by the hospitals and hospital associations. The hospitals, after all, have that much more at stake. Of the total national budget for health care, home health (in the year 2000) will absorb roughly 2.7 percent. Hospitals, by contrast, will account for roughly 32 percent of it—the largest single share—projected at $424 billion.[6] The prospect of the nation's hospitals being forced to adopt more conservative billing practices carries, for them, enormous financial implications.

From 1994 onwards, hospital billing practices came under greater and greater scrutiny. Most threatening of all, from the industry's perspective, was that the abusive billing practices discovered in one or more hospitals gave rise to major trawls of the hospital industry for similar false billings—termed "national initiatives." By 1996, the Department of Justice and the OIG were coordinating two major national initiatives, plus the continuing investigation of teaching hospitals under the "PATH" audits. In January 1999, the Department of Justice announced two additional national initiatives. That brought five areas of hospital billings into the spotlight—a relatively small portion of the hospitals' business—but certainly enough to get under the industry's skin and make them worry just where all this might be heading. Here is a summary of the five billing issues so far subject to national projects:[7]

- *Physicians at Teaching Hospitals ("PATH" Audits):* Medicare pays the costs of training residents and interns at teaching hospitals through the Graduate Medical Education Program (GME), and through "Indirect Medical Education" (IME) payments to the hospitals. Medicare pays over $8 billion per year in GME and IME grants which are designed to cover the costs associated with training residents. The basis for the PATH audits is a rule that determines when teaching physicians can charge for their services to patients within the teaching hospital setting. Teaching physicians are supposed to charge only if they have provided the service to the patient themselves, or if they were physically present when the resident furnished the care. If teaching physicians claim fees when absent and the work was performed by residents unaccompanied, Medicare is in effect being billed twice, having already paid for the residents' work through the grant structure. As of March 1999, four teaching institutions have entered into settlements with the government to resolve potential liability under the False Claims Act, paying $67 million between them. (Reviews of four other similar institutions showed up no substantive billing issues—which suggests that the rules were perfectly clear and that following them was not so difficult.)

- *Hospital Outpatient Laboratory Project:* This project, started in Ohio in 1994 before being extended nationwide, addresses improper and excessive claims for hematology and automated blood chemistry tests by hospital outpatient laboratories. Such claims involve improper unbundling (billing the components of a composite test as if they had been separate tests), double billing for lab tests, and billing for medically unnecessary tests. So far, 206 hospitals have entered settlements totaling more than $47 million.

- *Diagnosis-Related Group 72-Hour Window Project:* Launched in 1995, this project examines hospitals' billings for outpatient services when those services should already be covered by a DRG (Diagnosis Related Group) payment for an associated inpatient procedure. For example, if a patient is admitted for a surgical operation but receives preparatory services in the seventy-two hours preceding admission, all those associated outpatient services should be covered by the fee for the surgery, and billing for them separately amounts to double billing. The project, coordinated by the U.S. Attorney's Office in the Middle District, Pennsylvania, has identified 4,660 hospitals submitting improper billings for outpatient services. As of March 1999, settlements had been reached with 2,550 of them, with $66 million recovered.

- *Patient Transfer Project:* Announced as a national project by the Department of Justice in January 1999, this project focuses on transfer of patients between two hospitals. If both hospitals are being paid on a PPS basis, only the second of the two hospitals—presumed to be the one that delivered the bulk of the services—is entitled to the full payment. The transferring hospital receives a per diem payment based upon length of stay before the transfer. Many transferring hospitals, however, were charging the full diagnosis-related payment instead of the per diem payment (Medicare was effectively paying both hospitals for the patient's treatment). Considerable concern also surrounded the establishment of some hospital partnerships or business arrangements whereby patients were transferred between hospitals much more frequently and apparently by design (a practice referred to as "ping-ponging" the patients). An OIG report on this issue in 1996 identified $227 million in recoveries and savings, and a follow-up analysis identified additional overpayments of $202 million.

- *Pneumonia Upcoding Project:* Also announced in January 1999, this project focuses on the way hospitals bill for treatment of pneumonia. Most pneumonia cases are grouped into four different DRG codes, one of which (relating to bacterial pneumonia) pays much more than the others (which relate to viral pneumonia). Although most cases of pneumonia are viral, many hospitals use the higher paying DRG more often than one would expect. The OIG is investigating the coding for bacterial pneumonia at more than one hundred hospitals. To date, five have settled their liability for such coding, paying $7.7 million between them.

Most irksome to the hospital industry as these projects unfold has been the government's increased use of the False Claims Act. Enacted in 1986, the federal False Claims Act updated laws from the Civil War that were originally designed to prevent procurement frauds against the Union Army. The False Claims Act imposed substantial civil penalties for false claims made against federal funds; this created a mechanism for addressing false claims in health care (amongst other areas) without first having to prove criminal intent. The penalties—which were further enhanced by HIPAA in 1996—apply to anyone who "knowingly" presents, or causes to be presented, a false or fraudulent claim for approval to the U.S. Government. The standard of proof relating to the necessary "knowledge" is lower than that required for proof of a deliberate criminal deception. Under the False Claims Act, false claims are submitted "knowingly" if the provider had actual knowledge of their falsity, or acted with deliberate ignorance, or with reckless disregard for their truth or falsity.

This standard of proof brings patterns of false claims, where a provider has failed to implement any kind of reasonable controls to prevent such claims from being submitted, within the scope of the Act. Each false claim carries penalties of triple damages, plus between $5,000 and $10,000 per claim.

Within the context of the national initiatives, U.S. attorneys drew heavily on the hospitals' potential false claims liability in urging them to make repayments. Through data analysis, they would identify potential overpayments and then send the hospital a "demand letter" asking them to repay the money and pointing out that they might otherwise face investigation and action, possibly with significant financial penalties, under the False Claims Act.

Many hospitals, and the AHA, saw the Department of Justice's use of these demand letters as threatening and complained bitterly about them. The majority of hospitals receiving such demand letters did not dispute the findings and paid up without a fight. The industry characterized these hospitals as victims of the government's campaign of blackmail and extortion. Faced with the option of repaying or of facing protracted and costly litigation, hospitals paid up—according to industry lobbyists— simply as a prudent risk-management decision, not because they thought they had done anything wrong.

Of the national initiatives to date, the 72-hour window project has had the widest reach. Data analysis suggested that 4,700 of the nation's roughly 5,000 hospitals had engaged in this one particular, improper, billing practice. Spokespersons for the industry maintained the 72-hour window project was all about innocent billing errors that the government was unfairly characterizing as fraud. As Mary Grealy, general counsel for the AHA put it: "Yes, there are billing mistakes . . . but we're saying 'let's move beyond characterizing this as fraud.'" Richard Davidson, president of the AHA, pointed out, "There's something wrong with the system itself when most hospitals are found to be fraudulent."[8]

The government, however, was not generally characterizing this as fraud, and had no need to. By using the False Claims Act, they had only to show that the claims were false and that providers had the requisite degree of knowledge (which is quite carefully defined by the act). The government did not need to prove criminal intent, nor deliberate deception, nor that the claims were "fraudulent." Thus the appeal of using civil remedies: The government could apply them quite broadly and reach resolutions comparatively quickly once inappropriate billing patterns had been identified. That avoided the need, in the majority of cases, for protracted and expensive criminal proceedings.

It suited the industry, however, to equate the government's use of the False Claims Act with accusations of fraud. The idea that the majority of the nation's hospitals—through years of neglectful oversight—might have fallen into illegal but lucrative billing practices might seem shocking yet plausible. But the idea that the majority of these highly respected institutions were engaging in deliberate criminal fraud was surely *not* plausible. The industry preferred to characterize the government's accusations in these more serious and less plausible terms. By characterizing the government's actions as tantamount to accusations of fraud, the industry hoped to undermine the credibility of the government's position, garner sympathy for themselves, and paint the "national initiatives" as misguided witch-hunts perpetrated by overzealous, bounty-seeking U.S. attorneys, who were seizing upon the moneymaking opportunities presented by a small number of innocent billing errors.

The AHA embarked on an outreach campaign that included the mass faxing of periodic bulletins, headlined "Guilty Until Proven Innocent," that highlighted hospitals the AHA felt had been unfairly targeted.[9] Armed with their story about hospitals victimized by law enforcement and prosecutors, the hospital associations turned to the courts and to the legislature for relief.

In October 1997, the Association of American Medical Colleges, the American Medical Association (AMA), and a number of other associations representing teaching hospitals filed a lawsuit in California to end the PATH audit program as currently conducted. The lawsuit involved a total of forty-five complainants. (In April 1998, the District Court for the Central District of California granted the government's motion to dismiss the suit.)

In March 1998 and April 1998 respectively, the New Jersey and Greater New York Hospital Associations sued the government to stop the 72-hour window and PATH initiatives against their member hospitals. These lawsuits were based on the contention that the government's attempt to impose its view on which billings were correct or incorrect amounted to retroactive rulemaking, and that such rulemaking had been conducted without the benefit of the appropriate notice and comment provisions of the Administrative Procedures Act.[10]

In April 1998, hospital industry officials and some supportive members of Congress met with the Justice Department to press for an enforcement moratorium until August 1, 1998. (It was not granted.)

The most serious threat to the government's campaign came in the form of a direct assault on the provisions of the False Claims Act itself. In March 1998, Congressman Bill McCollum (R-Florida) introduced a bill to amend the provisions of the False Claims Act as they applied to the health care industry.[11] Through an extraordinary behind-the-scenes lobbying effort, the hospital associations secured more than 200 cosponsors for the bill even though it would have crippled the use of the act in health care matters. Three provisions of the McCollum bill would have done particular damage. First, with respect to the necessary degree of "knowledge," the bill would have changed the burden of proof from "preponderance of evidence" to "clear and convincing evidence." Second, the bill would have required that false claims constituted more than 10 percent of a provider's total Medicare billings before they could be considered material enough to warrant an action. Third, providers who set up a "corporate compliance plan" would gain immunity against false claims lawsuits.

Supporters of the False Claims Act fought hard to save it. In particular, Senator Charles Grassley (R-Iowa)—who had cosponsored the Federal False Claims Act in 1986—worked to win over his colleagues. And "Taxpayers Against Fraud," an advocacy group based in Washington, D.C., fought energetically to save the act. They argued that there was absolutely no reason for the health care industry to be treated differently (with respect to the burden of proof) from defense contractors, or anyone else in a position to cheat government programs. They argued that the 10 percent materiality provision would, in effect, grant providers the license to steal with impunity up to 10 percent of their legitimate volume. Moreover, given the lack of investigative resources, the government would almost never be able to examine enough claims to establish that more than 10 percent of total billings were false. Under such a provision, none of the previous actions would have been brought. Finally, in relation to the immunity provision, the last thing the Department of Justice needed was to be sucked into endless and complex debates over what did or did not constitute an adequate compliance plan.

Testimony by administration officials helped to persuade lawmakers that the AHA's characterization of the issues had been somewhat misleading. For example, in the case of the 72-hour window project, industry representatives conveniently seemed to forget some pertinent history as they portrayed the hospitals as innocent victims hit without warning for minor billing errors. Lewis Morris, Assistant Inspector General for Legal Affairs, laid out the relevant history in congressional testimony in April 1998.[12]

The OIG had conducted a number of previous audits of hospital billing for outpatient services. Each one had revealed widespread violation of the DRG 72-hour window rule. The first such audit covered the period from October 1983 to January 1986. The OIG supplied HCFA a computer listing of such claims paid improperly. HCFA, through its contractors, sought reimbursement and put the hospitals on formal notice of their noncompliance.

The second OIG audit examined the period between February 1986 and November 1987. Over $40 million in improper payments were identified; again, HCFA sought repayment and put the hospitals on notice. The third audit covered the period between December 1987 and October 1990. This time, $38.5 million in overpayments were identified. HCFA worked hard to recover them. Each time, HCFA instructed its contractors to educate the hospitals regarding the 72-hour rule. The fourth audit in 1993 still revealed noncompliance and identified $8.6 million in improper billings. A fifth audit, in 1996, identified an additional $27 million in potential improper payments for the period January 1992 through December 1994. Morris testified:

> Incredibly, even after all of the previous public OIG audit reports and HCFA's repeated efforts to remind hospitals of the requirements, OIG's fifth audit revealed that with respect to the hospitals' claims processing systems, the necessary edits at hospitals were not sufficient, or were nonexistent. All of this left the question: What would it take to get hospitals to comply with the "DRG 72 Hour Window" rule?
> . . . Innocent mistakes? Perhaps initially. But at some point, repeated failure to abide by explicit notice becomes, at a minimum, reckless behavior. We had every reason to believe that without this remedy [selective use of the false claims act] false claims would continue. And the Medicare program could not depend on the OIG to repeatedly audit compliance. Yet, without the continued audits, the program and taxpayers would suffer annual improper losses in the millions of dollars due to this abuse.[13]

Morris also described the system the OIG had used for grouping hospitals into tiers according to the ratio of their improper billings to their size. The majority of hospitals identified, placed in lower tiers, had been asked to pay no penalty whatsoever—merely to repay the overpayments. Only the serious and repeat violators had had enforcement action launched against them.

Launching a national project, and using the False Claims Act, appeared necessary to alter the cynical economic calculation that these worst offenders seemed to be making; that is, from a business perspective, it was better to persist in improper billings, and worth running the risk of audits. After all, the worst that would normally happen—even if you were caught by an audit—was that you would be required to pay back the overpayments; interest would be calculated only from the date the overpayments were discovered! Such an economic calculus had to be altered.

Eventually, the McCollum bill was dropped when the Department of Justice offered to issue new guidelines to its officers regarding the use of the False Claims Act. The department would urge U.S. attorneys to be more discriminating and to take greater care to assess the necessary degree of "knowledge" to warrant a false claims action. Under national initiatives, *demand* letters would be replaced with *contact* letters informing the provider of the problem and requesting a dialogue before proceeding further. The department would reserve stronger actions for those cases where the pervasiveness and magnitude of the overpayments supported an inference of deliberate ignorance or intentional or reckless conduct.[14] In accepting the compromise, many Justice officials claimed that the adoption of the guidelines really represented no change because such criteria should have been evaluated anyway. Others acknowledged that some letters had been overly harsh.[15]

In any case, when the Justice Department issued the new guidelines regarding the use of the False Claims Act, support for change to the act itself died down. The hospital associations, at least for the time being, acquiesced. This particular skirmish was over.

Both sides suffered casualties. The hospitals had failed to halt the national initiatives, two more of which were announced in January 1999. They had also failed in their attempt to weaken the provisions of the False Claims Act.

But the administration had also taken some losses. They had been reminded of the political power of the health care industrial complex. Investigators and prosecutors had learned how their slightest misstep would be seized upon, and how costly it could be to the overall campaign. Officials responsible for program integrity—at HCFA, the OIG, and the Department of Justice—had seen the lobbying power of the industry associations mobilized against them. They had not enjoyed being portrayed as ignoramuses blundering about in the medical profession, failing to understand its subtleties. They feared being labeled overly aggressive, "jack-booted thugs," or "the next IRS." Efforts they were making to save benefits had been recast as efforts to destroy them. The industry was not so much on the defensive as on the counteroffensive. The administration had been forced to soften its rhetoric and to adopt a more conciliatory and cooperative tone. Perhaps their resolve was weakened, too. Only time will tell.

By the Numbers

The Clinton administration has unquestionably paid more attention to health care fraud and abuse and launched more initiatives designed to counter it than have previous administrations. The account above recognizes some of their battles and legislative achievements—many of them embodied in HIPAA (1996) and the Balanced Budget Act (1997).

The numbers also tell a convincing story, revealing higher levels of investigative activity, criminal prosecutions, civil actions, settlements, exclusions, and increases in resources for prevention. Most visible (and alarming for the industry) has been the steady rise in civil and criminal enforcement outputs since 1993, and the fact that the various output metrics continue to rise at an annual pace of 15 percent or so.

Here are some of the statistics that indicate greater resource commitments for various aspects of fraud control:

- Between 1993 and 1998, the Department of Justice increased the overall level of human resources devoted to health care fraud by 236 percent. The number of FBI agents dedicated to it rose from 147 to 442 (measured in full-time-agent-equivalents); the number of work years devoted to the area by U.S. attorney's offices increased from 43 to 185; and the number of Civil Division attorneys from 6 to 40.[16]

- Since the False Claims Act was updated and amended for use within Medicare and Medicaid (i.e., from 1986 to 1998), over $2 billion has been recovered in matters relating to the HHS. Fiscal Year 1997 was the bumper year, with over $1 billion in settlements, penalties, and recoveries. (This included the SmithKline Beecham Clinical Labs' settlement of $325 million.) In Fiscal Year (FY) 1998, $480 million was awarded or negotiated in health care fraud matters at the federal level.[17] In Fiscal Year (FY) 1999, $524 million.

- During Financial Year 1997 and 1998, roughly 5,700 individuals and entities were excluded from participating in the Medicare and Medicaid programs, doubling the rate from the previous two years. The higher rate was maintained in Financial Year 1999 with a further 2,976 individuals or entities being excluded.[18]

- Partly due to the new funding stream provided under HIPAA, the OIG was able to place personnel in an additional 12 states, raising the OIG "presence" from 26 states to 38.

- Expenditures for Medicare program safeguards, with scheduled increases guaranteed under HIPAA, will rise from $428 million in 1995 to $630 million in 2000, and then to $720 million in 2003.[19]

- More health care provider institutions are voluntarily disclosing problematic billing situations than ever before. The OIG increasingly uses "Corporate Integrity Agreements" both as a component of settlements and as a method of resolving billing problems voluntarily declared. In 1998, 231 institutions entered into Corporate Integrity Agreements (oddly enough, over a third of these agreements involved providers in Ohio).[20] Fourteen percent of these agreements accompanied settlements of over $1 million.[21]

This self-evident ratcheting up might easily lead observers to assume that the problem of health care fraud and abuse, if not solved already, must surely be solved soon—especially if government enforcement operations sustain their growth trajectory for a few more years. It is easy for policymakers to equate increased efforts with program security, which perhaps explains why HCFA's Comprehensive Plan for Program Integrity (issued in February 1999) confidently declares, "In summary, the program integrity aspects of Medicare and Medicaid operations are robust and improving every day." [22]

Count the Zeroes

To see just how robust these protections really are, you have to match them up against the enormity of health care costs, and the potential losses. To do that, you have to count the zeroes quite carefully. Health care costs (in 2000) will run over 1.3 trillion. One trillion has twelve zeroes. The health care fraud problem (which might be as little as 10 percent or as much as 40 percent of that) is therefore counted in hundreds of billions of dollars: maybe only *one* hundred billion, more likely two or three, conceivably five. No matter which digit turns out to be the right one, it has eleven zeroes following it, and that does not include the cents.

Investments of a few million dollars here and fifty million dollars there (with six or seven zeroes) cannot possibly mean all that much in the bigger picture. Even if the combined enforcement operations of federal and state governments could produce one billion dollars every year in settlements and recoveries (with nine zeroes), that figure would represent only one sixth of one percent (i.e., 0.17 percent) of the annual amount spent on public sector health programs (projected at $594 billion for 2000).[23]

The facts and figures presented above may indeed represent a "ratcheting up" when compared with previous investments. When compared with the size of the issue, however, they pale almost into insignificance. Consider the following:

- Yes, the government has collected more than $2 billion in settlements and judgments since 1986. And the best year was 1997, with over $1 billion. But consider the context. During the period 1986 to 1998, total federal expenditures on health care exceeded $3 *trillion,* so the aggregate recoveries represent less than 0.07 percent of the federal outlays during this period.

- Note, also, that the Health Care Financing Administration now pays out (for Medicare, plus the federal share of the Medicaid program costs) $1.4 billion, every single working day of the year.[24] If you add in the states' share of Medicaid, the total for these two programs runs above $1.8 billion each working day.

- The percentage of Medicare claims routinely reviewed has dropped from 17 percent in 1989 to around 9 or 10 percent in 2000.[25] Virtually none of these routine reviews (less than 0.10 percent) involves external validation techniques such as calling the patients to verify the services were actually delivered.

- Even with the guaranteed and steadily increasing funding provided under HIPAA, program safeguard expenditures in the Medicare program for 2003, adjusted for the number of claims processed and for the effects of inflation, will be about one half the level of 1989.[26]

- Program Integrity funding for the Medicare program in 2000 (roughly $630 million) represents about one quarter of 1 percent of program costs (i.e., 0.25 percent). The "benefit integrity" component (the piece that funds fraud units and handles beneficiary complaints of fraud) is only $78 million for FY 2000, or 0.03 percent of program costs (i.e., $.03 for each $100 dollars spent).[27]

- The Medicaid program, in FY 1998 (the most recent year for which aggregate figures are available) spent a total of $114.2 million on the Medicaid Fraud Control Units (MFCUs) around the country. Seventy-five percent of this comes from the federal government, which matches state spending on these units at a ratio of 3-to-1. Despite the federal support, most states invest way below the cap for the matching funds (set at 0.25 percent of program costs). Nationally, the fraud unit budgets represent roughly 0.06 percent of program outlays (i.e., $0.06 per $100 spent).[28] In FY 2000, even with projected increases in funding, the total spending on fraud units will not exceed 0.07 percent of program outlays.[29]

- In November 1998, the OIG published a review of the staffing and performance of the fraud units at Medicare's fiscal intermediaries.

The review covered forty-one intermediaries that had been under contract with HCFA in 1996 and were still under contract in 1998 (i.e., the more stable, long-term contractors). These fiscal intermediaries process claims for Medicare Part A, which covers home health care and inpatient hospital and institutional care. Since 1993, they have been required to operate separate and distinct fraud units. After reviewing the operations of the fraud units, the OIG reported: [30]

- In the period of operation studied (FY 1996), ten out of the forty-one units referred *no cases* of fraud to the OIG.
- Despite HCFA's expectation that fraud units proactively identify fraud, half the fraud units did not open any cases proactively.
- Despite HCFA's expectation that fraud units identify and address program vulnerabilities, more than one third of fraud units did not identify program vulnerabilities.

• Even more telling were the statistics compiled by the OIG relating to these units. Medicare payments for FY 1996, made through these forty-one intermediaries, totaled $113 billion. The corresponding fraud unit budgets, in total, were just $7.6 million (i.e., 0.007 percent of the payment rate). The total number of personnel allocated to these fraud units, measured in full-time equivalents (FTEs), was 112.75. These 112 or 113 brave souls, scattered across forty-one massive claims processing operations, were therefore each responsible on average for watching over one billion dollars of Medicare spending every year. (These staffing numbers included clerical staff as well as investigators.)[31]

The latest Medicare overpayment study estimates "improper payments" at 7.1 percent of program costs. Because of the measurement protocols used (discussed in Chapter 3), we know that the majority of Medicare fraud would not be included within that measured 7.1 percent. Fraud losses come on top of the 7.1 percent improper payments, and they may add a further 10 percent, or 30 percent, to the losses.

Consider the potential scale of the problem and the actual scale of the interventions. Although the problem may run between 10 percent and 30 percent of program costs, the majority of interventions and control investments come in around one tenth of 1 percent. Or lower. Fraud units handling Medicare's hospital claims funded at less than one hundredth of

1 percent. Personnel responsible for watching over hundreds of millions of dollars—even billions—each. Here lies madness. Recent efforts may exceed what went before, but the doses of response and the scale of interventions, to date, remain ridiculously low.

The industry probably fears that fraud control-efforts might sometime become serious. Perhaps they figure that by objecting strenuously enough to the small number of projects launched to date they could squash the administration's war on fraud before it gathered any real momentum. For the government, getting serious—in terms of investments and staffing—would mean multiplying everything by a factor of twenty, for starters. Of course, that is unlikely to happen anytime soon. But this is certainly not the time to back off; the real war has scarcely yet begun. For every case we've seen to date, there are probably a hundred we have not seen.

Medicare Contractors

Within the Medicare program, there is yet more bad news. HCFA relies heavily upon its contractors (called *fiscal intermediaries* and *carriers*) to control fraud and abuse. These contractors pay claims, monitor them, audit providers, deal with beneficiary inquiries and complaints, and run the majority of the HCFA-prescribed program integrity functions.

In an alarming number of recent cases, the integrity of these contractors themselves has been found seriously lacking. Thanks mostly to whistle-blowers, HCFA and the OIG have discovered several of them lying, cheating and stealing in the course of their duties under Medicare. And these contractors are supposed to be HCFA's first line of defense for preserving program integrity.

Cases closed to date (i.e., either settled out of court, or judgments handed down in court) are summarized here. The figures quoted include criminal fines and civil settlements; the dates given show when the case was closed.[32]

- 1993. Blue Cross/Blue Shield (BCBS) of Florida (created physicians' orders): $10 million.

- 1994. BCBS Massachusetts (fraud in Performance Education Program): $2.75 million.

- 1995. BCBS Michigan (falsified documents to support audits): $27.6 million.

- 1995. BCBS Michigan (used Medicare trust funds to pay private claims): $24 million.
- 1995. BCBS California (impeded Performance Education Program, falsified documents, hid errors): $12 million.
- 1997. BCBS Massachusetts (falsified statements on Health Maintenance Organization (HMO) applications): $700,000.
- 1998. BCBS Illinois (altered documents to increase evaluation scores): $144 million.
- 1998. Pennsylvania Blue Shield (falsified documents for evaluation, falsified administrative costs and number of claims processed): $38.5 million.
- 1999. BCBS Massachusetts (paid private insurance claims with Medicare funds): $4.75 million.
- 1999. BCBS Colorado (obstructed a federal audit to conceal poor performance): $7.3 million.
- 1999. BCBS New Mexico (obstructed a federal audit, concealed evidence): $6.3 million.
- 1999. Rocky Mountain Care Corp. (a joint venture of New Mexico and Colorado Blues plans) (obstructed a federal audit, concealed poor performance): $500,000.

According to a GAO report, these deceptions and improprieties became a way of doing business and went undetected for long periods because, when it came time to review contractor performance, HCFA relied too heavily on information supplied by the contractors without verifying it. In addition, HCFA's audit methodology was so transparent and predictable (and was even communicated in advance) that contractors found it quite easy to cheat on their performance reviews.[33]

To date, by far the most significant of these settlements was reached in 1998 with Health Care Service Corporation (HCSC), also known as Blue Cross/Blue Shield of Illinois. HCSC, which served as the Medicare contractor for Illinois and Michigan, agreed to plead guilty to eight felony counts and pay $4 million in criminal fines and $140 million in settlement of its liability under the False Claims Act following a whistle-blower suit. False statements to conceal evidence of HCSC's poor performance in processing Medicare claims comprised six counts and the other two counts related to obstructing and conspiring to obstruct federal auditors. Officials had falsified documents, manipulated samples of claims, and failed to handle inquiries from beneficiaries and physicians in a timely manner. According to the government's suit, one night in 1993 the company simply destroyed 10,000 Medicare claims that had been sitting in the mail room for three months. As of December, 1997, HCSC agreed to withdraw from the Medicare program and, by September 1, 1998, was no longer a Medicare contractor.[34]

Ironically, HCSC had been brought in by HCFA to replace another contractor with integrity problems—BCBS of Michigan—when it settled allegations for $51 million in 1995. BCBS of Michigan had been accused of paying private insurance claims with Medicare funds, and falsifying documents relating to their evaluations.

Many of Medicare's contractors—companies that also function as private insurers or managed care plans—would seem to have inherent conflicts of interest with respect to their work under Medicare. The same doctors and provider institutions they are supposed to monitor and whose billings they police for Medicare are corporate partners in their private businesses. This concern has been pointed out numerous times, not least by the GAO, and forms in part the basis for HCFA's shift of integrity functions to separate contractors (a shift that is just getting underway).

According to Deputy Inspector General George Grob (HHS), as of September 1999 his office was investigating nineteen current and former Medicare contractors.[35]

Medicaid Operations at the State Level

Judging by reports from the state Medicaid agencies, the war does not go particularly well there, either.

During the fall of 1998 and spring of 1999, I had the privilege of working with HCFA in conducting a series of regional workshops on fraud and abuse within the Medicaid program. Each state (forty-nine attended) was invited to send senior representatives from the Medicaid agency and from the Medicaid Fraud-Control Units. The workshops gave the participants the opportunity to discuss recent innovations in fraud control and to share their frustrations. The resulting report, published by HCFA, summarizes the issues raised by Medicaid officials across the country.[36] Principal among the issues to emerge was what many participants experienced as a persistent lack of commitment to effective fraud-control. Twenty-one of the states represented raised this subject explicitly in advance written submissions. In particular, participants expressed the following frustrations:[37]

- legislatures and senior management (particularly of the Medicaid agencies) appeared either not to recognize the problem of Medicaid fraud and abuse or, if they did, they seemed not to treat it as a serious or central issue in program administration;
- providers and provider associations exerted powerful political influence at the state level; these thwarted efforts to bring them into compliance and to impose sensible controls on billing behavior;
- resources available for program integrity functions (including fraud detection and investigation) appeared minuscule compared to the potential losses to the program;
- "separation of funds" (program funds from administrative funds) prevented consideration of the returns on investment available from investments in fraud and abuse-control activities. This leaves program integrity funding at the mercy of other inescapable administrative requirements (in a zero-sum game) and normally last in line;
- the constrained capacity of the justice system, which created backlogs, and often led to abandonment of significant cases;
- the culture of social service agencies and claims processing operations, which appeared to be adverse and in some cases openly hostile to the purposes and methods of effective fraud control.

The following six comments—a sample of the seminar participants' advance written submissions on this subject—give a flavor of these concerns. These six comments were presented by senior Medicaid officials from six different states:

- "We are a provider-driven agency. Our agency operates directly under the governor's office and primarily by executive order and therefore is subject to political pressure by providers and associations. This creates difficulty in introducing new programs, new checks and balances, changing rates, policies and punitive actions. The agency's attitude for units within Medicaid that uncover mistakes, or even potentially fraudulent behavior, is negative."
- "Because most public health insurance programs are administered at a fraction of the administrative cost of private health insurance, there is a tremendous internal struggle over limited administrative resources. The program integrity budget is always at risk of the agency's other administrative needs. A long-term budget commit-

ment to program integrity is always a problem. The program integrity budget commitment tends to be crisis-driven."

- "The largest obstacle we have is top-level management of the division. The manager does not want anything to do with the fraud unit or referrals." [In presentation, later clarified: "The new director does not tolerate the fraud unit. He has announced internally that there will be no referrals to the fraud unit."]

- "The most substantial obstacle facing Medicaid Program Integrity operations is the lack of awareness and understanding of the extent of the problem. Senior management have limited time and resources to deal with antifraud and abuse issues. Provider fraud and abuse issues take second place to productivity and service delivery priorities . . . over the past several years the department's Program Integrity operation's resources were reduced in order to staff up [other] efforts . . . [our state's] antifraud and abuse efforts are minute in relationship to the size of its program; [the state's] response is simply not proportional to the problem."

- "The most serious problem in combating fraud in [the state] is the loss of resources and the aging of the systems used to identify and combat fraud. With the advent of the managed care delivery system, many of the resources previously devoted to fraud and abuse detection have been diverted to support managed care."

- "The most serious obstacle to fraud control in our state is, I think, the single state agency's lack of interest in and commitment to it, despite the cordial and cooperative day-to-day working relationship which exists between our agencies. . . . This lack of concern manifests itself in myriad ways."

One might be tempted to dismiss such concerns as the predictable complaints of specialists, more attuned to their own program responsibilities than to others'. And one might reasonably expect officials who chose to attend a "fraud and abuse" seminar to care a lot more about the subject than other officials who chose not to attend. Some might draw comfort from these observations.

However, as an outsider, I would observe that the concerns expressed on these matters had an earnestness, a gravity, and a prevalence that would lead anyone who heard it all—as I did—to conclude that those who are dedicated to controlling Medicaid fraud and abuse feel, quite genuinely (and despite recent improvements), that they are "up against it" almost every way they turn.

How Goes the War?

Fraud control, by its very nature, carries with it a certain underlying pathology. Elements of that pathology include the fact that fraud is always invisible unless detected, which means that the majority of fraud remains invisible in perpetuity; that finding integrity problems is never good news, and can therefore be an unpopular occupation; and that massive underinvestment in controls is the norm in almost any fraud-control setting.

Most insurers, both public and private, do no systematic measurement of their fraud losses. They therefore fly blind, remaining largely oblivious of the true magnitude of the problem. (In the case of the Medicare measurement studies, a weak audit protocol produces results that are actually deceptive.) No insurers, as far as I have seen, make resource-allocation decisions based upon valid estimates of the size of the problem and thus continue to underinvest in controls by a factor of twenty or more.

In terms of explicit strategy, most fraud units are bogged down in a reactive, casemaking mode, unable to see the forest for the trees. They see only what whistle-blowers report, or what systems detect. Software generally available within the industry supports utilization review, but not fraud detection. Most insurers, even when they believe in the value of proactive outreach and intelligence-gathering (to find out what's happening out there) cannot find or protect resources for it. They operate with a distorted and fragmentary picture of fraud, revealed by largely ineffective detection and referral systems.

Among those who perpetrate fraud, the ones who come to light are largely those who make enemies, or get too greedy, or forget to bill their lies correctly, or forget to aim their lies in the center of medical orthodoxy. And then, when the greedy and unsophisticated ones get caught, we comfort ourselves because they got caught.

The most significant parts of the campaign ahead concern what we have not yet seen and some areas we have not yet properly understood. The next two chapters describe problem areas where control systems utterly fail, where policymakers seem not to have grasped the issue, and where major battles urgently need to be fought.

PART TWO

New Frontiers for Control

3

False Claims

Patient: "There's a problem with this bill. I never received these services."
Provider: "Why should you worry? Medicare is paying."

This chapter focuses on the submission and payment of false claims—an area that crooks seem to understand perfectly well; which the health care industry fails to condemn, and often seems to defend; and against which insurance programs, public and private alike, lack adequate defense.

I use the term "false claims" here in its simplest (i.e., nonlegal) sense. I use it to mean claims that are false (i.e., they contain a material falsehood) and which are nevertheless billed correctly, processed perfectly, and paid. Never mind how the falsehood entered in; whether it was an accidental error or part of a criminal conspiracy. Let us put off, for as long as possible, consideration of how the claim came to be false. Let us put aside judgments about what might have been happening, or not happening, inside the mind of whoever submitted the false claim and subsequently received payment. It is enough, for the purposes of this discussion, that the claim was *false*: The diagnosis was false, or the services were not provided as billed, or the procedures were inflated or exaggerated (upcoded) to something more expensive.

Payments for such false claims constitute the most basic, central, and obvious form of inappropriate health care payments. Focusing on this rather simple, uncomplicated phenomenon turns out to be quite instructive in advancing the art of fraud control. Why? Because this remarkably commonplace phenomenon—where false claims are billed, processed correctly, and paid—exposes some major holes in existing control systems. The false claims phenomenon shows the principal remaining weakness in the fee-for-service structure; it debunks the administration's claims to have slashed Medicare's improper payment rate; it exposes the subterfuge industry uses to dodge the issue; and it connects directly with one of the major sources of consumer outrage. False claims, then, are *useful* to consider. In the battle against fraud and abuse, they are one of the most important things to consider *next*.

Fixing the vulnerabilities of fee-for-service systems seems all the more important now, as the transition to capitated managed care systems slows down. Within the Medicare and Medicaid programs in particular, managed care organizations are pulling out as the authorities struggle to keep the lid on capitation rates. A wave of industry mergers and consolidations has sharply reduced competition in many managed care markets. Consumers are angry with their Health Maintenance Organizations (HMOs) and want the right to sue them. Regulators find it increasingly difficult to exert their will over fewer and bigger companies. In some parts of the country, the conversion of insured populations into managed care plans has not only stopped, but gone into reverse. How serious this faltering will turn out to be, in the long term, is hard to predict; clearly, though, fee-for-service systems will be around for much longer than many were predicting a few years ago. In the Medicare program, fee-for-service payments still account for more than 80 percent of total costs. Fixing up the fee-for-service structure remains critical.

Fraud perpetrators understand the dynamics of false claims extremely well: They lie about diagnoses, falsify the record of services, and in some cases fabricate entire medical episodes for patients they have never seen. They bill their lies correctly, aiming for the sweet spot—smack in the middle of medical orthodoxy, policy coverage, and price. Then, having found combinations that pay, they replicate them (electronically) thousands of times, spreading the activity across hundreds of patients' accounts, and preferably across different insurers, to evade detection. Fraud perpetrators focus on claims that do not trigger the dispatch of a statement to the patient; they choose patient populations whose mail they can control; and they target patients who are not capable of spotting discrepancies or are not in a position to report them. When the perpetrators are caught through some miscalculation or misfortune, they quickly pay back the claims in question, apologize profusely for the billing error, and continue to steal.

By contrast, policymakers seem not to understand these dynamics so well. In the 1999 and 2000 budget and performance requirements for Medicare contractors, the Health Care Financing Administration (HCFA) emphasizes that it expects contractors to maximize the number of prepayment reviews they conduct, and encourages contractors to develop and implement as many automated edits as possible—in order to deny services that are excluded by statute, are never medically reasonable and necessary, or are not covered on the basis of medical review policies.[1] Of course, all that is important work and should be done. But it doesn't touch the problem of false claims *at all.*

The Consumer's Perspective

From the consumers' perspective, "billing for services not furnished" is the most common type of fraud they experience.[2] While government seems preoccupied with undocumented claims and medically unnecessary treatments (which are, of course, important), consumers are mostly furious about well-documented lies.

Nothing irritates consumers more than discovering that their insurer paid for services that they are quite certain did not happen; except, perhaps, complaining about it and finding out that the relevant authorities either don't care very much or lack the investigative resources to determine how such a strange thing could have occurred.

The following stories all relate to complaints received over the "Fraud Hotline" (1–800-HHS-TIPS) run by the Office of Inspector General (OIG). They were compiled as part of a press release for a news conference about Medicare fraud in February 1999, hosted jointly by the American Association of Retired Persons (AARP), the Department of Justice, and the Department of Health and Human Services (HHS).[3] The following examples all relate to false claims as I have defined them here—quite without my making a judgment as to what was in the mind of the provider at the time. These stories are typical for this phenomenon. Note particularly what happens in each case when the claim is established as false:

- *Hospital bills, after a visit to a diabetes clinic:* A Medicare beneficiary from Sacramento saw that a Sacramento hospital had billed Medicare over $31,000 for her treatment and was paid $3,758; she had never received treatment at that hospital and was irate to discover that Medicare had paid for services not rendered. When the beneficiary obtained an itemized hospital bill, the only item she recognized was a visit to a diabetes clinic (which was part of the hospital chain) where she had once gone to learn how to use her sugar machine. There was no charge for that clinic's service, but the clinic had taken the patients' Medicare number, address, and phone number. A review of the hospital charges resulted in repayment of the $3,758 to the Medicare program.

- *Which hospital, and what treatment?:* A Texas man received an explanation of medical benefits (EOMB) on which he noticed Medicare payments to a hospital in Denver, Colorado. He had never heard of the hospital, nor had he visited it for treatment. A "review" by Blue Cross/Blue Shield (BCBS) of Texas substantiated the improper charges, and Medicare recovered $748.

- *The cost of "Hello":* A beneficiary from Georgia contacted the OIG Fraud Hotline. He had convalesced for a short time in a rehabilitation center, where an osteopath from Macon, Georgia, dropped by to say hello. The beneficiary suspected the osteopath was visiting rehab centers, collecting names and Medicare numbers, and moving on. An investigation into this patient's alleged "treatment" from the osteopath determined that the services claimed had not been rendered; the osteopath returned the money, which amounted to $2,800.47 for that one patient.

- *The long reach of anesthesia:* A New York woman called the OIG Fraud Hotline when several of her Medicare statements listed charges for surgery and anesthesia from medical practices in Florida. She had never had medical treatment in Florida. The local Medicare insurance company reviewed the case and discovered that the provider had billed "in error." Medicare was refunded $1,607.

From a thief's perspective, what a beautiful target! The worst that happened in these examples (and in countless thousands of other instances) is that the provider had to repay the one false claim detected, without penalties, and usually without even paying interest on the government's "loan."

From the perspective of a taxpayer or premium-payer, this pattern is extremely disturbing. When a consumer sees a fabricated medical episode, complete with multiple visits and procedures all billed and paid, and when inquiries confirm that the services were *not* provided, that consumer is never satisfied with a simple repayment of the money. In the minds of consumers, repayment alone ought not to be the end of such matters; consumers want to know how such billings happen. They want to know whether this one spurious claim falls within a pattern of systematic abuse. They want to know how many other patients have been exploited in the same way. They want to know whether it could happen again. They think someone should figure out at what point and through what mechanism false information entered the provider's billing system. When they are told, as happens often, that the provider merely entered the wrong patient's identification number by mistake, they want to know if the real patient was charged at the same time and whether many other patients also ended up sharing the same medical episode. These are the questions for which taxpayers and consumers properly expect answers. They seldom get them.

Sometimes, investigators do take the time to look deeper into the business practices of providers who generate false claims. Here are two more stories from the OIG Fraud Hotline, but with a different twist in the tale:[4]

- *Orthopedic improprieties:* A beneficiary from Miami called the Fraud Hotline after reviewing Medicare statements and discovering that a local medical equipment company had billed $367 for orthopedic supplies. The beneficiary had never received these supplies and had not heard of the company. A review by the Medicare insurance company turned up considerable improprieties and lead to a demand for the return of $102,393 in overpayments. The supplier fled before the Medicare insurance company received the money.

- *DME supplies billed but never received:* A Medicare beneficiary identified equipment and supplies that Medicare had paid for, but which had never been delivered to him. Following an investigation into the business practices of the supplier, the owner of the company was prosecuted and sentenced to prison for seventy-two months and ordered to pay restitution to Medicare in the amount of $11 million.

Traditionally, the Medicaid program has not routinely sent patients EOMBs. Medicare, traditionally, dispatched EOMBs only to beneficiaries under certain circumstances—when a payment was refused, or when it involved a copayment. If a service was 100 percent covered and paid, the beneficiary would not be sent a statement. The Health Insurance Portability and Accountability Act (HIPPA) of 1996 requires HCFA to substantially increase the use of EOMBs within the Medicare program. Eventually, beneficiaries will receive statements for every service. With roughly 900 million Medicare claims being processed each year, that constitutes a massive increase in EOMB mailings—which is now being phased in.

As well as dramatically increasing the volume of EOMBs mailed out, the administration is devoting some effort to helping beneficiaries interpret them and report discrepancies, even providing limited financial incentives for beneficiaries who identify fraud. In 1997, the Administration on Aging awarded $2 million in grants to twelve states for the recruitment and training of thousands of retired professionals to serve as health care "fraud busters." These trained volunteers work with older people in their communities to review benefit statements and report potential cases of waste, fraud, and abuse.[5] In 1999, this "fraud buster" program budget was expanded to $7 million. A separate program, sponsored under HIPAA, has spent $1.4 million to train existing aging network staff and volunteers to educate Medicare beneficiaries about fraud, waste, and abuse as a part of their ongoing activities.[6]

What happens when a major program, like Medicare, substantially increases the volume of EOMBs mailed out, raises the general level of awareness, and provides phone numbers for people to call? According to HCFA officials, the result is an avalanche of complaints—far more than they can deal with—as thousands and thousands of people call to say "it didn't happen." It is not at all clear that the administration needed to boost the volume of complaints. Medicare beneficiaries, somewhat enraged, already reported false claims faster than government could keep up. According to surveys conducted by the American Association of Retired Persons (AARP), rewards or monetary incentives would not make the majority of consumers more likely to report fraud than they have been already.[7] Patients already report plenty; the real issue is what happens when they report it.

In 1992, the General Accounting Office (GAO) examined the procedures Medicare contractors followed when beneficiaries called to report discrepancies.[8] According to the GAO's report, what happens is quite surprising. If a beneficiary says a service, reported on an EOMB, was not provided as billed, the investigative unit mails a form or letter to the provider asking for confirmation that the service was, in fact, provided. Depending on the practice of the Medicare contractor, providers might be asked to produce medical records or merely to sign a declaration that the service was provided. Assuming the provider confirms the service, the unit then sends the complainant a letter explaining that the service has been confirmed. That is the end of the matter, unless the beneficiary chooses to appeal the finding. To a complaining beneficiary, such actions make the government appear extraordinarily stupid. Most beneficiaries drop their complaints at that stage, many of them no doubt feeling the government does not deserve help; some, however, according to investigators, "go ape, call the media, or call their congressman."

The same GAO report cites the example of one Medicare beneficiary who was visited in her home by a nurse and doctor, neither of whom she knew. They claimed Medicare had sent them. Later that day, a supplier delivered several medical items. The woman had neither ordered nor needed the supplies and told the supplier to take them away. Later, she received notification (an EOMB) that Medicare had paid the physician for a home visit and the supplier for the equipment. The beneficiary complained immediately to the Medicare contractor who, upon receipt of the complaint, requested the refund of the payments from the physician and the supplier (totaling roughly $700) and took no further action.[9] The complaint had been adequately "disposed of."

The GAO reviewed the case later and pushed the contractor to investigate further. With a little deeper inquiry, the contractor discovered over $450,000 in potential overpayments to these same providers. The contractor also found another medical supply company operating at the same address as the first but under a different name and Medicare provider number.

It seemed, in 1992, that the units responsible for investigating such complaints had fallen into a case-disposition mode whereby they merely processed isolated "billing disputes" and resolved them by recouping the overpayments identified.

How much have things improved? The OIG Fraud Hotline number is now being printed on some EOMBs in some parts of the country.[10] They can't do it everywhere because the lines could not handle the volume. But let us suppose that you had heard about the fraud hotline, either from your Medicare statements or through the government's publicity campaign, and you called to report a false claim. What happens?

The OIG Fraud Hotline appears to treat reports of false claims as routine billing disputes, rather than reports of potential fraud. When I last called the hotline (January 2000), I first had to "press 1" to choose the English language. Then, in presenting a list of menu options, a recorded female voice cautioned, right up front, that many problems are better handled by calling your health care provider first, and your Medicare insurance company (whose number is printed on the bottom of the EOMB form), second. What types of problems are better handled that way? The recorded message details three:

1. billing for services that the caller believes were not provided;
2. billing for equipment that the caller or their doctor did not order;
3. billing more than once for the same services.

The message continues that if you have already called both of those other parties and still wish to talk to a representative, or if you have "information about fraud," then stay on the line.

Now, let's imagine that a patient receives an EOMB detailing a course of treatment in a hospital that the patient has never been anywhere near. With respect to the false claims, the advice given to the patient by the OIG is quite specific and unambiguous: Take it up with the provider yourself. (Bear in mind, this may put patients directly in conflict with potential fraud perpetrators. This is certainly not wise, and in some cases may not be safe.) Even the EOMBs have been modified by HCFA so that beneficiaries are told to check with their physicians before reporting suspected billing errors to the government.[11]

If, after taking it up with the provider, the patient is still not satisfied, he or she should take it up with the Medicare contractor. In the case of a hospital bill, that would be one of those fiscal intermediaries that fund their fraud units at an average level of around 0.007 percent of the claims volume! The patient's complaint, if the patient can get through at all, is going to sit in a pile with hundreds or thousands of others. The best the consumer can generally hope for is that the ordinary "billing dispute resolution procedures" will confirm the claims as false and that the government will recover the particular overpayment.

Most consumers who call a fraud hotline to report false claims will be somewhat taken aback to find their complaints immediately reclassified as billing disputes, and treated as such. For the majority of consumers, evidence in their hands that someone has been paid for services not provided is the strongest indication of fraud they are ever likely to see. When they try to report the fraud to the relevant authorities, they learn that the control apparatus *assumes* false claims to be billing errors. From the consumer's point of view, that response is simply not adequate. Routine controls, and even the OIG's fraud hotline, fail to treat false claims with the seriousness they deserve.

The Medicare Overpayment Measurement Studies

The OIG's measurement program for improper Medicare payments also fails to take false claims into account. The Government Management Reform Act, passed in 1994, requires an annual audit of all government programs according to private sector accounting principles. With respect to Medicare, HHS has placed responsibility for this audit with the OIG. (In the future, HCFA may take over the conduct of the audit. For the Medicaid program, no national audit has yet been performed.)

The OIG instituted the audit of Medicare in 1997, and repeated it in 1998 and 1999. To estimate the extent of Medicare overpayments, the OIG draws a stratified random sample of Medicare beneficiaries and reviews all the claims submitted on their behalf during a selected three-month period. From the sample, the OIG determines an overpayment rate (a percentage), which is then extrapolated over the entire Medicare fee-for-service budget to provide an overall estimate of what they call "improper payments."

The first study, reported in July 1997 and based on claims paid during 1996, produced an overpayment estimate of $23.2 billion, or 14 percent of Medicare payments. The next year's study, based on claims paid during 1997, brought the estimates down to $20.3 billion, or 11 percent. Another year later, the OIG announced that the overpayment rate had been reduced further, to $12.6 billion (7.1 percent of payments). This is how the OIG reported the change:

> In a recent audit of the Health Care Financing Administration's financial statements, OIG found that improper Medicare payments to health care providers dropped dramatically last year. The error rate in Fiscal Year (FY) 1998 was 7.1 percent; that amounts to a remarkable 45 percent reduction in overpayments in just 2 years.[12]

This series of three measurement studies form the basis for the administration's oft-repeated claim to have "cut the Medicare improper payments rate by 45 percent in just two years."

To understand what *kinds* of overpayments might be included within the measured loss rate (most recently, 7.1 percent), and which ones might be left out, one has to examine the procedures the OIG used in auditing the claims within their samples. For all three years, they employed essentially the same audit protocol, described in their report of February 1999:[13]

> *Audit Procedures.* We reviewed all claims processed for payment for each selected beneficiary during the [relevant] three-month period. We contacted each provider in our sample by letter requesting copies of all medical records supporting services billed. In the event that we did not receive a response from our initial letter, we made numerous follow-up contacts by let-

ter and, in most instances, by telephone calls. At selected providers, we also made onsite visits to collect requested documentation.

Medical review personnel from HCFA's Medicare contractors and peer review organizations (PROs) assessed the medical records to determine whether the services billed were reasonable, medically necessary, adequately documented, and coded in accordance with Medicare reimbursement rules and regulations.

Note that these procedures do not include contact with the patients.[14] Note, too, that requests for supporting documentation were made by letter. This audit procedure essentially replicates a standard *Medical Review* audit. Such audits will not uncover the majority of fraud schemes. There is no reason, either, to believe they will uncover false claims whenever false documentation is supplied to match the false claims.

In April 1998, the *Reader's Digest* published a "Special Report" on Medicare fraud, written by Randy Fitzgerald for the *Digest's* audience of over 100 million readers. It is one of the best available short lay-expositions of the nature of health care fraud. In describing the deficiencies of existing control systems, Fitzgerald wanted to communicate the inadequacy of focusing only on correct processing and adequate documentation. He got that message across quite effectively by recounting the experience of one scam artist:[15]

> John Watts, Jr., described to a Senate committee how simple it was for him to open a home health care agency, even though 13 months before going into business, he had been in prison, and his prior business experience was as owner of a nightclub. He opened his agency in Culver City, California, received Medicare certification and within the year began sending in bogus claims for clients, some of whom were dead.
>
> All Watts needed for these claims was the patient's name, a health insurance number and a code for diagnosis. During a 17-month period Watts billed Medicare $5.6 million for over 80,000 home health visits—of which he estimates $1.5 million to $2.5 million was fraudulent.
>
> *When Medicare finally sought documentation, Watts paid nurses to create fraudulent medical records.*[16] Only after an anonymous complaint was Watts investigated.

Even a relatively unsophisticated crook, like Watts, quickly figured out that if all the government ever did was compare the claims submitted with the medical documentation provided—and did not verify the services with the patient—then all he needed to do, when asked, was fabricate documents to match.

Even back in the 1980s, crooks had learned the importance of generating phony medical records to match their phony bills. Take the case of Sheldon Weinberg, a physician, and his two sons, in New York. In 1988, they were convicted of stealing $17 million from Medicaid. When they billed Medicaid for close to 400,000 phantom patient visits, they had their medical center's computer produce the claims and the backup medical charts for as many as 12,000 fictitious visits per month.[17]

A *Medical Review* audit (which accepts all documents as "true," and focuses on their medical significance) would seldom reveal claims as false. Only a more rigorous *fraud audit* could do that. A fraud audit would have to include, at a minimum, substantial efforts to contact patients or their relatives to verify the services were delivered. Preferably, the patient interviews would be done before any approach to the provider. If the patient disputed the services, a rigorous audit protocol would call for an unannounced visit to the provider's offices to examine medical and billing records, minimizing their opportunity to tinker with them.

Because the OIG measurement studies fail to capture the majority of fraudulent claims that might have fallen into the samples, the series of overpayment error rates these studies have produced *do not cover fraudulent claims*. Fraud might add another 10 percent (or 20 percent, or 30 percent) on top of the estimated overpayment rate. Nobody knows exactly how much because the *fraud* rate has not yet been measured.

The lack of rigor in these audits also calls into question the reported declines. Why did the rate drop from 14 percent to 7.1 percent in two years? Perhaps because billing practices did improve. Or perhaps, because word got around in the industry that if you received one of these OIG audit letters, all you had to do was fill out the medical record and send it in and that would be the end of the matter. The decline is probably due to a mixture of the two effects. The OIG's 1999 report (of the 1998 study) did comment that most of the improvement from year to year involved better documentation rather than changed billing practices. Even when payments were ineligible, they had become better documented.

Fraud Audits

In 1997, the Texas Legislature required the Texas Comptroller of Public Accounts to study the size and nature of fraud and overpayments in three of the state's health care programs—Medicaid, the Worker's Compensation program, and the state employees' benefits program. (Texas and Illinois, to date, are the only two states to attempt to measure overpayments within the Medicaid program.)

The comptroller's staff employed an outside consulting firm to design a sampling strategy for each of the three health programs and to audit the claims drawn in the samples. Together they designed a rigorous fraud audit protocol that included patient interviews before the providers were approached.[18] In December 1998, the comptroller's staff, in conjunction with the contractors, produced a draft report containing the findings. These findings were so disturbing that they were fiercely contested by some of the programs studied, particularly the state employees' benefits program. Partly as a result of the ensuing controversy and partly because of changes in the political landscape, a final report was never issued.

During the study, the comptroller's staff learned that a significant number of claims in the samples had been presented and processed correctly and then paid; yet when the patients were interviewed, a number of them said, "Not me." These patients stuck with their denials even when given repeated opportunities to recall the treatments in question. Several parents, interviewed about their children's treatment, stated adamantly that their children had never had the sickness in question, nor had they seen the provider.

The methods used in the Texas study *would* have identified false claims. The methods used in the OIG's Medicare studies, to date, would not. Perhaps the OIG will adopt a more rigorous approach for their 1999 study, to be reported early in 2000. Or perhaps, "for the sake of making valid comparisons," they will stick with what they have done before; in this case, we may have to wait until 2001 to find out how much fraud is costing the Medicare program.

The Industry's Perspective on False Claims

One possible reason that control systems classify and treat false claims as billing errors is that major industry associations ridicule the government's position when it tries to classify them or treat them any other way.

When the OIG first published its Medicare overpayment estimates (of $23 billion for Fiscal Year [FY] 1996) the American Medical Association (AMA) took offense. A report from the AMA's board of trustees complained:[19]

The Inspector General of the U.S. Department of Health and Human Services (HHS IG) released an audit in July, 1997 suggesting that fraud and abuse in the Medicare program totals $23 billion a year or 14 percent of the traditional Medicare program. The IG audit substantially stretched the definition of fraud and abuse. Physician claims which were not fully documented and initial medical necessity denials that are frequently overturned on appeal (up to 70 percent are reversed), were labeled as "evidence" of fraud and abuse. The Board of Trustees has expressed strong concerns that fraud and abuse estimates should be confined to proven cases of fraudulent intent and acts which are inconsistent with accepted medical practices.

In other words, unless criminal intent has been proved in court, leave out the word "fraud." All overpayments (other than those proved to be fraud) stem merely from errors and sloppy documentation—to be regarded as regrettable, but as prerogatives of the profession. The same report also claims that the AMA "has defeated repeated attempts by the Department of Justice and HHS IG to lower the current knowing and willful standard for fraud prosecutions."[20] (I think this would come as a surprise to the Department of Justice, who have neither made nor attempted to make any incursions on normal standards of proof required in criminal cases. Presumably this is a reference to increased use of the *civil* provisions of the False Claims Act [FCA].) Also, portending the AMA's lobbying efforts to gain immunity for providers under the FCA, the report indicates:

> The existence of an effective compliance plan provides evidence that any mistakes were inadvertent, and this evidence could be considered by the federal government in determining whether reasonable efforts have been taken to avoid and detect fraud and other misbehavior.[21]

The report recommends that the AMA leadership "should intensify efforts to urge federal policymakers to apply traditional definitions of fraud and abuse which focus on intentional acts of misconduct and activities inconsistent with accepted medical practice." Also, that the AMA "continue to work within a coalition of other health care organizations to lobby for restrictions on the use of the False Claims Act."[22]

Perhaps the AMA leadership should be reminded that, until the 1950s, the AMA regarded a financial incentive (to prescribe one course of treatment instead of another) as an inherent conflict of interest for physicians. But then, with the decline of individual physician's clinics and the growth of more complex business relationships within the industry, the medical profession grew considerably in wealth and power. Now, it seems, the AMA is intent on insulating their members' financial interests from government scrutiny or regulation.[23] Their strategy: Recast government reporting of false claims or overpayments as sweeping allegations of criminal fraud (which they think would be self-evidently lacking in credibility). The obvious truth, by the industry's account, is that false claims and overpayments all stem from innocent billing errors.

During the hospitals' battle over the False Claims Act, Mary Grealy, counsel for the American Hospital Association (AHA), complained, "The environment has changed from zero tolerance for fraud to zero tolerance for errors. It's been a dramatic sea change, and this wide net has been cast with these indiscriminate letters to hospitals."[24] In other words, by using the False Claims Act to go after false claims, the government had ceased to distinguish between errors and fraud.

Of course, if things get really sticky, providers can always blame the computer. In a recently published discussion of compliance issues, the chief compliance officer for the Medaphis Corporation in Atlanta pointed out, "We submit 50 million claims a year. It only takes one computer glitch to make 50,000 of those claims bad."[25] That's why taxpayers get so worried about false claims. Computerized billing systems—attached, through various health care programs, to the U.S. Treasury—represent extraordinarily powerful instruments for self-enrichment at the taxpayer's expense, whether intentional, reckless, careless, or purely accidental. Yes, 50,000 false claims can be dispatched in an instant. If, by some fluke or mischance, they are discovered, then blame the computer! What particularly bothers investigators and analysts in this field, is that they observe upwards of 95 percent of computer glitches working to the financial advantage of the provider. From that, the more cynical among them might impute some less than honorable motive. They might even be tempted to label the false claims produced by such glitches as fraud. Stepping too eagerly over that line and implying what you cannot prove, however, merely plays into the hands of the industry's propaganda machine.

Let's just leave them as false claims. Let's not make any judgment about criminal intent, or reckless disregard. Let's put aside the assumptions embedded in many control systems, and promulgated by industry, that these are all errors. Let's consider instead what *taxpayers* expect with respect to false claims.

From the public's perspective, providers who want to work for government programs ought to take sufficient care over their billings to prevent false claims. If they operate huge automated billing systems that carry the risk of producing many thousands of false claims through the slip of a finger, consumers expect those providers to treat the consequent financial risk to the government just as seriously, or more so, than the company would treat such a financial risk to itself. Sophisticated systems should have sophisticated controls. Massive corporations using such systems—given their enormous potential for facilitating theft—should exert proper control over them. "Computer glitch" is no excuse.

From the public's perspective, if providers cannot ensure that their billings are fair and true representations of services provided, the government should not do business with them. They should be *excluded* because they take insufficient care of public funds and their bleeding of the system is intolerable. Investigators and auditors should not be required to get inside the heads of the providers and to prove criminal intent beyond reasonable doubt before they can stem the flow of public funds. No homeowner in his or her right mind would continue to do business with plumbers or electricians or roofing contractors who showered them with bills for services never provided. Taxpayers expect government to apply the same ordinary prudence and to develop the audit programs and policies necessary to put such common sense into action.

If the Clinton administration claims to have cut the false claims problem (the central fraud problem) "almost in half in just under two years," they, too, make a *false claim*. Work on this one has hardly begun. False claims have yet to be measured. Control systems fail to treat them seriously, shuffling them off as billing errors. And the industry has so far refused to take responsibility for them, preferring to cloud the issue by fussing about what might or might not have been in providers' minds at the time.

4

Managed Care

The second area requiring urgent attention, and a much higher level of understanding, is the issue of fraud and abuse under capitated managed care systems. As capitated systems continue to expand, so we must understand how the nature of fraud will change and how the new forms of fraud might be controlled.

Many within the industry still believe that managed care structurally eliminates the fraud problem. Many times, during interviews with senior managers at both private and public payers, I found that they would acknowledge some of the more serious weaknesses in their fee-for-service controls and then close the discussion by pronouncing it irrelevant anyway: The inevitable expansion of managed care would eventually consign fee-for-service, with all its associated problems, to the history books.

Managed care systems certainly alter the financial incentives for providers. Under capitation—where a fixed fee is paid each month for each patient, regardless of usage—the traditional financial incentives for overutilization are indeed eliminated. Capitation, therefore, should eliminate the incentives for provision of medically unnecessary services. Capitation fees, moreover, are paid regardless of the level of service provided and thus eliminate the possibility of false claims.

By eliminating the incentive for overutilization and the possibility of false claims, managed care—so the argument goes—should eliminate fraud. This chapter tests that hypothesis and clarifies the impacts that managed care will have on opportunities for fraud and on methods for fraud control.

Expansion of Managed Care

The growth of managed care continues, although the growth rate has slowed since 1997. Roughly three out of every ten Americans are now enrolled in some sort of Health Maintenance Organization (HMO). In June 1998, the proportion of the Medicaid population enrolled in managed care plans passed the 50 percent mark.[1] For the Medicare population, which lags considerably behind the general population in switching over, the proportion was roughly 17 percent, or 6.8 million people, as of the end of 1998.[2]

The fastest-growing type of contract under the major public programs is the "risk" program (fully capitated), where the payer (e.g., Medicare or Medicaid) pays a per capita premium for an agreed-upon package of benefits. The package generally includes services such as routine physical examinations, immunizations, and eye and ear examinations not traditionally covered by Medicare fee-for-service. Additional services available within a smaller number of plans include outpatient drugs, dental care, foot care, and health education. The attractiveness of managed care plans for beneficiaries stems from inclusion of these extra (preventive) services, a minimal paperwork burden, and small or no out-of-pocket expenses.

Major Types of Managed Care Plans

Managed care comes in many shapes and forms, with a seemingly endless variety of financial arrangements. The major categories are summarized here:[3]

- *Preferred Provider Organizations (PPO):* These are basically fee-for-service organizations with incentives for the beneficiary to stay within a defined pool of providers. Providers discount their rates in exchange for a guaranteed, steady stream of business.
- *Exclusive Provider Organizations (EPO):* An EPO is the same as a PPO, but with tougher restrictions on out-of-network services. There may be a stricter utilization review and no coverage at all for out-of-network services.
- *Health Maintenance Organizations (HMO):* The HMO receives capitated payments—a set premium for each patient each month. Enrollees designate a primary care physician and subsequently pay a small fixed fee for each office visit. Some HMOs (open-ended HMOs) provide some benefits with respect to use of out-of-network providers. Others (network model HMOs) do not. HMOs sometimes bear all the financial risk, compensating their network physicians on a claims-submitted basis (usually at discounted

rates). Alternatively, the HMO might share the risk with its providers, or distribute it to providers entirely, paying them at least in part on a capitated basis.

- *Individual Physician Association Model HMO (IPA):* An HMO receives capitation payments and bears the financial risks. The HMO then contracts with a network of physicians (as does a PPO or an EPO) to provide services on a discounted fee-for-service basis. There may be year-end bonuses (in the form of cash disbursements) or penalties (usually in the form of reduced fee schedules) depending on whether aggregate cost-control goals were met across the network.

- *Staff Model HMOs:* Staff model HMOs are hospital- or clinic-based HMOs whose providers are salaried employees working almost exclusively with HMO enrollees.

Structural Solution to the Fraud Problem?

Those who believe that managed care solves the fraud problem assume that the solution is structural. In other words, they believe that the contractual and financial arrangements peculiar to managed care plans remove the opportunity for fraud; and that detection, investigation, or any other dedicated fraud-control functions consequently become unnecessary.

The National Health Care Anti-Fraud Association (NHCAA) commissioned a task force to examine managed health care and to address the hypothesis that the structure of managed care plans eliminates the opportunity for fraud. Their report, published in November 1994, works through each of the major managed care plan categories in turn and then roundly rejects the idea: "Experience of managed care organizations contradicts the myth that managed care, by its nature, eliminates incentives to commit fraud. It merely eliminates some of the more familiar methods of committing fraud, and replaces them with others." [4] The NHCAA report explained logically the different forms of fraud that might appear under each type of plan; it pointed out that, under capitated fees, the predominant nature of fraud will involve diversion of capitation fees away from frontline delivery of health care services, resulting in underutilization.[5]

In practical terms, however, the myth that managed care provides a structural solution lives on. Relatively few cases of fraud relating to capitated payment systems have been prosecuted. The paucity of cases, by itself, leaves open the question of whether levels of fraud have been reduced. As always with fraud control, you see only what you detect. The dearth of cases under managed care could mean that either fraud has become less prevalent or that existing detection methods fail to detect the new forms of fraud, leaving them invisible. If fraud has merely changed its form, the industry needs to understand why existing detection systems fail to find it and move quickly to design alternatives that might work better.

Early Experience

The National Association of Medicaid Fraud Control Units prepared a report for the president's task force on health care reform in 1993. They summarized nationwide fraud-control units' early experience with fraud under managed care:

> No health plan is immune from fraud and indeed fraud does occur in managed care plans. Rather, fraud simply takes different forms, in response to the way the program is structured.
>
> While the traditional Medicaid provider fraud investigation focuses on overutilization of services and fraudulent billing . . . in managed care organizations the evil more likely lies in the underutilization of services. Unlike the typical Medicaid provider fraud case, the human cost in terms of reduced access to quality care may be tremendous.[6]

In June 1995, fraud under managed care finally followed where so many fee-for-service frauds had gone before: the front page of the *New York Times*.[7] The story concerned high-pressure, misleading, and illegal marketing practices that some HMOs had begun targeting at Medicaid recipients in New York. Marketers had told recipients "Medicaid is coming to an end. Sign up for this HMO now or lose your medical coverage." The HMO, of course, protected itself by firing the saleswoman subject of the story, saying she had acted out of line.

Also in June 1995, Maryland's attorney general, J. Joseph Curran Jr., announced charges against fourteen HMO marketing representatives, two HMO supervisors, and eight employees of the Department of Social Services. The state employees had accepted bribes to disclose confidential information to the HMO marketing agents, who then used the information to enroll Medicaid recipients into HMOs (who then began collecting capitation fees) without the recipients' knowledge.[8] The state employees received roughly $0.50 to $1 for the name, address, dependents, and welfare status of each patient. The marketing agents received around $28 commission for each patient enrolled.

A few months later, another front-page story in the *New York Times* (November 17, 1995) began to drive home the dangers of underutilization:

> Posing as patients, New York State health investigators called the 18 largest managed care programs that serve Medicaid recipients in the state and asked to see doctors for such basic but essential services as prenatal care, immunizations of babies, and annual checkups. At 13 of the 18, the investigators had so much trouble just getting an initial appointment, that the Department of Health cited them for providing substandard care.[9]

More Recent Experience Within the Medicaid Program

Given the more rapid penetration of managed care within the Medicaid program, we should look there, first, to understand how things are going now.

During the recent series of seminar discussions on Medicaid fraud, executives from Medicaid agencies across the country described their experiences as their programs had begun to shift recipients into managed care plans. (I refer specifically to the "Executive Seminars on Fraud and Abuse in Medicaid," sponsored by the Health Care Financing Administration (HCFA) and held between December 1998 and May 1999, in which I participated as moderator.) These seminar discussions revealed a vast range of divergent opinion and some measure of confusion, with Medicaid officials still struggling to understand the implications of capitation on fraud and abuse control.[10] It was clear that the residual confusion and difficulties outweighed the limited progress that a handful of states had made. The pervasive impression from seminar recipients was that they did not feel their agencies had really grasped this issue yet.

This sense of widespread uncertainty resonates with the findings of a June 1999 report from the Office of Inspector General, Department of Health and Human Services (OIG, HHS).[11] That report, titled "Medicaid Managed Care Fraud and Abuse," examined the first ten states to obtain Medicaid Section 1115 Waivers (which permit them to restrict patients' choices) for Managed Care.[12] The report describes vast differences in perception among states about the possibility and nature of fraud and abuse in a capitated setting, the need for control, the locus for control, the nature of detection and referral systems, and the necessary elements of a control strategy. The report's findings include the observation:

> There is no general agreement about roles and requirements to detect and refer fraud and abuse in the managed care setting.[13]

Examining case detection and referral mechanisms, the OIG report found that two states, out of the ten examined, now had "active programs which result in case detection and referral of fraud and abuse; others do not." And these two (Arizona and Tennessee), which both employed proactive outreach mechanisms, accounted for 490 out of the 504 cases of managed care case referrals, or 97 percent within the group during the period studied.[14] However, despite the concentration of cases, neither in Arizona nor in Tennessee did the fraud units receive any case referrals from the Managed Care Organizations(MCOs).[15]

In survey responses, three of the ten Medicaid State agencies indicated that they thought they were no longer responsible for detection and referral of cases; and two others indicated that, because the monies were capitated, there was no longer any reason to worry about fraud and abuse.[16]

The overall impression one gets from this OIG report is that Arizona and Tennessee—as pioneers in the introduction of capitated managed care within the Medicaid Program—have learned certain lessons the hard way, through their early and somewhat bitter experience. Unfortunately, it appears that many other states, following along later, have not been quick to learn the same lessons; if they have, they too are learning them the hard way, beset by scandal, uncertainty, and confusion. As the OIG report puts it:

> Overall, there is confusion and disagreement on how to address fraud and abuse and there is limited activity in developing or actively pursuing and referring cases in the Medicaid managed care program.[17]

The body of law, policy, and operational knowledge required for control in this environment has apparently not yet been sufficiently well codified and communicated to give states that are moving their programs in this direction a sound basis upon which to construct effective controls.[18]

During the Medicaid fraud and abuse seminars, several participants stressed the need for HCFA, or others, to provide greater assistance in this area, particularly with the business of educating state legislators and senior program officials about the nature of the risks. The seminar discussions (involving forty-nine states) validate and extend the findings of the OIG study (which examined only ten states, but in a much more systematic fashion). States, presenting this issue area as a major obstacle for them, drew attention to the following central problems concerning fraud and abuse under capitated arrangements:

- the apparent persistence of the assumption that "managed care takes care of the problem," and the accompanying conclusion that Medicaid agencies who introduce capitated systems "don't have to worry about fraud and abuse anymore." As one participant put it:

  Program managers of the State's managed care program believe that there is no fraud and/or potential fraud in their programs . . . Although the managed care program reviews quality of care issues, it believes fraud is unlikely and if existent, the problem of the contracted entity.

- the inadequacy of encounter data as a basis for assessing quality of care issues;
- the lack of awareness or cooperation within MCOs regarding fraud and abuse detection and referral;
- the loss of program integrity resources within Medicaid agencies as these are transferred over to help administer the managed care programs;
- the absence of relevant performance measures for fraud and abuse controls (the traditional measures from the fee-for-service environment—dollars recovered or payments prevented—are clearly not relevant here);[19]
- the difficulties of establishing and maintaining an investigative capacity for fraud under managed care (with few referrals or sources, unfamiliar investigative environment, little cooperation, etc.);
- the absence of model fraud statutes for the managed care setting.

One of the basic points of confusion is a continuing general failure to distinguish carefully enough between frauds committed *against* the Managed Care Organizations (MCOs) and frauds committed *by* the MCOs themselves. Frauds committed against the MCOs by providers or recipients would hurt the MCO's bottom line. One might expect them to have a natural incentive to control these; and therein lies the basis for the widespread assumption that "managed care takes care of the problem."

But fraudulent or abusive practices *by the MCOs themselves* principally involve improper diversion of capitation payments away from frontline health care delivery, resulting in poor treatment for recipients, and enriching the MCOs and their affiliates. The idea that the "MCOs have the financial incentive to control fraud" (with its natural corollary—that program officials therefore need worry less about it) clearly applies to the first category (to some limited degree), but doesn't apply to this second category at all.

Potential Frauds Committed Against Managed Care Plans

The first category of abuses includes inaccurate billing, unbundling, upcoding, billing for services not provided, kickback schemes, false claims, balance billing or double billing, excessive utilization, and falsification of diagnoses to support such behaviors. These are traditional fee-for-service frauds committed by providers; they occur at the expense of the MCOs or intervening MCO subcontractors paid on a capitated basis.

Medicaid executives report (as did the OIG's study) that even in this area the managed care organizations seem either unconcerned, ineffective, or uncooperative. They generally seem reluctant to appear hard-nosed with their provider networks, preferring to shuffle troublesome providers quietly out of the system or to constrain them administratively. MCOs seem more willing to report fraud by recipients than they are to impune any part of their valuable provider networks.

The consequent failure to control even this kind (the traditional kind) of fraud results in diminished profits for the MCOs. Dwindling profit margins may, in turn, lead to:

1. lack of adequate competition for MCO contracts (which, in turn, diminishes the leverage the Medicaid agency might have had over these organizations);
2. MCOs pulling out of the business;
3. MCO bankruptcies; and
4. higher capitation rates in the future.

All four of these phenomena, which occur with increasing frequency, damage the Medicaid program. Hence the inadequacy of a control strategy that relies too heavily on the natural propensities and capabilities of MCOs in this domain.

Fraud and Abuse Committed by the Plans

The much greater and more pervasive weakness, however, is in failing to understand the myriad ways in which MCOs and their corporate affiliates can take advantage of lax systems for control and accountability. Many of these methods have already been observed and chronicled by organizations such as the National Association of Medicaid Fraud Control Units, the National Health Care Anti-Fraud Association, President Clinton's task force on health care reform, the General Accounting Office (GAO), the OIG (HHS), and others. Such practices include

- withholding or unreasonably delaying payments to subcontractors, providers, or provider networks;
- destruction of claims;
- embezzlement of capitation funds paid by the state;
- theft of funds, equipment, and services;
- fraudulent subcontracts (for example, where no services are provided, or phony management contracts);
- fraudulent related-party transactions;
- excessive salaries and fees to owners or their close associates;
- "bust-outs" (money goes in, no money goes out to the vendors, then the entrepreneur claims bankruptcy or simply disappears);
- collusive bid-rigging (between plans, and potentially involving collusion with state personnel);
- improper enrollment practices (attracting good risks or refusing bad risks);
- improper disenrollment practices (deliberately eliminating bad risks—persuading or forcing sicker patients to leave);
- disenrolling beneficiaries prior to hospital treatment (so hospital fees are paid under fee-for-service system), then re-enrolling them once they have recovered;
- or, conversely, presenting bureaucratic obstacles to prevent dissatisfied patients from disenrolling;

- falsification of new enrollee registrations (either fictitious patients or fictitious enrollments);
- kickbacks for primary care physicians for referrals of sicker patients to "out-of-network" specialists;
- arbitrarily excluding identifiable groups of beneficiaries (e.g., those with mental health problems, children, infants, the elderly) from service;
- regularly denying treatment requests without regard to legitimate medical evaluation;
- establishing policies that require an appeal before treatment will be given;
- measuring performance only in terms of absence of specific breaches of the contract language;
- failing to notify assigned beneficiaries of their rights, yet retaining the capitation payments;
- failing to procure health practitioners so that no service is ultimately provided;
- retaining exorbitant "administrative fees" and leaving inadequate provision for services;
- assigning unreasonably high numbers of beneficiaries to providers of service, making adequate service impossible.

Most of these methods center on diversion of capitation fees into the pockets of entrepreneurs. None of them involve false claims in the traditional sense. Most of them are *corporate* frauds, committed somewhere within the complex layers of intervening businesses which now separate payers (e.g., the Medicaid agencies) from frontline providers and their patients. The existence of so many abusive practices, which have been uncovered and reported all around the country, rebuts the notion that Medicaid agencies no longer need to pay attention, and demonstrates quite convincingly that the kinds of detection and investigative capacities developed under fee-for-service simply do not match the nature of these corporate abuses. A different kind of monitoring, different forms of accountability, and a new set of investigative skills must be established to ensure the integrity of these contracts.

Many federal and state programs require MCOs—either by statute or as a condition of their contracts—to report any instances of such fraudulent or improper practices. But it would be naïve to imagine these corporations would report *themselves* with any regularity. The need for Medicare program integrity units and Medicaid Fraud-Control Units (MFCUs) to focus on these issues and to develop a broad range of other methods for uncovering such abuses seems clear enough. Even as MFCUs and program integrity units work with the MCOs to improve performance with respect to provider fraud, they need to develop their capacity for monitoring the behaviors of the MCOs themselves, their subcontractors, and their agents. Thus the institutional arrangements necessary to promote control of fraud committed against the MCOs will be quite different (and maybe organizationally separate) from the apparatus developed to control fraud committed by the MCOs and their corporate affiliates.

Difficulties with Detection of Underutilization

Many state Medicaid programs rely heavily on the analysis of *encounter data* for detecting patterns of underutilization. A few have attempted to feed encounter data through the same sets of edits and audits used for fee-for-service claims. Most states report that the encounter data they currently receive (if any) is simply unreliable as a basis for monitoring anything. Executives cite the following difficulties:

- To establish underutilization, a broad pattern of encounters (or absence of encounters) has to be established. A case can no longer be built around one false claim.

- MCOs generally fail to submit encounter data as required by their contracts. Data is often late, of poor quality, incomplete, or totally missing. Falsification of encounter data is generally not a crime because it does not act as the basis for payment.[20]

- Even where contracts clearly require submission of encounter data, most MCOs do not comply. Medicaid agencies, worried about losing yet another MCO, seem unable or unwilling to press the issue too hard.

- Encounter data that is not passed through the claims-processing system (even if submitted in the same form as a fee-for-service [FFS] claim), is subsequently not available through the Surveillance and Utilization Review Subsystem (SURS).

- Analytic tools developed in the SURS environment are not suitable for detecting the kinds of anomalies one might expect to represent underutilization. Tools tailor-made for this task have been slow to emerge on the market; they would in any case be useless given the current quality of encounter data submission.

- Investigators of managed care fraud have few natural complainants or allies. The MCOs' corporate world will remain a closed system with respect to useful information, and difficult for investigators and auditors to penetrate.[21]
- Proving fraud or abuse is inextricably intertwined with questions of medical quality—a poorly developed field even amongst medical experts.
- Investigative units lack some of the investigative skills required in this domain; these include the ability to explore complex webs of contractual arrangements, to "follow the money," and to understand the effects of complex incentive and financial systems.[22]

In light of all these difficulties, and in light of all the current inadequacies of encounter data as a basis for monitoring service quality, some officials question the usefulness of continuing to press for reasonable quality encounter data submissions. Within the Medicaid program, however, HCFA continues to *require* the submission of encounter data; efforts to improve the quality, completeness, and timely submission will undoubtedly continue. Nevertheless, with these persistent difficulties, this avenue seems unlikely to provide effective monitoring anytime soon; hence the importance of developing a much broader range of techniques to gather data on MCOs' policies and practices, including focus groups, patient satisfaction surveys, monitoring of grievance procedures, and sample record reviews. Meanwhile, many states remain frustrated by the poor quality of encounter data; perhaps—at least in part—because they rely upon it so heavily.

Shifting Locus for Fraud

When the MCOs are paid on a capitated basis, but reimburse the frontline providers on a fee-for-service basis, then the frontline service providers, in theory, retain the capacity to commit all the regular forms of fee-for-service fraud. However, as a practical matter, commission of fraud by physicians would make them expensive to the plans, and the plans are not of a mind to tolerate providers who become expensive for any reason. Providers can generally be discharged from a plan, without cause, within ninety days or less. If cause can be established, discharge can be even quicker.

Therefore, expensive frontline providers will soon find that managed care plans either constrain them or throw them out. It makes no difference whether the reason for the high expense was pure greed or professional diligence. A thoroughly conscientious doctor who, under constrained resources, does more thorough testing than normal will meet the same fate as a dishonest colleague who tries to steal from the plan through excessive billing. Fee-for-service frauds (at least, the egregious ones) committed by frontline physicians against the plans will probably be controlled. Curiously, though, such frauds will be controlled not because they represent dishonesty, but because they are expensive. Fraud control, in this context, is subsumed under the goal of cost control.

One investigator, noting the ability of the plans to control fraud by frontline providers, remarked that this heralded a new form of fraud control. He defined it as "having the ability to control *who* can commit fraud." Managed care plans clearly have this power, and those so inclined will keep the opportunities for committing fraud to themselves. Hence the locus for commission of fraud moves upward, from the frontline service provider to the corporate middle layer.

Shifting Locus for Fraud Control

The locus for fraud control shifts, too. The responsibility for fraud control used to rest with the payers; but now when payers see the plans assuming the financial risk, they may assume that fraud will hurt the plans, not themselves. Payers may then pass the responsibility for fraud control down to the level of the plans. The plans, after all, should have a financial incentive to control fraud and protect their profit margins. If the plans allow their providers to defraud them, the loss will be primarily theirs. (If enough plans fail this way, the entire managed care structure may fail.) This argument holds up provided false billings remain the predominant form of fraud, as they were under fee-for-service arrangements.

But payers make a major mistake if they allow the responsibility for fraud control to pass into the hands of the contracting MCOs. Mindful only of the old forms of fraud, the payers recognize the MCO's financial incentives to control it. They relax their scrutiny of the plans, thinking the plans are the ones to suffer the consequences of fraud. What payers fail to realize is that the locus for fraud *control* has now shifted to precisely the same place as the locus for fraud *commission*: to the intervening corporate middle layers. Those with myriad opportunities to commit new types of fraud are also the ones being trusted or expected to police the system. The payers end up leaving the fox watching the henhouse.

Hence the stunning lack of fraud referrals from MCOs. One senior Medicaid investigator told me she was not the least bit surprised at the lack of referrals: "Now why would you want to create a situation where the middlemen, who are in league with the providers and working with them, are responsible for oversight? It's unbelievable." Another said the fraud-monitoring capacity at his state Medicaid agency had been gutted with the advent of managed care, and that those responsible for fraud control remembered only false claims and consequently focused on entirely the wrong things. As he put it:

> Whenever they talk about fraud they focus on *claims*. But the kinds of fraud that arise now are more white-collar, corporate fraud: bid-rigging, public corruption, conflicts of interest . . . and so on. Monitoring by [the state agency] is superficial and focused upon claims. The other mistake everybody makes is to assume that the pressure to control costs will act to control fraud. In fact, fraud merely results in worse underutilization than we would have had without it.

Corporate Middlemen
Not Bound by Professional Ethics

The locus for fraud and the locus for fraud control come together, in the middle. And who are these middlemen? They are corporations, not bound by medical ethics; in the health care business, for profit. In 1994, for-profit HMOs overtook not-for-profit HMOs as the dominant force in the market.[23] Arnold S. Relman, physician and editor emeritus of the *New England Journal of Medicine*, has said, "There's never been a time in the history of American medicine when the independence and autonomy of medical practitioners was as uncertain as it is now. I think that in this process businessmen and their agents will begin to exercise unprecedented control over the allocation of medical resources."[24] Managed care brings allocation of medical resources more under the control of businessmen than ever before and also shifts health care fraud firmly into the domain of big business.

At the same time, fraud will become much harder to detect, investigate, and prosecute. Investigators will have few natural allies or informants, except perhaps disgruntled providers or whistle-blowers within the MCOs. Frauds will involve complex webs of contractual arrangements, requiring an entire new set of investigative skills. Fraud will not rest on a single false claim but will be revealed only in patterns (e.g., of underutilization). Proving fraud under managed care will depend upon the ability of the courts to assess the significance of corporate policies and procedures, and patterns of outcomes, rather than specific individual acts. Many prosecutors remain reluctant to accept such complex cases. Investigators complain "they want a false claim." As a result, many complex and sophisticated fraud schemes will never make it to court. The data required to establish such patterns is of extremely poor quality, if available at all. And proving fraud will hinge on questions of medical quality, which remains a poorly developed and inexact science. Fraud prosecutions will require proof of systematic and conscious failure to provide adequate medical care—with the money being improperly diverted. And criminal diversion of funds will be difficult to distinguish from inflated administrative overhead. Investigators will find themselves lacking for information, for opportunities to get involved, and for the necessary investigative skills. Many prosecutors will fight shy of cases that have no central fraudulent transaction and that rely upon expert medical testimony. Over time, the criminal justice system will become less and less relevant to fraud control.

Reevaluating the Health Care Consequences of Fraud

Many of the prevalent forms of traditional fee-for-service fraud do not affect patient care at all. Billing for services not rendered, entering fictitious diagnoses, and "upcoding" often pass without the involvement or even the knowledge of the patient. Fraud, under fee-for-service, is predominantly a financial crime.

Under managed care, fraud will carry a much higher price in terms of human health. Fraud under managed care will claim lives. Testing will not be conducted when it should. Operations will not be performed when they should. Procedures will be carried out by inadequately qualified staff. Bureaucratic obstacles will be erected to deter patients from seeking treatment (and some patients will be deterred). Sick patients will be driven away.

During the honeymoon period for managed care, now drawing to a close, HMOs enjoyed high capitation rates based upon historical costs under fee-for-service structures. They also enjoyed the extra profitability that resulted from favorable selection, as they enrolled younger, healthier patients. As the penetration of managed care increases, so risk-bearing contractors will be forced to accept a broader mix, including sicker, costlier categories of patients. And major payers will squeeze capitation rates to reflect more accurately the cost of providing reasonable service. Once the opportunities for favorable selection diminish, whatever fraud takes place will become progressively more dangerous. Previously, managed care fraud may have sucked the money out of the cushion; but once the cushion has gone, it can only suck the money away from care. Then, more than ever before, the victims of fraud will be the patients.

Given the penetration of capitated systems into the industry, no time is left for policymakers to remain confused. They need to be crystal clear about the dangers of capitated systems, as most of the work of constructing adequate control systems still lies ahead.

PART THREE

The Nature of the Fraud-Control Challenge

5

The Pathology of Fraud Control

This part of the book is for those who want to understand the nature of the fraud-control business and who may have already discovered that there is precious little instruction in that art available. To contemplate the underlying nature of the beast, let us for a while step back from the immediate issues of the day. The objective for this chapter is to develop some understanding of what makes fraud control *in general* so difficult, and what makes fraud control within the health care industry even more so.

Essential Character of Fraud Control

Fraud control is a miserable business. Failure to detect fraud is bad news; finding fraud is bad news, too. Because news about fraud is never good, senior managers seldom want to hear it.

Institutional denial of the scope and seriousness of fraud losses is the norm. In the course of my field work within the health industry, many interviewees explained how their own views differed from "the official position" of their organizations and how uncomfortable they felt telling what they saw as "the truth," even to their own management. Investigators in Florida described how only recently, after years of media attention to the concentration of fraud problems in southern Florida, has it become acceptable to "speak up" during interagency meetings. Previously, they explained, if you talked honestly about the prevalence of fraud, you immediately got blamed for having failed to prevent it.

Employees closest to the work of fraud control habitually feel frustrated, unappreciated, sometimes ostracized by their own organizations, and deeply resentful of management's deaf ears to the entire subject. As one industry consultant, James Guzzi, told me:

> Senior management does not want to take the time to deal with the issue. It's too troublesome, and with too many other things on their plate to attend to, fraud always gets pushed to the bottom. The only time they pay attention is when there's a scandal involving them, or close to them. If they see a headline case, then they just want to know if their company was involved and whether or not they are going to be embarrassed.

Fraud-control policy tends to be scandal-driven. Management pays little attention to fraud control provided everything is quiet. They finally pay attention when scandal hits, either at home or close to home; even then they pay attention for a remarkably short time and with short-term damage control as the primary motivation.

Fraud control—as a science or art—is scarcely developed and little understood. Little instruction is available from academia, nor is there much expert guidance in the field. Guiding principles or practical approaches to fraud control are almost impossible to find in literature.

The discipline of *Managerial Accounting* gives the subject some attention but treats it as a rare subspecialty. Even specialist texts readily acknowledge the vacuum. Howard Davia (author of *Management Accountant's Guide to Fraud Discovery and Control*) confesses:

> There is no existing, established methodology for fraud auditing. Furthermore, there are no generally accepted fraud audit field standards, or generally available criteria that normally guide traditional auditors in the pursuit of their craft. Why is this so? There is a lack of such methodology and standards because effective fraud auditing is generally not being practiced.[1]

Under the heading, "Fraud—Pernicious and Largely Ignored," Davia describes the inevitable consequence:

> We cannot overemphasize the fact that entities throughout the world do not adequately recognize the seriousness of their exposure to fraud. The result is that he or she who would commit fraud has, more or less, carte blanche to do so. All entities are at risk, but few perceive the serious gravity of that risk.

Unfortunately, even when accounting or audit textbooks tackle fraud, they deal with it almost exclusively from the point of view of defense against internal corruption (employee embezzlement), rather than from the point of view of institutions defending their payment systems against concerted criminal attacks from outside.[2]

Those who commit to the task of controlling fraud, then, throw themselves into an area that academic literature has virtually ignored[3] and where practitioners often feel isolated and abandoned. As one investigator testified to Congress: "You have to have guts. . . . There is no body of law or procedure, and you are . . . going out in an area relatively unexplored."[4]

Before turning to the particular difficulties of the health care industry, what do we know about fraud control in general? What makes fraud control—in any environment—such a difficult and depressing business? Why do so many managers prefer to leave it alone? Why do organizations routinely underestimate or deny the existence of fraud? Why do organizations routinely fail to make proper investment in fraud-control apparatus?

We must understand the general pathology of fraud control as a backdrop before considering the health care industry more specifically. The following seven points represent common experience in fraud control, across many different professions. They represent the core, the harsh realities, that an effective approach to fraud control must confront.

What You See Is Never the Problem

Frauds can be categorized as self-revealing or not self-revealing, depending on whether or not fraud shows up by itself some time after the commission of the offense.

Credit card fraud that involves usurping somebody else's account is generally self-revealing: Account holders usually report unauthorized activities when they show up on their monthly statements. Tax refund fraud, where the perpetrator files a return and claims a refund by using another person's identity, also shows up by itself if the real person subsequently files a return. Tax administration systems will notice the duplicate submission. Check fraud, also, usually reveals itself ultimately, provided the legitimate account holder is alive and well and paying enough attention to bank statements to spot illegitimate activity.

Some fraud schemes fall between the two extremes, showing up, but showing up as something other than fraud. For example, many organized credit card frauds are based on fraudulent applications for cardholder accounts. Perpetrators using fictitious names run their cards up to the credit limit, and then discontinue use of those personal identities. From the credit card company's point of view, the "cardholder" has simply become untraceable—a common phenomenon with a variety of possible explanations. Because they are unable to establish fraudulent intent, most credit card companies classify such losses as "credit losses."

Most white-collar fraud schemes do not reveal themselves. Examples include most categories of insurance fraud, bankruptcy fraud, and tax refund fraud where the perpetrator uses his own identity or that of a nonfiler. All these frauds, provided they go undetected at the time of commission, and provided they escape postpayment audit, will remain invisible forever.

In relation to non-self-revealing frauds, therefore, *you see only what you detect.* Whatever fraud-control systems do not detect, no one will ever know about (although the aggregate economic impact might become apparent if the volume of fraud grows large enough). The consequent danger, of course, is that organizations vulnerable to fraud lull themselves into a false sense of security by imagining that their "caseload" (i.e., what they detect) reflects the scope and nature of the fraud perpetrated against them. Often it represents only a tiny fraction, and a biased sample, of the frauds being perpetrated. A 1980 study of white-collar crime expressed this basic truth.

> Conceptually and empirically, the records of individual events themselves are products of socially organized means of perceiving, defining, evaluating, recording and organizing information.[5]

In plainer language: The number and type of fraud schemes that become visible depends as much upon the effectiveness and biases of the detection systems as upon the underlying patterns of fraud.

Detection rates for non-self-revealing fraud types are usually extremely low, typically ranging from a high of 10 percent all the way down to zero. Some organizations simply have no idea they are vulnerable to fraud at all. Seeing no problem, they create no detection apparatus; having no detection apparatus, they see no problem. Thus some organizations remain completely oblivious to the truth about fraud losses until some outside source surprises them by showing them what they have lost.

Other organizations see a problem, but make the serious mistake of allowing the performance of their detection systems (often exceedingly poor) to shape their understanding of the problem and their sense of its magnitude. The inevitable consequence, with extremely serious long-term effect, is that they allow what they see to determine the level of resources allocated to fraud control or prevention. Quite naturally, everyone focuses on the visible part of the fraud problem. The real battle in fraud control is always over the invisible part.

Available Performance Indicators Are All Ambiguous

Nearly every available statistic in a fraud-control environment is ambiguous. At best, ambiguous; at worst, perverse and misleading.

If the amount of detected fraud increases, that can mean one of two things: Either the detection apparatus improved or the underlying incidence of fraud increased. Few organizations can tell for sure which, or how much of each, is happening. The resulting ambiguity pervades much fraud-control reporting, as noted by Larry Morey, deputy inspector general for investigations, Office of Inspector General, Department of Health and Human Services (OIG, HHS), testifying to Congress in 1993:

> Fraud is invisible until detected. Because of that fact, it is extremely difficult to estimate the total monetary loss as a result of fraud in the health care industry. While we cannot assign a dollar figure to the monetary loss to the Medicare and Medicaid programs as a result of fraud, we can tell you that we have noticed a dramatic increase in our investigative workload. This is caused, in part, by the ever expanding size of these programs. The increase in administrative and prosecutable authorities that the Congress has enacted is also a contributing factor. Finally, there may also be an increase in fraud in absolute terms.[6]

One private insurer, the Travelers, had observed steady increases in their levels of detected fraud from 1987 through 1990. Unable to tell whether this meant more fraud or better detection, they used an interesting technique to try to separate the two factors.[7] They carefully re-created the old set of detection tools (i.e., as of 1987) and then passed a subset of each subsequent year's claims through that same set of controls.[8] Having eliminated improved detection from the experiment, they still observed a 14 percent increase each successive year; they concluded that the level of fraudulent claims being submitted was actually increasing, even in areas for which defenses had been in place for some time. Without such careful analysis, it generally remains impossible to say whether an increase in detected fraud is good news or bad news.[9]

Many other quantitative measures of fraud-control success are ambiguous, too. Reactive successes can equally be viewed as preventive failures. Some organizations boast of "record recoveries"; others say they prefer to stop the fraud up front and regard chasing monetary recovery after the fact as a poor second best to prevention. Some organizations emphasize prevention simply to avoid having to admit that their detection systems are ineffective. If detection systems detect next to nothing, one can always claim preventive success.

The introduction of fingerprinting as a welfare-fraud control in the state of New York serves as a case in point. New York City and thirty-seven other counties in the state adopted a fingerprint system for welfare recipients; it was designed to detect "double dipping"—claiming the benefit multiple times using multiple identities—by recipients of home relief. In the summer of 1995, during the first two months of the operation, the system only identified forty-three cases out of 148,502 claimants. The *New York Times* reported the story under the headline "Welfare Fingerprinting Finds Most People Are Telling the Truth." [10] There are two quite plausible explanations for the unexpectedly low number of cases; one suggests the system accomplished its goal; the other suggests the system was a waste of money: "While the Giuliani administration hailed the low number of double dippers as proof that fingerprinting was scaring off cheats, advocates for the poor said the results showed that welfare fraud was an overblown issue." The Giuliani administration, which had introduced the measure as part of a more comprehensive crackdown on welfare fraud, pointed out that the number of claimants of home relief had dropped by 30,000 since January 1995 as a result of tougher investigative procedures and the institution of a work requirement.

The article raises the question, unanswerable without much more serious analysis, "Did the creation of a system to fight fraud stop it? Or was there little to begin with?"[11] Either way, any administration will likely have trouble maintaining a budget for a fingerprint system that prevents fraud but does not detect much, because nobody can say for sure what a preventive system does or does not accomplish.

To complicate things further: Fraud controls usually come in a sequence of phases or stages. The phases of fraud control typically parallel various phases of the claims-processing operation. Detection successes late in the sequence often represent failure at earlier points in the process.

For example, auditors at one Medicaid Fraud-Control Unit (MFCU) described what could be called "last-ditch controls," just before checks were sent out. Following the entire claims adjudication process, a magnetic tape was sent over to the state controller's office to generate the weekly payments to providers. Two employees within the controller's office took the trouble to examine the "big checks" and identify providers or services that appeared problematic. The auditors reported that these two employees typically saved the state "between 30 and 60 million dollars each year" and suggested that 30 to 60 million dollars per year, as an error rate, indicated "surprisingly accurate payment for a $15-billion program."

Well, that is one way of looking at it. When you realize that two employees (maybe costing the state $100,000 a year each) were saving up to $60 million a year, you have to ask how much *ten* employees might have saved. With a savings-to-cost ratio exceeding 150 to 1, it would seem wise to invest additional resources.

The ratio of direct dollar savings to cost for virtually all fraud-control activities normally ranges from a low of 2 to 1 to a high of 50 to 1 or 80 to 1. Savings-to-cost ratios are frequently used as a method of justifying the budgets for fraud control expenditures. In calculating the *savings,* companies typically combine prepayment savings with postpayment recoveries. (The indirect and nonmeasurable deterrent effects are never included in the calculation.) Of course these ratios, as measures of fraud-control effectiveness, are also ambiguous. Higher ratios may reflect unusually effective operations or may result from the existence of huge, untapped reservoirs of fraud.

A ratio of 150 to 1 is unusually high, though. The program integrity efforts of the Health Care Financing Administration (HCFA) typically produce returns of 10 to 1 or 12 to 1 each year. Officials claim a return rate for Operation Restore Trust of 23 to 1. To find a return rate of 150 to 1 so late in the process suggests serious weaknesses earlier in the process. The existence of such rich pickings so late in the day should surely lead officials to question the adequacy of preceding controls. Still, when it comes to saving $30 or $60 million in taxpayers' money, better late than never!

Thirty million dollars is indeed a small fraction (0.2 percent) of a $15 billion program. If $30 million was really all the fraud left at this last stage of the process, the payment system would indeed be "unusually accurate." But a savings ratio of 150:1 suggests nowhere near optimal levels of investment in detection; the low detection figure (0.2 percent) more likely represents massive underinvestment in controls rather than low fraud rates.

Another type of measure also deserves comment. The deterrent effect of a prosecution or set of prosecutions is often measured by a sudden subsequent drop in the level of claims within that category of services. In the health care industry, precipitous declines in claims rates often follow well-publicized cases. One can interpret this phenomenon as the sign of extraordinarily well-targeted investigative effort.

Conversely, one can interpret the drop in claims level as an indication of the previous level of fraud. If the Medicaid claims for medical transportation, for example, drop by 75 percent in an area following a handful of ambulance company prosecutions, what does that tell us about the level of fraud just prior to the enforcement action? That it was probably 75 percent of total billings, or higher.

When enforcement actions produce dramatic reductions in claims levels, should we be encouraged or disheartened? We should feel encouraged because of the skillful targeting and effectiveness of an enforcement response. At the same time, we should feel disheartened because the evidence has shown up yet another segment of the health system apparently riddled with fraud.

Finally, how should the industry interpret its major investigative successes? Many investigators derive great satisfaction from what they refer to as "tip of the iceberg cases"—where an apparently insignificant tip-off or lead is developed, through diligent and painstaking investigative work, into a major case on a massive fraud scheme. Investigators are most satisfied when they know they could easily have dropped the case, or not pressed so hard, because it looked somewhat trivial at the outset. As one investigator put it, "I love it when one [telephone] call blossoms into a massive investigation."

Although these cases represent excellence in investigation, they also reveal chronic failures of routine detection systems. If major scams are only uncovered through tip-of-the-iceberg-style investigations, routine monitoring is missing the mark. Such cases suggest that discovery of major fraud schemes is more a matter of luck than judgment.

Fraud Control Flies in the Face of
Productivity and Service and Competes for Resources

A third feature common to most fraud-control situations is the inevitable tension between those officials responsible for fraud control and those responsible for productivity. Additional fraud controls tend to slow down or complicate routine processes and create too many categories for exceptional treatment.

To the fraud investigators, the *process-oriented* appear narrow-minded, obstructive, blind to the reality of the fraud threat, and self-serving. The process-oriented seem to be preoccupied with processing efficiencies and appear not to care at all about the dollar losses through fraud that might completely eclipse savings achieved through automation or other processing enhancements.

Officials whose job it is to make processes more efficient or streamlined or predictable resent the obstacles to performance placed in their way by those who concentrate on exception monitoring. To the managers of the high-volume processes, the fraud investigators seem irritatingly obsessed with an apparently small (and, to them, insignificant) segment of a colossal transaction load. The processors want to think about the best way to handle the entire load. The investigators or fraud analysts want to think about the best way to handle the exceptions. These are two different agendas. In some organizations, these two groups work hard to destroy each other's careers, each convinced that they are working in the best interests of the organization. Where does this tension lead? The savings from processing efficiencies may be small, but they are concrete and tangible. By comparison, the potential savings from enhanced fraud controls may be massive, but they remain uncertain and invisible. Bureaucracies always choose concrete and immediate monetary returns over longer term, uncertain ones. Processing efficiency invariably wins the battle for resources, and the process-oriented normally get their way.

The late Congressman Ted Weiss, calling for creation of a national commission to map out a health care fraud strategy, said, "I do not understand how we can be cutting funds to oversee federal health insurance programs at a time when costs are rising at the speed of light." [12] The reason "funds to oversee" get cut is because they represent the easiest, least painful, and most obvious opportunity to cut costs.

The head of the fraud-investigation unit at one major Medicare contractor explained how her most powerful weapon against fraudulent providers was to require documentary evidence, before approving payment, in support of every claim submitted. Because electronic submission cannot handle accompanying documentation, that pits her interests directly against those of the claims-processing division, which has to accommodate all the extra claims coming in on paper rather than electronically:

> The real weapon is putting people on prepay (which, if they are committing fraud, is the equivalent of putting them out of business), but that hits me hard here within the company. If I require supporting documentation, I get killed inside the organization for increasing processing costs. Over $3 per

claim for paper, rather than 5.5 cents for electronic claims submission. They all hate me, inside and out. It's a great job.

Relentless pursuit of processing efficiencies can seriously undermine payment safeguards. As one senior HCFA official succinctly put it, "Of course the cheapest way to process a claim is to pay it, without question."

The Dynamic Nature of the Game

The fraud-control game is dynamic, not static. Fraud control is played against opponents: opponents who think creatively and adapt continuously and who relish devising complex strategies; this means that a set of fraud controls that is perfectly satisfactory today may be of no use at all tomorrow, once the game has progressed a little. One commentator on the health care reform debate noted: "About ten minutes after the president signs a bill, Americans will figure out how to 'game' the new system. The cleverest doctors and lawyers in the country will match wits with bureaucrats. Guess who will win?" [13] Maintaining effective fraud controls demands continuous assessment of emerging fraud trends and constant, rapid revision of controls.

Officials responsible for fraud control often complain that, for every loophole they find and close, the providers seem to find another.[14] Some even respond to this realization by suggesting that closing loopholes merely displaces fraud rather than eliminates it and is therefore a waste of time. (This tends to be their private, pessimistic, somewhat embittered view; never the official position.)

These complaints suggest a lack of understanding of the fundamental nature of the fraud-control business. Fraud control is like chess. You play against opponents who watch everything you do and adapt accordingly. To win the game, you must watch everything they do and counter every play they make.

In numerous fraud-control situations, I have found people spending inordinate amounts of time fruitlessly searching for the "golden bullet"; that is, the perfect, final, detection methodology (or econometric model) that will forever hereafter distinguish legitimate from illegitimate transactions. The health care industry, preferring medical terminology, searches not for the "golden bullet" of fraud detection, but the "magic pill." One may as well search for one perfect, final configuration of chess pieces that—without the need ever to make another move—will guarantee complete defense. All too often, organizations vulnerable to fraud make some investment in new edits or auditing systems and then sit back, relax, and convince themselves that they have taken care of the problem. Placing faith in a static set of controls and failing to appreciate the paramount importance of watching how the opponents respond is as foolish as trying to play chess blindfolded, your pieces bolted to the table.

In the fraud-control business, intelligence counts. One investigator, tackling extensive webs of corruption in the hospital construction business, pointed out that the fraud perpetrators know the value of watching their opponents: "Counterintelligence is a serious business. They have their own network and talk about what we're up to." Enforcement priorities and current targeting strategies are frequent topics of conversation, formally and informally, at conferences for provider specialties. At some such conferences, the doors are closed and careful checks are made to ensure that no government or law-enforcement officials are present before the conversation proceeds. (Investigators hear this, eventually, from honest providers alarmed by their own profession's behavior.)

Generally, it takes committed fraud perpetrators less than a week to figure out how fraud-control defenses have changed and only three months to a year for a new, successful fraud strategy to become known all across the country. Many defending organizations, by contrast, take a year or more to consider and adopt even the most straightforward adjustments in their claims processes.

Overreliance upon Traditional Enforcement Approaches

Another common problem is confusion between the art of fraud investigation and the art of fraud control. Many organizations treat these as the same. They assume that vigorous pursuit of individual offenders, with well-publicized prosecutions, will produce control through deterrence— which it does, to some extent. The strength of the deterrent effect, though, depends upon the probability of getting caught, the probability of being convicted once caught, and the seriousness of the punishment once convicted. For white-collar crimes, all three are notoriously low.

Feeding the justice system (criminal or civil) is a slow, constrained approach to control. Control strategies must incorporate a much broader set of tools. Insurers vary in the degree to which they rely on the process of referring cases to the justice system. In general, the more the members of a fraud unit view their jobs purely in terms of *making cases,* the more frustrating they find their jobs.

Effectiveness of New Fraud Controls Is Always Overestimated

Another common problem is that the next set of fraud-control enhancements to be adopted always look as though they will solve the problem. Why? Because the new set of controls properly reflects the most recent experience of fraud. The new controls, provided they work as expected, should eliminate most of the instances of recently observed fraud.

The hope that elimination of the types of scams seen most recently spells the defeat of fraud produces a false optimism. Unfortunately, this assumption fails to take into account the adaptability of the opponents, who take only a few days, or weeks at most, to change their tactics once they find a particular method thwarted. Often officials deliberately point to some minor recent change as a way of dismissing allegations of vulnerability. No matter how bad the situation was, an adaptation in controls—no matter how minor—casts uncertainty over how bad the situation is or will be. Note the predictable last sentence in so many news stories about health care fraud losses: "Some officials say that recently enacted controls should help curb abuses in the program." [15]

Officials place unwarranted faith in new controls. Even the designers of new controls, if asked, "What would *you* do, as a criminal, if you were trying to get around these new controls?" can immediately describe methods of circumventing them. The designers' mistake is to fail to think more than one move ahead, or to imagine that the opponents will easily lose interest and move on to some other target. Having learned the claims-submission business, having developed the necessary cooperative arrangements, and having invested in billing apparatus (people, systems, and software), few criminals will be easily deterred. They move on only when they are made to adapt so much and so continuously that the target begins to appear unprofitable for them. They have to be harassed out of the game.

Often, fraud artists move on only when a noticeably easier, more profitable, slower-moving target comes into their sights. For many well-established and sophisticated criminal rings, health care payment systems are exactly that: fat, rich, and slow-moving.

Fraud Control Arrangements Fail to Appreciate the Multilevel Nature of the Fraud-Control Game

In many institutions the type of fraud control that is implemented is determined—or, at least, strongly influenced—by the type of transaction-processing environment within which they operate. These can be characterized as high-volume, repetitive, transaction-oriented processes. Fraud controls implemented within such processes tend to acquire certain characteristics. The underlying transaction-processing system deals with the work in the same form and usually in the same order in which it arrives: claim by claim (insurance), return by return (tax), or charge by charge (credit cards). Fraud controls, superimposed upon or embedded within the process, most naturally do the same, that is, they examine the claims, returns, or transactions one at a time and usually in the same order in which they arrive. Thus the fraud-detection systems most naturally use the same unit of work as the underlying processes; this means they operate principally at the level of the *transaction.*

Fraud-control systems operate within environments committed to efficiency and productivity. For fraud controls to fit (and to cause no more disruption to the production process than necessary), they also become high-volume, repetitive, transaction-oriented processes. Many institutions, realizing the inadequacy of relying upon service-oriented clerks for fraud control, turn instead to automated controls. Certain variables or ratios known to be indicators of fraud are calculated and checked automatically so that claims fitting suspicious profiles can be filtered out from the mass for closer inspection, investigation, or rejection.

Whether it be humans or machines that do the monitoring, developing good-quality fraud controls is, for many institutions, synonymous with having a finely adjusted set of filters or branch points embedded within the transaction-processing operation. The most obvious way to improve existing fraud controls is to improve the filters, making them better discriminators through the use of more variables or ratios, or by using sophisticated forms of econometric modeling, discriminant analysis, or "expert" rule-based systems.

Two major problems arise with the fraud-control mind-set that puts its faith in perfecting the transaction-level filters. The first problem is that the fraud-control game is dynamic, not static (as already discussed); a static set of filters has only short-term utility. When the opposition makes its next move, a set of fraud controls that is satisfactory today may be of no use at all tomorrow. Maintaining effective fraud controls demands continuous assessment of emerging fraud trends and constant revision of controls.

The second problem is that most sophisticated fraud schemes are devised by perpetrators who assume the existence of transaction-level filters and who therefore design their fraud schemes so that each transaction comfortably fits a legitimate profile and passes through unchallenged. The perpetrators of such schemes accept the constraints imposed by having to fashion each claim to fit a legitimate profile; they then make their millions by operating on hundreds or thousands of accounts simultaneously, often using computers to generate multiple claims and to incorporate sufficient randomness or variation to minimize the risk of detection.

The opening moves in the fraud-control game consist, therefore, of the defending institution's implementing transaction-level filters; the fraudsters then adapt all their subsequent strategies to circumvent those controls. These moves could be regarded as a "standard opening" in a game that, like chess, is complex, dynamic, and rich in strategy.

Unfortunately, many of the institutions most vulnerable to fraud have not progressed past these standard opening moves. They enjoy a false sense of security based upon the operation of their transaction-level filters; that sense of security is reinforced through the observation that the process-based filters do reject claims from time to time. A proportion of these rejects indeed turn out to be fraudulent—an observation that demonstrates that transaction-level controls have their usefulness. But such controls generally detect only the casual, careless, and opportunistic fraud attempts, not the serious, dedicated criminal groups who quickly progress to a higher level of sophistication.

Medical providers deliberately spread fraudulent activity across multiple patient identities and craft each claim to pass all the transaction-level tests (eligibility checks, pricing controls, diagnosis/procedure code combination, etc.). The smarter criminals are usually careful not to claim too much, or too fast, for any one patient, knowing that most systems use some patient-level monitoring to check for sudden jumps in utilization. They also devise methods for spreading their billings across numerous different provider numbers to avoid detection by the provider-profiling techniques standard in the industry.

Investigators report that dishonest providers in the health care industry have become adept at using multiple corporate identities to further frustrate monitoring. One Medicaid fraud-control unit recently made a case against an organization fraudulently billing for sonograms (ultrasound images). A small number of patients would have a large number of sonograms performed; the organization would then bill Medicaid using a long list of Medicaid recipients, none of whom had received a sonogram. The perpetrators, if asked, could usually provide a sonogram to go with each claim, but the pictures were either entirely fake or were of someone else. One organization used nine different corporate identities to conceal the billing pattern. They were detected through undercover operations conducted by the MFCU, which acted on ample intelligence that the sonogram business was rotten to the core.

The Smushkevitch brothers' "rolling labs scheme" in southern California used more than 500 corporate identities and tens of thousands of patient identities over a ten-year period of operation.[16]

To defend against these kinds of schemes, payment integrity programs need to escape the natural tendency to concentrate on transaction-level controls. Transaction-level controls, embedded in the claims-processing sequence, accomplish very little for fraud control. They are important and necessary—like the opening moves in chess. The game, for the most part, is no longer played at that level.

Particular Challenges in the Health Care Field

The general pathology of fraud control, discussed above, makes the job hard enough. Some particular characteristics of the health care profession make effective control harder still.

Insurers as Socially Acceptable Targets

A 1990 study of insurance fraud compared fraud and fraud-control trends in eight different Western countries, including the United States, Canada, and Britain. In all these countries, the study reports, "a significant minority [of the public] regard insurance companies as large, rich, anonymous, and as fair game for fraud in much the same way as tax authorities." [17]

In the United States, the prevalence of opportunistic insurance fraud—readily acknowledged by the insurance industry at large—is astonishing. Nevertheless, the nation was just a little shocked by what it saw when the state of New Jersey staged a series of fake bus accidents in a variety of urban locations. State officials arranged ten minor bus accidents, in each case employing actors to pose as passengers. After each impact, hidden video cameras recorded opportunistic passersby scrambling to get aboard before the police arrived so they could claim to have been injured in the crash.

In six such accidents around New Jersey, a total of fifty-one people boarded the buses and had their names recorded as having been aboard during the crash. Doctors and lawyers, or "runners" soliciting business for them, were videotaped boarding the buses, coaching passengers on how to feign injury, and handing out business cards. Eleven additional individuals submitted injury claims for injuries supposedly sustained in these six accidents, without even bothering to board the bus at the scene.[18]

One genuine accident, not part of the sting operation, occurred when a truck and a car collided just behind another New Jersey bus. Passengers, hearing the bang, assumed the bus had been hit (which it had not). No fewer than twenty-seven of the bus passengers subsequently submitted injury claims.

The rest of the country displays a surprisingly high tolerance for insurance fraud, even though things are not quite as bad elsewhere as they are in the cities of New Jersey. A 1993 public attitude survey conducted by the Insurance Research Council asked members of the general public all across the country whether they thought it was all right to pad insurance claims to make up for past premiums. Nationwide, 19 percent of respondents said they regarded the practice as acceptable, but residents of the mid-Atlantic states (New York, New Jersey, and Pennsylvania) were more than twice as likely (41 percent) to regard the practice as acceptable.[19]

Another question on the survey asked whether it was all right to continue to receive medical treatment after an injury had healed to increase the size of an insurance settlement. Nationwide, 9 percent thought it was all right. In the mid-Atlantic states, 20 percent, and among residents of big cities, 25 percent of those surveyed said it was all right.[20] The Newark sting operation, conducted in dense urban areas of New Jersey, apparently played to an unusually dishonest audience. More broadly, however, a significant proportion of the U.S. population sees insurance companies as fair game. With health care fraud, financial losses accrue primarily to insurance companies and to massive government bureaucracies. It is hard to imagine targets that would engender less public sympathy. Tales of insurers (or their claims-processing contractors) who behave less than honorably themselves certainly do not help. More broadly, many believe the cost-control practices of insurers to be punitive, even immoral, and consequently regard them as having forsaken any claim on honesty in their dealings with policyholders. One physician told the Senate Committee on Aging:

> The insurance companies, particularly Worker's Compensation carriers, appear to create an almost adversarial climate between themselves and honest doctors. Legitimate services rendered by honest providers are often going unpaid. Some honest doctors feel as though they are being encouraged by the insurance companies to break the rules in order to get paid.[21]

Health Care Fraud Schemes Not Self-Revealing

Virtually all health care fraud schemes fall into the non-self-revealing category. Many members of the public believe that EOMBs (explanations of medical benefits) provide protection against fraud. Patients, receiving EOMBs, would surely spot the appearance of services not rendered and would report the activity, just as credit card holders would report unauthorized activity when they saw it on their monthly statements. Health care fraud advisories continually remind patients to check their EOMBs carefully.

Bill Mahon, the executive director of NHCAA (The National Health Care Anti-Fraud Association), in answer to congressional questions, encouraged the same kind of sensible, prudent, consumer behavior: "I would respond . . . by simply saying we all need to pay as close attention to the insurer's statements of what was paid on our behalf as we would to a monthly credit card bill or a Sears bill to make sure that what was paid for was, in fact, what was provided. No question, we need to be better consumers."[22] Unfortunately, EOMBs do not have the effect one would hope, for a number of reasons. First, in many circumstances they are not sent at all. Use of EOMBs is not routine within the Medicaid program. Under Medicare, EOMBs have traditionally been sent out only when services require a copayment, or where the Medicare program refuses to cover a service. Only recently has HCFA begun phasing in expanded use of EOMBs, as required by the Health Insurance Portability and Accountability Act (HIPAA). Many commercial insurers do not routinely mail out statements to patients.

Second, recipients of EOMBs have little or no financial incentive to pay attention to them. Recipients are not, as in the case of a credit card statement, being asked to pay a bill. Third, many recipients cannot decipher the strange computer-generated forms and they see no reason to try.

Fourth, fraudulent suppliers find innovative ways to stop patients from reading their EOMBs. In Florida, DME (durable medical equipment) suppliers have paid Medicare recipients $5 for each *unopened* EOMB envelope. And investigators at major Medicare contractors described how providers were altering beneficiaries' addresses on their claim forms and switching them to post office boxes under their own control, knowing that the claims-processing system would automatically update the beneficiaries' addresses before dispatching the EOMB. Typical schemes, these investigators reported, would use around thirty post office boxes and switch twenty to thirty beneficiaries to each box. (The fraudulent activity

in such schemes is routinely spread across upwards of six hundred beneficiaries, none of whom would ever see their EOMBs.)

Fifth, as Louis Freeh, director of the FBI, testified in March 1995, many
fraud schemes deliberately target vulnerable populations:

> Nursing home and hospice operators exploit the elderly and Alzheimer's pa-
> tients by fraudulently billing for services, incontinence supplies and med-
> ications; tragically choosing patients who have difficulty understanding or
> remembering what was and what was not done, much less complaining to
> their insurer or alerting law enforcement.[23]

Despite all these obstacles, beneficiaries in significant numbers do call
their Medicare carriers to complain about bogus or questionable charges.
HCFA mandates that such calls go directly into the fraud and abuse unit
within the carrier, and "beneficiary complaints" are, for many of those
units, the bulk of their work. As we saw in Chapter 3, the resources available to investigate a discrepancy and the manner in which such complaints are handled remain inadequate.

It turns out that, for these reasons, EOMBs are *not* the automatic
fraud-discovery mechanism many naturally assume. EOMBs are only issued with respect to certain categories of services and generate notoriously low response rates. Moreover, the handling of beneficiary complaints, even when they do arise, often lacks the rigor required to
uncover fraud.

What about Certificates of Medical Necessity (CMNs)? Within the
durable medical equipment segment of the industry, one would imagine that CMNs would play a major role in guaranteeing the validity of
DME claims. The majority of DME services require a CMN signed by
the prescribing physician. The provider must provide his or her unique
physician identification number (UPIN). Surely these physicians would
be able to confirm whether or not they had actually prescribed an expensive piece of equipment—such as a hospital bed or motorized
wheelchair?

In theory, the prescribing physicians could help verify DME claims, but
in practice they are seldom, if ever, asked. There is no routine or random
verification of CMNs with the signing physicians. And, even once a claim
is under review, investigators report that going back and trying to check
on CMNs can be frustrating. The director of the investigative unit at one
of Medicare's regional contractors for durable medical equipment described CMNs as "totally useless":

Doctors sign them to get rid of suppliers. No sense of responsibility. They are not getting paid for signing or not signing them. And often physicians do not respond to queries when we check up, as it doesn't relate to any claim of theirs. So they say, "Why should we? Are you going to pay us?"

Moreover, DME suppliers intent on fraud tend to submit CMNs under the names of prescribing physicians who are corrupt, lazy, sick, absent, desperate for cash, or dead. They forge signatures where necessary.

The non-self-revealing nature of nearly all health care fraud schemes exacerbates the difficulty of seeing the fraud problem clearly. It makes the design and operation of instruments or systems to *uncover the invisible* all that much more crucial.

Separation Between Administrative Budgets and "Funds"

Fraud controls also suffer significantly because *program administration* costs are budgeted separately from *program* costs (i.e., claims paid). This budgetary separation makes it virtually impossible to consider the notion of return on investment in allocating resources for fraud control. Particularly within government programs, even substantial returns cannot justify investments in control if the program funds (which stand to gain from better safeguards) are administratively or legally separate from administrative costs.

In May 1995, the Senate Appropriations Subcommittee on Labor, Health and Human Services held a hearing to consider the findings of the latest General Accounting Office (GAO) study. This particular study had explored the savings to the Medicare program that might accrue if the government purchased commercially available "code manipulation" software packages and installed them within Medicare payment systems. These commercial packages rebundle improperly unbundled procedures and automatically correct a variety of other improper or erroneous billing practices. Senator Tom Harkin opened the hearing with this statement:

> The GAO indicates that it would cost around $20 million to install the private sector technology in Medicare. And they have clearly demonstrated that such an investment would save Medicare taxpayers and beneficiaries over $3.9 billion in five years. So, for every dollar we invest, taxpayers will get $200 return. I call that a bargain. For every day we fail to invest, taxpayers will lose $2.5 million. I call that a scandal. The time to change is now and I will be introducing legislation today to mandate that Medicare discard its

outdated system to detect billing abuses and take advantage of this cost-saving technology.[24]

The particular merits and limitations of this GAO study are not the issue here. HCFA contested the conclusions at the time, but has since initiated projects to test such software packages within the Medicare program.

What Harkin's statement reveals, however, is the obvious public appeal of notions such as "value for money" and "return on investment" when considering additional fraud controls. A $200 return for every $1 invested looks irresistible. Unfortunately, the practical workings of the budget process cannot even consider such ratios. The Medicare trust fund (for Medicare payments under Part A) is sacred to the AARP (American Association of Retired Persons); woe betide the politician who suggests taking any of it for administrative purposes. The Medicare trust fund is maintained by the 2.9 percent Medicare payroll tax, paid half by employers and half by employees.[25] The Medicare program's administrative expenses, by contrast, come out of the discretionary budget from general tax revenues. Even private insurance companies, whom one might expect to be more focused on the aggregate bottom line, use structures that budget claims processing separately from claims. And that separation, if fraud control is regarded as a component of the administrative budget, essentially eliminates consideration of returns on marginal investments.

Given the prevalence of such segregations, extra investments in fraud controls must come from discretionary or administrative budgets, whereas savings directly benefit the funds. Whether the separation is legal, budgetary, or organizational, it forces fraud and abuse control into a zero-sum game with other parts of the processing apparatus. Every extra dollar spent on prudent controls means one dollar less spent on processing, automation, customer service, due process, beneficiary services, or a variety of other inescapable obligations. Fraud controls, once in this zero-sum game, invariably lose. Whenever the administrative budget comes under pressure, program integrity controls (given the uncertain nature of the dividends they bring) are always first on the chopping block.

Minor fluctuations in administrative budgets cause major fluctuations in control resources. These fluctuations, say senior HCFA officials, have disastrous effects on the capacity of investigative units. "It takes a long time to train a Medicare investigator. First they have to learn their way around the program. Then they have to learn their craft. Usually they become productive after around three years. But every time we take a budget cut, we lose investigators. Then we have to start over. It's *very* frustrating." (Thus the significance of the Fraud and Abuse Control Fund, created under HIPAA in 1996, which guarantees steady and increasing levels of funding for fraud and abuse control operations at the federal level.)

Such separation, whether statutory or merely administrative, is powerfully manifested in employee culture and attitudes. Most officials care a great deal, *either* about the costs per claim (where their goals and incentives all relate to efficiency) *or* about payment accuracy. Which one they care about depends on their specific functional responsibilities. Virtually nobody cares about both, and virtually nobody working within insurance organizations is in a position to act upon the important relationship between them.

Respectability of the Health Care Profession

Society places enormous trust in health care professionals, and rightly so. People must be able to trust their doctors. Lacking expert medical training, most consumers of medical services are in a poor position to assess the quality or appropriateness of those services. Society acknowledges the rigor and intensity of physicians' training and honors them in many ways.

Society has traditionally paid physicians the compliment, as a profession, of subjecting medical judgment to scrutiny only by another physician. Physicians expect to be granted exemption from outside scrutiny and strenuously oppose efforts by administrators, investigators, or even managed care companies to question or influence their professional judgment. Defense of the profession, by the profession, is serious business—as the power, wealth, and political influence of the medical associations attest. Physicians, therefore, are willing to censure only the most outrageous acts of their colleagues, and even then with remarkable reluctance. Revelations about fraud by medical practitioners are perceived by their peers as a slur on the integrity of the profession and on its ability to police itself.

Some commentators have noted the peculiar defensiveness of the medical profession: "If one reports on the frauds committed by doctors, the vast majority of doctors, whose conduct is honest and aboveboard, nonetheless are tempted to complain that their whole profession is being unfairly besmirched."[26]

The unwillingness of doctors to condemn their own has also been commented upon by judges in criminal court. In 1984, a California ophthalmologist was convicted of performing unnecessary cataract operations on Medicaid patients; he stole more than a million dollars over five years and left several patients blind or with unnecessarily impaired eyesight. The judge, disgusted by the letters of support the court had received from other physicians appealing for leniency, commented that not one of the letters paid attention to the true victims in the case, which he described as "uneducated, Spanish-speaking people, some of whom will never see a sunrise or a sunset again." Rather, the letters of support painted the entire trial as "a contrivance by the attorney general's office." [27]

Some physicians, even when convicted by a jury of a criminal offense, seem to show remarkably little regret or remorse. They often cling to the moral high ground, viewing and presenting themselves as innocent victims of unreasonably complex and meddlesome bureaucratic rules, too busy caring for their patients to watch their own backs:

> Convicted physicians often insist that their crimes were merely the consequence of their being too involved in heady medical matters to attend to the niggling red tape of the programs that were paying them. This not uncommon strain of professional arrogance among medical practitioners may help the guilty deflect the disgrace of criminal prosecutions, the accompanying unpleasant publicity, and assaults on their self-esteem.[28]

With regard to fraud and abuse, some physicians still imagine (or pretend to imagine) that all the integrity problems lie elsewhere. The *New England Journal of Medicine's* review of the first edition of this book, written by a physician, stated:

> A careful reading makes clear what almost anyone in the fraud-detection business knows: the worst fraud these days involves those removed from the mainstream of medicine, such as independent laboratories, suppliers of durable medical equipment, home health care, and home infusion services.[29]

And medical boards, too, seem remarkably reluctant to recognize the seriousness of fraud and abuse, especially when the offenses are financial in nature, rather than involving bad medicine. In 1998, the Coalition Against Insurance Fraud conducted a study of the disciplinary actions taken by twelve state medical boards against 251 medical providers convicted of criminal fraud or excluded from participation in public health programs such as Medicare and Medicaid between 1993–1995.[30] The choice of period was designed to allow long enough for all appeals processes to have since ended. The study report, titled "Licensed to Steal: Action and Inaction by State Medical Boards," showed that 57.4 percent of these providers had *no action* taken against them by the appropriate licensing authorities and actions taken were sufficiently lenient that, overall, 81.7 percent of these practitioners retained their licenses to practice. One explanation for this apparent leniency is that medical boards might deliberately not concern themselves with financial matters or issues of honesty, focusing more narrowly on medical judgments. That may be an appropriate role for them. If so, they have little to offer in support of fraud control.

The desire for members of the medical profession to protect their professional status is perfectly understandable. Their resulting defensiveness, however, has historically inclined the profession and its associations to play down the extent and seriousness of health care fraud and to oppose quite strenuously provision of additional resources for the purposes of investigation and review.

Extension to Other Provider Groups

Investigators concede society's need to trust physicians and acknowledge the integrity of the majority of physicians. Many, however, express outrage when they see the same kind of professional immunity or trust being extended to, or claimed by, all kinds of other provider groups not bound by any code of professional ethics. Investigators view these other provider groups—DME suppliers, home health agencies (HHA), medical transportation companies, physiological laboratories, behavioral health clinics, billing agencies, and so on—quite starkly as businesses, run by business people, for profit. Investigators believe health care insurers and payers are naïve to assume, as they do with physicians, that for these provider groups the drive for self-enrichment might be subordinated to higher professional obligations. In these other provider groups, investigators see no such professionalism.

Nevertheless, payers accord such groups surprising latitude, paying claims on trust without routine verification of services provided. In some cases, payments are made on the basis of prevailing fees, a practice that began as a compliment to the integrity of professional physicians. Prevailing fees, in many of these industry segments, are "whatever you can get away with."

Despite the absence of an identifiable code of professional ethics, these segments of the health care industry, dominated by big business, acquire aggressive political lobbies and wield enormous power. Home health care suppliers, for instance, are renowned for the aggressiveness and effectiveness of their political lobbies, despite the prevalence of fraud in that segment.

Fraud investigators have no trouble naming the most significant trend in health care fraud today: increased involvement in the health care industry of big business with powerful political allies and no code of professional medical ethics.

Unclear Distinctions Between
Fraud, Abuse, and Overutilization

Criminal fraud is defined clearly enough. It requires a deliberate misrepresentation or deception, leading to some kind of improper pecuniary advantage. If the deception relates to some objective fact (e.g., if the services were not provided as billed, or were billed as something else), the boundaries of fraud are fairly clear. When the deception or misrepresentation relates to the question of medical necessity, however, the distinctions between fraud and abuse (or between fraud and defensive medicine, or between fraud and well-intentioned overzealousness) become quite muddy. To establish fraud, many argue, you would have to get inside the head of the physician to ascertain the motivation, or, at least, establish such a blatant and persistent pattern of behavior that criminal motivation could be inferred.

No one would categorize phantom providers billing millions of dollars, with never a service rendered, as anything other than fraud. Many other blatant scams, equally, would present neither the public, nor physicians, nor juries with definitional problems. Although there is plenty of obvious fraud, the fuzziness of the boundaries, away from the extremes, produces a problem: It becomes extraordinarily difficult to mobilize unequivocal condemnation of fraud, even when the fraud is blatant. Providers, and the provider associations, could never be quite sure exactly where along the continuum that condemnation, once mobilized, would end. Physicians may find it hard to condemn fraudulent practice among their peers if they cannot construct satisfactory dividing walls between behavior they might condemn in others and the way they behave themselves.

Neat dividing walls are hard to construct, even among objective realities such as false claims. Even if the services were not provided as billed, what was the reason? Was it a genuine, isolated mistake? Was it part of a persistent pattern of mistakes resulting from a genuine misunderstanding of the regulations? Was it reckless disregard for the rules? Or was it a deliberate attempt to steal?

These ambiguities do not always appear in other fraud-control situations. If unauthorized activity appears on a credit card bill or a bank statement, there are few plausible explanations other than fraud. In most contexts, determining whether a transaction is fraudulent is a relatively straightforward affair when the objective facts are known. The definitional ambiguities within health care hamper fraud-control efforts in a number of ways:

- First, they contribute to the medical profession's reluctance to unequivocally condemn fraudulent practice, even of the most egregious kind.

- Second, definitional ambiguities make it much more difficult to measure the problem systematically, because measurement methodology would have to establish clear outcome classifications. For practical reasons, outcome classifications would have to be based on objective, verifiable realities, none of which precisely fits legal definitions of fraud.

- Third, definitional ambiguities provide an excuse for anyone who would prefer, for whatever reason, not to refer suspected fraud cases to an investigative unit. For a wide range of reasons, many officials within payer organizations display a marked reluctance to refer cases to fraud-control units (which are organizationally separate). Conscious of the need to protect and maintain their provider network, the paying agencies generally prefer to deal with suspicious claims or billing practices through administrative action rather than through fraud referrals. The difficulty of distinguishing fraud from other, grayer behaviors enables anyone so inclined to avoid the obligation to refer suspected cases of fraud. They say, "I'll refer it when I know it's fraud," but that could not be definitely established until after a criminal trial!

- Fourth, definitional ambiguities weaken fraud controls. For example, within the Medicare program, many staff at carriers and intermediaries generally accept the rule that, to prove a provider guilty of fraud, you have to demonstrate that the provider had been previously "educated" about a particular billing practice. Only that way, the logic goes, can a court be sure the provider intentionally committed fraud. This rule is commonly applied for all but the most blatant forms of fraud. In practical terms, then, when a contractor discovers that a provider is cheating, the most common ac-

tion is to write to the provider and explain what wrongdoing occurred and request that it not happen again. Only if the provider
persists in the same practice, following education, is investigation
and prosecution for fraud likely. This practical rule substitutes ob-
jectively verifiable facts—in this instance, previous education—for
the need to probe the mind of the provider in search of criminal
intent. It serves to protect honest providers who make honest mistakes. But it protects fraudulent providers too, enabling all but the
most stupid and greedy to eliminate their vulnerability to prosecution entirely, simply by heeding warnings if and when they come.

These impediments to effective fraud control—the social acceptability
of government and insurers as targets, the invisible nature of the crime,
the separation of administrative budgets from funds, the trust placed in
providers, and the difficulties of separating fraud from other behaviors—
are substantial. Add them to the seven elements of the general fraud-control pathology, and the task of controlling fraud begins to seem complex,
amorphous, and overwhelming.

Perhaps this helps explain why health care fraud has not gone away despite all the attention paid to it, and why strenuous political and administrative efforts to bolster defenses have so far failed to provide a cure. Many
dedicated, intelligent people—administrators, reviewers, analysts, auditors, investigators, and prosecutors—work long hours seeking to combat
the problem; at the end of the day, almost none of them feel the problem
is under control. Most feel that their efforts barely dent the surface.

One reason is the underlying complexity of the task (which this chapter has laid out). Another reason—which the next two chapters will explore—is that the policies, systems, and machinery in place to combat
fraud do not work the way everyone thinks they do.

6

The Importance of Measurement

VISA International administers and operates the global network that handles VISA credit card transactions. On many days, the transaction volume on the network exceeds $1 billion. When considering potential investments in new fraud controls, VISA, like many other credit card operations, considers its "confirmed fraud rate" (which indicates the proportion of VISA card transaction dollars lost to fraud and never recovered.) They like to keep that rate below ten basis points (or 0.1 percent), a level the credit card industry generally regards as satisfactory for fraud in the system, the "acceptable price of doing business."

The health care industry, where the fraud rate might be 10 percent or higher—at least one hundred times worse than in the credit card industry—lacks precise instrumentation on which to base its control investment decisions and generally makes no serious attempt to measure the problem. Only in the last three years has the Office of Inspector General (OIG) instituted its annual audit program for Medicare, and that with a weak methodology that produces misleadingly low loss estimates. Only two states (Texas and Illinois) have so far attempted to measure the losses due to fraud, abuse, and errors in their Medicaid programs. Other major public programs do no measurement of the losses, nor do most commercial insurers. Given the general lack of such measurement efforts within the industry and the painfully slow development of them within the major public programs (even when they are required by law), it's worth pausing to stress the importance and effects of measurement; many believe measurement studies are a distraction, a waste of time, a research luxury with no practical benefit.

Basic decision theory teaches the value of information when choosing between alternative courses of action. Presumably the health care industry might consider different actions if the true level of fraud losses were 40 percent than if they were only 2 percent. Without knowing the true level, policymakers are liable to make enormously costly errors by either overinvesting or underinvesting in controls. To an outsider, therefore, for the health care industry to pay some attention to measurement of the problem would seem rational and reasonable, maybe even imperative.

Back in 1993, the General Accounting Office (GAO) reported that conventional wisdom among industry officials put the fraud and abuse loss rate around 10 percent, but commented, "Because of the hidden nature of fraudulent and abusive practices, however, the exact magnitude of the problem cannot be determined."[1] This means, of course, that the returns on new or marginal investments in fraud controls are uncertain; additional investments are therefore much less likely to be made. The same uncertainty existed even further back, in 1977, when the Medicaid Fraud-Control Units were originally created.[2] When the director of the Congressional Budget Office was asked to comment on the financial implications of the formation of these units, she replied, "The unknown magnitude of fraud and abuse presently extant in the programs makes it impracticable for the Congressional Budget Office to project the actual cost impact of this measure at this time."[3] In the late 1970s, as now, the absence of knowledge left different parties free to make their own, partially self-serving, estimates. In 1979, the OIG of the Department of Health and Human Services (HHS) estimated Medicaid fraud and abuse to be $468 million, with the caveat that the number was "incomplete and probably low." Responding, the Health Care Financing Administration (HCFA) recommended an estimate of only $100 million. The Inspector General (IG) diplomatically commented, "All agree numbers are soft. IG considers HCFA's estimate low."[4]

In the absence of hard facts, estimates from investigative units are normally at least double or triple the size of corresponding estimates from paying agencies, and much energy is wasted squabbling over the truth. Investigative units, closer to the realities of the streets and short of resources, aim high. Paying agencies, defensive about their own control systems, eager not to offend their network of providers, and protective of their program's public image, aim low.

The failure to systematically and routinely measure the scope of fraud is characteristic of the entire insurance industry—not just health care—and is not limited to the United States. Michael Clarke's comparative international study of the insurance industry, published in 1990, commented that

Despite the vigorous and extensive efforts of some insurers to detect and control fraud, there is no evidence that any insurer has undertaken research to establish the real extent of fraud in any given area of risk. It would certainly be possible to employ standard sampling techniques to pick out a representative set of insureds and to investigate each claim's history with exhaustive care, using the best available means of fraud detection (which, it should be said, are fairly effective).[5]

Given the absence of such systematic measurement, Clarke pointed out that

It is always likely, therefore, that the sophisticated fraudster is at least one move ahead in this process, and possible that entire categories of fraud are being ignored: beyond standard deterrent and defensive tactics, insurers are relying on the mistakes of fraudsters and on what they already know about them.[6]

Picking transactions at random and auditing them as thoroughly as possible is much more than an academic idea; for many regulatory and compliance agencies, it is a familiar operational tool for discovering what they do not know and for scanning the horizon in search of noncompliance problems that might have entirely escaped their attention. A program of rigorous random audits acts like the smoke or paint aimed at the invisible man in various Hollywood movies: It makes the invisible visible.

The IRS, for example, used to operate its Taxpayer Compliance Monitoring Program (TCMP) precisely for detecting patterns of noncompliance. Every three years or so, the IRS randomly selected 50,000 tax returns and subjected them to a rigorous line-by-line audit. The object was not to make cases but to obtain reliable information about patterns of noncompliance, of which the IRS might otherwise have remained oblivious.[7]

The danger of self-delusion threatens all agencies having to deal with non-self-revealing problems. Many issues of noncompliance fall in that category. The mechanism of delusion goes like this: The agencies focus on what they think are the central problems. As they do so, they learn more and more about those problems, and they become yet more central in their thinking. As time passes, the agencies work on the problems they know about and learn more about the problems they work on. Trapped by the circularity, agencies focus more and more carefully on things they have always focused on, just because those problems happen to be in their sights. They fish in the same place, year after year, because that is where they caught fish before. Meanwhile, new patterns and types of noncompliance emerge, all potentially out of sight. If there is no system or machinery to help uncover new problems, they may go unnoticed for years. TCMP, a piece of machinery whose strength lies in its random selection, is designed specifically to help the IRS identify new areas of noncompliance. The point is that the selection is not focused on known problems, nor is it influenced by existing IRS biases.

Conducting random audits is usually as unpopular internally as it is externally. Auditors often regard random audits (which they characterize as "studies") as a waste of time, claiming they could raise more revenue if only they were allowed to focus on known problem areas. Indeed, they *would* raise more revenue by focusing on known problem areas, but that argument misses the point. The principal value of random audits by the IRS (or, for that matter, random searches by customs or random audits of health care claims) is that random audits provide information about types of noncompliance that existing targeting mechanisms might be missing. Random audits provide the opportunity, over the long term, to reassess the level of resources devoted to control, to redirect those resources, to adjust audit selection formulas, to target investigations and audits more effectively, and to select enforcement actions that will have the greatest impact on significant areas of noncompliance.

In the 1970s, the Bureau of Health Insurance (a precursor of HCFA) ran a random audit program. Program validation teams conducted rigorous random validation audits guided by exactly the same philosophy as the IRS's TCMP program; however, the practice had disappeared by 1980. No doubt, when resources were tight, someone decided that the program of random audits did not pay for itself and it therefore became a prime target for elimination. The IRS also has not been able to conduct a TCMP program since 1988. Since then, proponents of the program have not been able to overcome congressional opposition to the random audits.

Within the health care industry, officials point to a wide variety of activities that seem, to them, to accomplish systematic measurement of the fraud problem. None of them, however, provides effective measurement of the size of the fraud problem.

Quality Controls in Claims Processing

Most insurers perform random sampling of processed claims. The purpose of the sampling is to measure the accuracy and consistency of the human claims examiners. These quality-control procedures test procedural compliance and accept the claim as presented; they do not attempt to check the veracity of the information in the claim itself. As one manager explained (within the context of a quality control program), "We regard the claim as a legal document and assume that what it says is true; we are measuring the performance of our staff."

A 1984 study of fraud control within the AFDC (Aid to Families with Dependent Children) and Medicaid programs expands this point:

> Thus, while the Quality Control data may be a measure of managerial accuracy and may reflect the types of mistakes which are being made, they are not a measure of fraud problems. The review process does little to distinguish between intentional and unintentional client errors, and the reviewers are given few opportunities to probe beyond the data contained in the files.
>
> The Medicaid quality control system checks a sample of Medicaid claims, but error findings indicate only that a payment violated a program rule (e.g., by paying for a service not covered, by paying an incorrect amount, etc.); QC reviewers do not check to see if the service was in fact provided as claimed.[8]

Quality-control processes check the consistency and accuracy either of the entire system or of individual claims examiners. In either case, the methodology employed involves a supervisor or senior claims examiner repeating the processing steps with respect to randomly selected claims; by comparing results, the supervisor then determines the original examiner's discrepancy rate. Quality-control procedures demonstrate that the role and value of *random selection* within measurement processes is understood and accepted. Quality controls, however, measure and detect internal processing errors, not fraud. A fraudulent claim will pop out of such a process only if, by some fluke, it was processed incorrectly. Even then, it would probably not be identified as fraudulent.

Accurate claims processing serves fraud perpetrators rather well. Perpetrators like to confront systems that are 100 percent predictable and that behave the same way, claim after claim, week after week, month after month. As Clarke points out, "the essence" of any fraudulent insurance claim "is to appear normal and to be processed and paid in a routine manner".[9] One of the surprising truths of the fraud control business is that *fraud works best when claims processing works perfectly.*

Surveys of Fraud Cases

Several interviewees have pointed me to industry surveys, such as those conducted by Health Insurers of America Association (HIAA), as "measurement" of the fraud problem. HIAA periodically surveys member organizations and publishes aggregate profiles of the fraud experience within the industry. But these profiles represent industry's aggregate investigative caseload, not the underlying universe of fraud. The profiles, therefore, reflect the biases and capacities of the detection systems and the policies and preferences of insurers as much as they reflect the nature or scope of the underlying problem.

Random Mailing of EOMBs

Insurers, for a variety of reasons, sometimes mail explanations of medical benefits (EOMBs) to consumers on a random basis. One state Medicaid agency showed me how they randomly mailed a small number of EOMBs, even though the response rate was low and scarcely ever resulted in the detection of fraud. They did it because they thought HCFA required them to do it, not as a measurement device. They made no attempt to interpret the aggregate response. Given the ineffectiveness of EOMBs in soliciting useful information (a widely shared opinion among officials within the Medicaid program), aggregate results would not have meant much anyway.

At one major commercial insurer, staff explained how they made a random selection of 200 claims per week (100 from the western half of the United States and 100 from the east) and dispatched payment verification letters. These letters, sent to the insurance certificate holder, included details of the provider, the date of service, and the dollar amount paid. Certificate holders were asked to reply only if there was a problem. Response rates averaged fifty per quarter (i.e., 2 percent), with twenty-five per quarter (1 percent) returned undelivered. Most responses resulted from misunderstandings or queries about genuine treatments and did not lead to financial recoveries or savings. Once again, little was made of the results, and no one was able to state a clear purpose for the practice.

The closest to a real explanation offered for the practice was that the payment verification letters provided management with a general sense of quality assurance. In other words, the failure of this practice to reveal extensive fraud or abuse was taken as reassuring evidence of the effectiveness of their control systems. This instrument's failure to reveal a substantial problem can be interpreted two ways: Either there was no big problem or the instrument was poor. Without rigorous follow-up on all the nonresponders (98 percent), one cannot possibly tell the difference.

The payment verification letters used by this company were more readable than most EOMBs, but still somewhat dense and bureaucratic. Few recipients would have had much incentive to respond, and little reason exists to believe that such letters produce better feedback than EOMBs. With low response rates and without rigorous follow-up on nonresponders, such systems provide little useful information and certainly no scientific measurement.

Without knowing the level of fraud in the system, it is extremely difficult to establish the appropriateness of particular fraud controls or to decide what level of resources should be invested in controls. Perhaps most important, without a sense of the magnitude of the problem, neither the medical profession nor society at large can determine what level of inconvenience (from additional verification procedures) should be tolerated for the sake of preserving or restoring program integrity. If the size of the problem cannot be accurately gauged, it is unlikely to be adequately addressed.

How Measurement Changes the Nature of the Discussion—Fraud in the IRS Refund Program

Without measurement, the debate focuses on the size of the problem, rather than on solutions. Different parties make their own estimates and expend considerable energy defending "their position" against others'. In the mid–1990s, the IRS discovered how measuring a fraud problem can transform the debate. By 1993, the IRS knew it had a tax refund fraud problem in the electronic filing program. The earned income tax credit (EITC) enabled low-income working families with dependent children to claim up to $2,200 or more, even if no tax had ever been withheld from their wages. The EITC was more a welfare payment than a tax refund, but was administered through the tax system. The advent of electronic claims processing, accompanied by the offer of refund anticipation loans from commercial banks, meant that tax return filers could receive the refund—cash in their hands—within forty-eight hours and without ever having paid taxes.

From the fraud perpetrator's point of view, this was just what they liked: easy money, fast. In April 1993, at the end of the 1993 filing season,

NBC's *Dateline* exposed massive EITC scams in which residents of housing projects, who would not normally file tax returns, were being paid $400 cash for the use of their names and social security numbers by scam artists. These perpetrators would then use the purchased identities and submit hundreds or thousands of fraudulent refund claims based upon the credit. Dependent children would be "borrowed" or "invented" as necessary. Through the circulation and use of lists by criminals, some children appeared as dependents on up to five hundred separate tax returns. The IRS electronic filing system, coupled with refund anticipation loans, paid up fast and reliably. There was little systematic check of the veracity of EITC claims.

In the worst scams, criminals set themselves up as electronic return originators (EROs) and submitted electronic claims themselves. One ERO submitted 18,000 individual tax returns during one filing season (roughly a $36 million scheme), every one of them based on fictitious taxpayers, fictitious earnings, fictitious children, or some combination of the three.

IRS detection systems did catch a certain number of fraudulent claims. As the "detected schemes" figures accelerated rapidly from $7.5 million in 1989 to $67 million in 1992, however, nobody knew whether the detection systems were getting better or the problem was getting worse. During the 1993 filing season, the detected fraud schemes jumped to over $136 million—more than double the volume for the previous year. Once again, nobody knew if that was good news or bad news.[10]

Inevitably, following the media revelations, Congress held a series of hearings during which IRS managers were condemned for their organization's apparent incompetence and, at the same time, asked to guarantee that the problem would be brought under control. The IRS was unable to state the magnitude of the problem with certainty and so was caught in the classic fraud-control dilemma: They could either play down the problem, claiming to have the situation under control (in which case they would get no additional resources to deal with the problem), or they could play *up* the seriousness of the problem (at the risk of making the service look incompetent) and ask for the necessary investments in controls.

As usual, in the absence of facts, the first option (play down the problem) seemed more attractive, but offered little hope for effective future control. The IRS needed significant systems improvements as well as reassignment of substantial examination and audit resources to bring the EITC problem under control. Without the facts on the table, the most likely prospect was for the IRS to be embarrassed year after year by revelations about fraud vulnerabilities in the filing system; the IRS would never be able deal with such problems because they could not obtain or devote the resources needed to solve them.

In the fall of 1993, the IRS resolved to measure the problem systematically, each year, beginning in 1994. In the first two weeks of the 1994 filing season (January), the IRS randomly selected over 1,000 of the returns claiming the EITC. They held up the refunds just long enough to send an IRS criminal investigator to the door of the taxpayer's home. The investigator, arriving with a simple survey form in hand, said, "We plan to issue your tax refund, but I'd appreciate it if you'd answer just a few simple questions." Did the dependent children really exist? If the filer fell in the category "Male: Head of Household," what evidence could be found that children lived in the house? Could the person's employment or earnings be confirmed? The investigators were not asked to make cases, just to use their common sense and obtain the basic facts so that the results could be compiled into a meaningful measure of the fraud problem. They were required to validate information the taxpayers provided by checking with third parties: They would verify the employment with the employer; they would talk to neighbors if there was doubt about the children's residency; they would make contact with a spouse or other relative who might also claim the children as dependents. After making their inquiries, the investigators were asked to make their own best judgment as to the nature of any error or omission and to classify any misrepresentation as intentional or unintentional. If the EITC was erroneous, the form was passed to the examination division for a formal review, after which a "best and final" judgment would be made in each case.

The results, once compiled, showed that 38.8 percent of the claims for the EITC were either inflated or entirely unmerited, with 26.1 percent of the total EITC budget going into the wrong hands.[11] Even with the most conservative definition of fraud, 19 percent of the EITC claims had been classified as outright fraud.[12] The EITC budget for the 1993 tax year (i.e., for the 1994 filing season) was roughly $15 billion. The survey results suggested, then, that roughly $4 *billion* of this was getting into the wrong hands; the piece of this loss resulting from outright criminal fraud exceeded $3 billion.

During the 1994 filing season, the IRS's detection systems found only $160 *million* worth of refund fraud. Had the IRS continued to rely on information coming from their detection systems, they would have underestimated the magnitude of the fraud problem *by a factor of twenty.* In other words, their detection systems showed them no more than 5 percent of the problem.

What changed, once systematic measurement of the problem had been instituted? Well, fortunately, IRS managers resisted the powerful temptation to discount or discredit their own study (the thought did cross their minds when they saw how bad the results were) and faced up to the true magnitude of the problem. They encouraged the Treasury Department and congressional overseers to do the same.

Now the nature of the discussion changed altogether. The debate was no longer over the size of the problem, but how to fix it. During the remainder of 1994, the IRS scurried to make some critical multimillion-dollar investments in control systems and a number of painful and difficult policy changes that would enable them to slow down payment of certain refunds to gain time for extra checking. They strengthened the eligibility requirements for electronic-return originators and devoted an extra 1,700 staff years to detecting and preventing refund fraud. [13] Having discovered how hard it was to recover EITC payments after the fact, the IRS instituted an entirely new operation; they used tax examiners in a pre-refund mode rather than in their traditional, more leisurely, retrospective mode. To avoid the impression of being "anti-EITC," the IRS also sent out notices to 420,000 taxpayers who appeared to qualify for the EITC but had failed to claim it. [14]

The policy changes were by no means easy. The lending banks and other tax filing intermediaries lobbied hard and mounted a well-orchestrated press campaign in an attempt to keep things just as they had been during 1994. For the refund anticipation loan (RAL) business to be profitable, IRS refund payments had to be fast and predictable. The new controls made them slower, much less certain, and many more of the refunds were stopped altogether, leaving the lending banks exposed on their loans.

Two months into the 1995 filing season, *USA Today* ran a front-page headline, "IRS Puts on the Brakes: Anti-Fraud Slowdown Angers Filers." The story was that the adoption of new IRS fraud-control measures claimed innocent filers and businesses as victims. [15] Deep within the text of that story, the simple facts emerged: "The [Earned Income Tax] credits have been a popular source of fraud. An IRS study last year found that 20 percent of 1.3 million returns claiming the EITC were fraudulent. Another 20 percent had mistakes that inflated the payments." The headline could have proclaimed, "Thirty-Nine Percent of $20 Billion Tax Credit Program Goes to Wrong People." Perhaps the media were not accustomed to such revelations coming from the defending agency itself and may not have known what to make of it. The norm, after all, was to have network TV or other outsiders blast the agency, and then for everyone to join in the spectator sport of watching agency management squirm in their seats as they tried to provide reassurance.

Valid scientific measurement of the problem enabled the IRS to hold up the problem for congressional overseers and other stakeholders to see. It allowed them to say, in effect, "This is the problem: What price—in terms of inconvenience as well as resources—are you prepared to pay to help us deal with it?" During the 1995 filing season, the IRS held true to their commitment and repeated the measurement survey. The problem had not gone away, but in just one year it had been cut almost in half. The 1995 survey not only provided feedback as to the effectiveness of the new controls; it also showed the IRS which categories of tax returns remained problematic, enabling them to focus additional resources in those areas ready for the 1996 season. In 1995, for the first time ever, the number of EITC filers claiming dependent children dropped when compared with the previous year. The total number of children claimed also dropped.[16] The Senate *Budget Bulletin* reported in July 1995 that "the refunded portion of the EITC is $2 billion lower than originally projected (perhaps due to increased IRS scrutiny of returns claiming the EITC this year)."[17] Nineteen ninety-five was the first year the EITC had ever come in under budget. All but the harshest congressional critics applauded the IRS's efforts in tackling EITC fraud.

Why Measurement Is Not Generally Done

Given the transforming effect of rigorous measurement, why does most of the health care industry fail to take it seriously, or even to consider it at all? Few officials say rigorous measurement shouldn't be done. Some say that it can't be done (i.e., it is technically too difficult). Most say they can't do it, and give a variety of explanations why not. One of the most common explanations is shortage of resources: "We don't have the time or the money." Another explanation stems from short-term, short-sighted, cost benefit analysis: "We'd get better return by focusing on known problem areas" (the same objection that IRS auditors raise to the TCMP). All available resources are consumed following leads. One senior investigator from a commercial insurer told me his company never did systematic measurement through random audits and could never do it because "we are all too busy . . . we'd have to hire outsiders to do it . . . we only have fourteen people here and plenty of work to keep us busy."

Paradoxically—assuming a fixed level of fraud-control resources—the worse the fraud problem, the less likely it is to be measured. The more fraud there is, the busier everyone will be; we will see less inclination to "waste time doing studies."

The technical objection—that scientific measurement couldn't be done—is often raised by senior managers. The same objection was raised by some when the IRS considered measuring the EITC problem. In the health care industry, definitional ambiguities (between fraud, abuse, waste, errors, differences of medical opinion, and overutilization) present substantial technical difficulties; these should not be treated lightly, but they are certainly not insurmountable.

Oddly enough, nobody at the field level raises the technical feasibility objection. Investigators and auditors accept readily that rigorous investigation of a random sample of claims would teach them a lot that they do not already know about the extent and nature of fraud. Many people at the field level say they would like to do it, but they never have the time.

Many senior managers are not so sure that they, or their companies, would really like to investigate random samples of claims. The vice president for audit of one major Medicare contractor explained carefully how all their various types of audit did something other than measure the fraud problem. External audit examined the procedures of external business affiliates. Internal audit focused on separation of functions, system security, and opportunities for employee corruption. Quality review processes were all aimed at procedural adherence. None of these procedures was designed to detect fraud attacks by claimants, or to measure the level of fraud in the system.

Faced with this glaring omission (which left the contractor with absolutely no idea whether their fraud problems were worse or better than anyone else's) and asked whether his company might consider instituting a program of random audits for fraud measurement purposes, the vice president for audit commented, "There is no reward for finding fraud. There are no out-of-pocket losses for us [as a Medicare contractor]. Why would we put ourselves in this painful position? We have to think about our shareholders." The head of the special investigative unit at the same company, explaining that no one within the company wanted to devote resources to a "study," added

> Let's not make a wave. No one's upset. No one here is complaining about [fraud]. Business is good. We're making money. [Fraud losses] are not operating expenses. It's just someone else's money that's passing through. Besides, what would happen if we did do such a study? What if this became known? The newspapers are watching us. They'd love a story like that.

Making the commitment to measurement demands enormous courage on the part of managers. In November 1993, when the leadership of the IRS gathered to consider whether to approve the random sampling of EITC-based refunds, the decision was far from painless.[18] Commissioner Richardson had been appointed by President Clinton and knew that the EITC program, which the president hoped to expand considerably, constituted a central plank in his welfare reform plans. If the IRS leadership discovered that the EITC program was riddled with fraud, that would be grim news indeed for the administration. Nevertheless, the commissioner was resolved to do whatever it took to restore the integrity of the program, even if that meant exposing its weaknesses.

What clinched the IRS executive committee's decision to approve the plan was a remark from the chief financial officer: "Let's see if I have got this right. It seems to me that the worst possible situation to be in—for *us* to be in—is to believe that we have a huge problem but not be able to prove it to anyone." That is precisely the condition within the health care industry.

Early Attempts at Measurement

Chapter 3 described the OIG's use of medical review audits to assess Medicare overpayment rates. Two states, Texas and Illinois, have so far attempted more rigorous measurement studies, using audit protocols sufficient to capture fraudulent claims as well as processing errors and insufficiently documented claims.

The Texas study was required by statute[19] and performed by the State Comptroller's Office. The study, completed in the fall of 1998, examined likely overpayments and fraud in Medicaid acute care, in medical services provided under the worker's compensation program for state employees, and in the health insurance program for state employees and retirees, during Fiscal Year 1997. The report, issued as a draft in December 1998, was hotly contested by some of the agencies concerned and is no longer available publicly.

Illinois has made a commitment to biennial measurement. The first study, based on a sample of over 1200 claims, examined claims paid for services during November 1997. The claims review protocol employed a four-part claims examination procedure: (1) medical record review, (2) client interview, (3) review of patient history seven days before and after the service, and (4) special review to make sure the diagnosis made sense given the patient's medical history. The findings from this first measurement study, extrapolated to the entire program, suggested that 13.5 percent of the services paid were in error, at least in part. The payment accuracy rate overall was 95.28 percent, suggesting an annual rate of roughly $113 million misspent in the fee-for-service (FFS) part of the Illinois Medicaid program. One provider, who surfaced through the sample, could not substantiate any of his claims. Officials also noticed that, among the claims pulled for transportation providers, an unnaturally high proportion of their transportation customers had suffered mental health problems, exacerbating the difficulties associated with claims verification. This raised the possibility that transportation providers deliberately targeted patients who would be less able to contradict them credibly. The Illinois report is available through the Inspector General's Web site.[20]

The Texas study, at least in draft form, produced significantly higher overpayment rate estimates. For the sake of others contemplating such studies who are unclear about the appropriate methodology, it is worth pointing out some differences between the protocols used by Texas and Illinois:

1. Texas used *patient days* as the sampling unit, rather than *claims.* Starting from randomly selected claims, analysts extracted all other claims for the same patient for the same day and added them to the sample. Thus duplicate submissions from *different* providers could be identified, as could incompatible services apparently delivered on the same date.
2. Texas used external consultants to review the claims and conduct patient interviews; Illinois used existing state employees (principally within the Medicaid agency).
3. The task for the Texas State Comptroller's Office was to find "certifiable savings" rather than just to set the baseline for future performance measurement. Hence they were required to show how various categories of overpayments (which the study identified) might be prevented, and at what cost.

Several other states are now considering some form of measurement program—partly to establish the parameters of the fraud and abuse problem, partly to determine appropriate investments in detection and control, and partly to establish benchmarks for performance monitoring with respect to their current and future fraud reduction programs. HCFA may soon require states to conduct such studies as a condition attached to federal funds. Despite a somewhat slow start in this area, over the next few years we might anticipate much greater attention being paid to this issue.

States may need some assistance in establishing protocols for overpayment measurement studies as well as guidance on handling the difficult politics of the issue. They will certainly need to understand the important differences between standard medical reviews and fraud audits.

A typical "Medical Review" audit protocol usually involves three stages:

1. *Claims examination,* focusing upon
   • medical orthodoxy (procedure code to diagnosis)
   • policy coverage
   • price guidelines
2. *Request for medical records by mail,* and then review, focusing on establishing medical necessity on the basis of the record provided (and accepting it as true).
3. *Further correspondence with the provider,* either by mail or telephone, as necessary to resolve issues of medical necessity or coding.

By contrast, a fraud audit should include at least the following four types of inquiry, preferably conducted in the order shown here, and rather soon after the date of the claimed services so that patients have a reasonably good chance of recalling the details of the encounter.

1. *Claims examination,* focusing on all the normal issues of medical orthodoxy, policy coverage, and price. Also focusing on anything else unusual or suspicious, for example, signs of deception and patterns reflective of scams known through intelligence reports.
2. *Contextual data analysis,* examining the claim within its broader data context. In particular, examining
   • the provider's aggregate billing behaviors and billing profile
   • the patient's aggregate treatment patterns and profile
   • duplicate, similar, or related claims
   • referral patterns, coincidences, clusters, or structures in surrounding billings
   • business relationships between providers and referring physicians, ownership arrangements, potential kickbacks, etc.
3. *Patient interview,* preferably in person, otherwise by telephone. To verify the relationship with the provider, the diagnosis, and the treatment provided. May require contact with relatives in some instances.

4. Then, if the steps above indicate grounds for suspicion, an *unannounced* visit to the provider by investigators, to examine the medical and billing records. If the above three steps indicate nothing abnormal, then less intrusive record review techniques can be applied at this stage.

Some officials, seeing the degree of inquiry required for these fraud audits, may immediately reject the idea of measurement studies as therefore infeasible, or too expensive. Using a fraud audit protocol (and assuming the existence of reasonably versatile claims-data analysis capabilities), one might expect to expend, on average, the equivalent of half a day (measured in aggregate staff time) per claim to determine its eventual classification. That need not be too expensive for multibillion-dollar programs because a lot can be learned from a relatively small number of claims (500 or 1000). To measure fraud, it is much better to audit fewer claims more rigorously than to audit more claims less rigorously. Auditing more claims with insufficient rigor only enables insurers to produce a more accurate estimate for *a part* of the problem. What they need, generally, is a much better sense of the overall problem.

Resource Allocation, in the Absence of Measurement

If the true scope of the health care fraud problem were actually known, one would expect resource allocation for controls to be based upon that knowledge. In the absence of such knowledge, how does the industry set the level of resources for fraud controls? Most industry officials agree that resources allocated for fraud control are pitifully small, but they fail to establish a rational basis for meaningful increases. In 1984, John Gardiner and Theodore Lyman stated that

> Our case studies, GAO reports, and Congressional hearings have found repeatedly that the agencies administering welfare programs [including Medicaid] place little emphasis on fraud control; when cases of fraud or abuse are discovered, the most common responses are to cut losses (terminating a recipient's enrollment or a provider's participation in Medicaid) and to try to recover overpayments. Rarely are defrauders prosecuted. More broadly, these studies indicate that fraud control efforts rarely approach a level of optimality, one at which further investments in control would exceed resulting benefits, or one at which additional control efforts would materially infringe on recipients' and providers' rights.[21]

One private insurer I visited, who operates nationwide, set the budget for their specialist fraud unit (special investigative unit [SIU]) at $800,000. The unit produced recoveries and direct savings of between $2 million and $3 million per year; a savings-to-cost ratio of roughly three to one. Company policy, according to the unit's director, was "zero tolerance for fraud"; they "aggressively pursue every case that comes up." The investigative unit was busy enough that they hardly ever had time to go out and search proactively for cases. They worked almost entirely in reactive mode.

This insurer's claims volume exceeded $2 billion per year, and management quoted the standard GAO 10-percent estimate when asked how much fraud they thought there might be within their system. In other words, they thought (but did not know for sure) that they might be losing around $200 million per year to fraud. Of that $200 million in potential losses, $2.5 million was recovered or saved by the SIU. They needed to *count the zeroes.* The obvious question, it seems, is why was this special investigative unit not forty or fifty times its size? Saving $2.5 million looks terrific when compared with the $800,000 budget, but looks terrible when compared with the estimated $200 million losses. What would have persuaded management to increase the size of the unit? Apparently management at this company would have been prepared to increase the size of unit, they said, if the existing unit were clearly unable to cope with its workload: a situation, they claimed, that did not exist.

Why was the SIU, if it was truly far too small, not overwhelmed? Two reasons surfaced. First, the SIU's reactive workload was driven by referral mechanisms that were ineffective. Most referrals received from claims processors or from medical review were quirky and unusual, often the product of fluke or coincidence rather than of system. Examiners or reviewers would notice something suspicious and make a referral, even though they were examining the claim for some entirely different reason. Keeping up with the relatively slow flow of referrals, therefore, was more a function of the size of the referral pipeline than the depth of the reservoir.

Second, evidence emerged of a dynamic equilibrium connecting proactive and reactive work. As soon as the investigators had a spare moment, they would go and "beat the bushes," that is, talk to claims examiners, educate medical reviewers, and hold discussions with law enforcement agencies or other insurers. When they engaged in these proactive activities, they were rewarded with a rash of cases and referrals that made them so busy that they had to suspend further proactive work for the time being.

Investigators described how just a little beating of the bushes produced a significant volume of high-quality fraud cases—which meant it would be a long time before they would get a chance to beat the bushes again. Had the SIU been able to dedicate some of its resources exclusively to proactive work, this SIU would soon have been completely overwhelmed with the resulting caseload.

Investigators had plenty of evidence for their conviction that a "huge, untapped reservoir of fraud is sitting out there." In support of that contention, they offered the following observations:

- Small investments in proactive outreach produce a large volume of high-quality cases. "The more we go out and ask and prod people, the more referrals we get. And when we do a presentation or something, and then we get a flood of calls over the next week or so, they are all good referrals. I mean they are *good* calls."

- Over the years, the number of referrals the unit has received from outside sources, such as the FBI, seems to rise in direct proportion to the resources invested in health care fraud by those outside agencies. They see absolutely no sign of diminishing returns on investment.

- Their own investigations reveal the weakness of the company's detection and referral systems. "When we get a report and look into it and start digging, it usually turns out that our exposure is huge compared with the little thing that was reported. And we didn't find it because we detected the big pattern; we found it because we got lucky with some little piece."

- The majority of cases they investigate involve blatant behavior, with little attempt at concealment or subtlety, and most are detected because the perpetrators were careless, excessively greedy, or stupid. Investigators are painfully aware that they lack both the time and the methods to tackle the professional white-collar versions of the crime. All their time and energy is consumed dealing with amateurs: "What scares me the most: how blatant it is. It's too easy. They are not careful about hiding their tracks. The stuff we detect is obvious. Not well hidden at all. It's just dumb junk."

- Finally, these investigators had obtained, from a law-enforcement agency, a list that had circulated among various telemarketing operations. The list showed which insurance companies were easy to defraud and which were tougher. Their company was listed on the "easy" side, perhaps in part because investigative resources were so limited.

The annual budget for their fraud unit ($800,000) represented 0.04 percent of the claims volume. They spend at the 0.04 percent level to deal with a problem they think might be costing them 10 percent.

Within the health care system, massive underinvestment in fraud-control resources seems to be the norm. These investments, small as they are, pay off handsomely. The special investigative units at Medicare contractors all save more than they cost. Some turn in savings-to-cost ratios as high as 14 to 1; nowhere is it less than 2 to 1.

A pattern begins to emerge, spanning both commercial and public health insurance programs. The extent of fraud is never measured, merely estimated. The estimates are too soft to act as a basis for serious resource-allocation decisions, so resources devoted to fraud control have to be based on something other than the perceived size of the problem. In practice, control resources are budgeted incrementally, with significant increases likely only when a fraud unit is visibly drowning under its caseload. Most such units are not drowning, and this is puzzling at first. Despite their tiny size, most fraud units manage to keep up with the volume of referred cases. How is that possible? If they are really far too small, why are they not overwhelmed with their work? The general answer, it seems, is that sufficient resources are allocated to handle the reactive workload, with little or no spare capacity for proactive work. And why then is the level of investment so low, scarcely ever reaching even 0.1 percent of program costs? Presumably because the reactive caseload is tiny compared with the size of the problem. And why is the reactive caseload so small if the fraud problem is so serious? The most likely explanation is that the referral and fraud-detection systems do not work very well. The next chapter examines them in detail to establish more precisely what they can and cannot accomplish.

7

Assessment of Existing Fraud-Control Systems

When news of scandalous fraud losses comes to the fore, industry executives often deflect criticism from their own agencies through what might be termed "defense by display of functional apparatus." They counter suggestions of wide-open vulnerability to fraud by listing all kinds of apparatus, in operational use, aimed at fraud prevention and detection. Defending the New York State Department of Social Services (which handles the state's Medicaid program) the executive deputy commissioner (in 1991) produced a fine example of defense by display of functional apparatus. He argued that the Department of Social Services used an impressive array of apparatus to control fraud, including identification processes (computer profiling and targeting, undercover investigations, and audits); front-end controls limiting program access (provider enrollment controls, prepayment edits, utilization thresholds); and extensive applications of technology, including Medicaid card-swiping and systems, and various computer matching programs.[1]

To see if the traditional mix of systems really works to detect or control fraud, we must inspect each one in turn. The traditional types of controls, commonly used throughout the industry, are claims processing (involving human claims examiners as well as automated edits and audits), prepayment medical review, postpayment utilization review, and audits of one kind or another. These systems are supposed either to reject fraudulent claims up front or to detect them after the fact and refer them to specialist fraud units for investigation.

Claims Processing

The bulk of today's health care claims are processed within high-volume, highly automated environments. (More than 85 percent of

Medicare's claims are processed electronically.) Claims are fed into the processing stream through one of three mechanisms; they are received either

- On paper forms, and data entry is performed by human data entry clerks
- On paper forms, but the forms are typed so they can be read by an optical character reader (OCR), eliminating much or all of the human data entry task
- In electronic form directly from the provider or billing agency, eliminating the paper forms altogether

Most payment systems can receive claims through more than one of these mechanisms; many payment systems can handle (and combine) all three. Once the claims have been fed into the processing stream, what happens to them thereafter is the same, regardless of the form in which they arrived. If the claim arrived on paper, the amount of data entered into the automated payment system is cut to the bare minimum required for processing and paying the claim; textual explanations or comments will not get beyond the data entry stage. (The original claim forms, or captured images of them, may be kept for inspection by claims reviewers when necessary.) The data entered from paper claims matches precisely the minimal data fields used for electronic claims submission; nearly all of them consist of numeric codes.

All claims then pass through a series of automated edits and audits. Edits generally test for data entry errors by checking that entries have been properly formatted and fall within acceptable ranges on a field-by-field basis. System audits test a variety of conditions to determine whether or not the claim should be paid. The automated audits are arranged as a sequence of separate software modules, each with a different function, although the precise sequence varies from system to system. The standard modules (in no particular order) are:

1. Data entered correctly? Have all the necessary fields been properly filled in? Do they pass basic syntactical and relational checks? Do the data fall in valid ranges?

2. Prior authorization? Was authorization required for this procedure? If so, does the system have a record that the necessary authorization was obtained for this procedure by this provider?

3. Procedure code matches diagnosis? Does the procedure make sense, given the diagnosis code entered? (Commercial software packages perform this function, providing a matrix of permissible combinations.)

4. Qualifying provider? Is the provider approved? Enrolled? Within the network? Qualified for this procedure? Is the provider on suspension or review? Is the provider required to submit supporting documentation for this procedure? Are the provider's rates approved and on file? (Involves "look-up" to provider record files.)

5. Qualifying recipient? Is the recipient enrolled? Eligible? Covered for this procedure? Subject to deductible? (Involves "look-up" to recipient record files.)

6. Pricing? Is the price within the approved range for this procedure? Is the price approved for this provider? Is the pricing for this procedure set on the basis of "prevailing rates within the industry?" Is this price within the approved range for this specialty and geographic area? (Again, commercial software packages provide tables of ranges, by zip code, by specialty, by procedure.)

7. Service limitations? Does the recipient's insurance provide coverage for this number of incidents of this type of service within a given period? (Involves interrogation of patients' claim-history files.)

8. Duplicate claims? Has this claim been submitted and paid already? Is there another claim for this patient for a sufficiently similar procedure at or around the same time that would cause this claim to be considered a duplicate submission?

9. Code manipulation? Does this claim present an unallowable combination of procedure codes either because the procedure items should be rebundled or because the combination of procedures does not seem medically appropriate? (Again, commercial packages provide two-dimensional tables of disallowable combinations.)

If a claim passes through all these modules without a problem, it will be paid automatically, without further human intervention. Most systems hold payments for a few days so they can be paid in a weekly batch cycle, when computers automatically dispatch direct deposits, or print and mail paper checks.

If the information content of a claim raises a flag within one of the nine audit modules, the processing system will do one of the following three things:

- *Auto-reject:* The system generates a notice of rejection; this is sent back to the submitter normally through the same medium—paper or electronic—as the claim submission. Rejection notices always include a summary explanation of the reasons for rejection.
- *Auto-adjust:* The system corrects an error, adjusts pricing or re-bundles procedures, and passes the claims through for payment.
- *Suspend the claim:* The system transfers the claim to a queue for human review. The claim is then examined by a claims examiner or by the medical review team, depending on the level of medical knowledge required for the review.

How do such systems contribute to fraud control? What do they not do? These audits and edits enable the system to pay the right amount to the right person for the service claimed; they serve to correct billing errors and inappropriate billing procedures; and they reject claims if one or more of the provider, the recipient, or the procedure is somehow ineligible.

Such systems do not do anything to verify that the service was provided as claimed, or that the diagnosis is genuine, or that the patient knows anything at all about the alleged treatment. Rather, they assume the information presented is true and consider whether that information justifies payment of the claim.

None of these nine standard modules is targeted on fraud. Generally no attempt is made to create rules or logic that would pick out suspicious claims for closer scrutiny or to detect claims containing some deception or misrepresentation. The industry generally does not use fraud-specific prepayment edits or audits; in most claims-processing operations, fraud-specific edits and audits do not exist.

Nevertheless, some fraudulent claims are rejected as a result of the system's prepayment edits and audits. Fraudulent claims are rejected if, and only if, they are billed incorrectly; that is, if the procedure does not match the diagnosis; if the provider, beneficiary, or procedure is ineligible; or if, by some mischance, the service billed overlapped with some other incompatible service (for example, inpatient hospital services overlapping with outpatient services).

In each of these cases, the most likely outcome is auto-rejection, with the reason carefully laid out in an explanatory note to the fraud perpetrator. The perpetrator appreciates the education and does not make the same mistake again. Although the perpetrator gets wiser, the paying organization generally does not. Because there is no system for monitoring *rejected* claims, no human within the paying organization notices the classic pattern used by fraud perpetrators of test a little, learn a little. Some insurers monitor aggregate rejection rates for providers so that they can pick out the ones that seem to be having a really bad time and offer them some extra special education (billing instruction). Provided the fraud perpetrators learn the billing rules as fast as anyone else, though, there is no reason why they should show up.

This is not to say that claims-processing operations produce no fraud referrals at all. They do produce some, but claims-processing operations produce fraud referrals only so far as they involve human beings in scrutinizing claims. These fraud referrals result from the extraordinary capability of the human brain to spot patterns that it was not looking for. Referrals come from data entry clerks, who notice such oddities as white-out on the claim form, misspellings of medical terms, signs of illiteracy, unnaturally round numbers, names spelled inconsistently, apparent relationships between provider and patient, and so on.

At none of the field sites I visited when studying these control systems did processing systems make fraud referrals. When the systems suspend certain claims for human review, the suspension leads to the possibility of a fraud referral. But the logic and criteria for suspension focus on billing procedures, not fraud. Fraud referrals, when they come from the claims-processing operation, generally come by accident. They come because, for one reason or another, a person looked at the claim form and became suspicious.

Claims-processing systems seldom incorporate effective fraud-referral mechanisms. The edits and audits do nothing to verify the information in the claims. And the opportunities for human beings to become suspicious are dwindling with every week that goes by. The proportion of claims coming in electronically rises constantly, and the majority of these go through auto-adjudication—which means there is no human intervention or inspection at any time between claims submission and payment. Even when claims do come in on paper, they increasingly come in neatly typed on standard forms that minimize the amount of textual information. Use of high-speed OCRs removes the human data entry function with the exception of the occasional correction of numbers that the OCR machine was not able to read reliably. Modern, high-speed claims-processing systems are not set up to detect or refer fraud; they are set up to process claims, fast and efficiently, and to ensure correct billing.

Even claims that are patently absurd will be paid, unless, of course, they happen to contain one of the specific procedural billing violations that trigger rejection. What follows is a case in point, described by a member of a fraud unit at a major private insurance company:

> The other day we had [a claim] come up here [to the fraud investigation unit] for some other mechanical reason, not because of the content of the claim. And [when we read the text of the claim] we rolled around. It was a guy who went to Africa and "fell out of a wet tree" and sustained an injury to his scrotum. So he spent thirty days in the hospital. But he never went to the hospital until two days after the accident. And we paid. Then he sent in a report some time later saying he'd really been in the hospital thirty-two days, so could we pay some more. So we paid. Now, what is a wet tree, and what was he doing up it?

No one could expect a highly automated claims-processing system to display common sense, to become suspicious, or to ask the kinds of questions that humans ask; and they don't, which is why they generally fail to detect fraud. The best one would hope for claims-processing systems is that they would ask all the questions that machines can ask. Sadly, there is good reason to believe they sometimes fail to ask even the questions they are supposed to ask, sometimes for good reasons, sometimes for bad.

One state Medicaid agency I visited showed the "diagnosis to procedure code" module in flowcharts of their system's edits and audits. When they were asked which commercial software package they were using for this function, they admitted that they had not yet purchased one and had not yet filled in the two-dimensional table connecting diagnoses with permissible procedure codes. They had been paying claims for years with this entire module missing.

System edits and audits are frequently turned off. Limited budgets for claim examination force managers to limit the claim-suspension rate by limiting the number of automatic edits and audits. Under the Medicare program, Health Care Financing Administration (HCFA) pays for a maximum suspension rate of roughly 9 percent of claims. Most contractors, if they turned all their edits and audits on, would easily exceed that percentage. Most Medicare contractors suspend claims at higher rates than HCFA budgets allow, making up the costs with savings elsewhere.

The various modules built into claims-processing systems, when they are all turned on, certainly help to ensure billing correctness and medical orthodoxy. However, these modules do little for fraud control. Overall, the model for claims suspension and review is this: *Systems select, humans inspect.* The criteria upon which systems select seldom have anything to do with fraud.

Claims Examination and Development

Once humans have a chance to inspect claims, the prospects for fraud detection and referral improve tremendously. Humans, given the opportunity, often notice the unusual or incongruous. The central task of claims examination and development turns out to be quite routine. Claims examiners mostly follow prescribed sequences of actions and decisions, usually specified in manuals on their desks. "If this, then look up that. If that, then do this." These prescribed procedures enable the examiner to resolve questions of eligibility, coverage, medical appropriateness, or whatever it was that caused the claim to be suspended. Examiners spend most of their time searching reference materials or interrogating other databases so that they can follow a decisionmaking path that was too complex or too unusual to be incorporated into the automated claims-processing system.

Claims examiners and developers, then, are required to resolve the more complex cases, but they focus on precisely the same issues as the edits and audits in the processing system; they just deal with the more complex cases.

Prepayment Medical Review

The term *medical review* is used in various ways. Usually it means "claims examination requiring medical knowledge." Medical review teams include senior examiners (who have picked up some medical knowledge), nurses, and a small number of doctors available for consultation (either in-house or externally as consultants). Medical review focuses on issues of medical appropriateness and medical necessity and does so within the confines of an insured's policy coverage. Medical review teams assume the information content of the claim to be true, even though they may request medical records to establish or substantiate medical necessity.

These are the actions open to examiners and medical reviewers:

1. Request additional medical documentation to support the diagnosis, or to establish medical necessity
2. Deny the claim, stating reasons, and have the system generate a rejection notice to the claimant
3. Approve the claim, accepting it as valid
4. Compromise, or cutback, based on the level or limitations of coverage and on the examiners' professional judgment as to what is reasonable in the circumstances

"Refer to fraud unit" does not normally appear on the reviewers' list of formal options. Their task is to resolve specific issues, but their list of issues does not include verifying the truthfulness of the claim. Nevertheless, medical reviewers do make fraud referrals from time to time—just like claims examiners—as an accidental by-product of human claims inspection.

Many senior managers expressed the belief that their medical review teams served as a major weapon in their efforts to combat fraud. Medical review and fraud detection, however, are distinct sciences. Medical review cannot act as a useful filter for fraud detection. When medical reviewers spot fraud, once again it is because they are human and because they are looking at the claim, not because it is their job. To illustrate how separate the sciences of medical review and fraud detection are, consider the use of the shotgun and rifle approach described in Chapter 1. Pick a genuine patient who suddenly became sick and developed an expensive but perfectly genuine medical history. Now take a thousand other patients' identities and replicate the same billing history, maybe a month later, claim by claim. For these thousand patients, provide no services. If the system paid all the original patient's claims without objection, the chances are it will pay the same medical history a thousand times over—for a thousand fake illnesses—without so much as a hiccup.

To escape attention from medical review, a fraud perpetrator has only to base false claims on medically plausible diagnoses and procedures and to stay comfortably within the confines of policy coverage.

An Experiment in Automated "Claims Examination"

The routineness and predictability of the claims-examination function was made vividly clear to me through an experimental application of personal computers at one of Medicare's regional durable medical equipment (DME) contractors. They had a roomful of personal computers neatly arranged around the walls; the contractors had programmed the computers to do the work of claims examiners and medical reviewers. They called the approach the "Automatic Transaction Processing System" (ATPS).

During my visit to the ATPS room, some of the computers were "sleeping," having resolved all of the suspended claims in their queue and having no work left to do. Others were working away, and, by watching the screen, one could just about keep up with what they were doing. The computers logged into various other mainframe systems, including Medicare's central database of beneficiary histories (HIMR);[2] they triggered an inquiry of some kind, waited for the response, and logged out; then they dialed up another system, and so on. These PCs were following claims-resolution procedures, as per the manual, just as claims examiners and medical reviewers do. They just did it faster, more reliably, and much more cheaply.

The designers of the ATPS had taken the list of suspension codes and picked off the ones whose resolution procedures were easiest to automate. Having demonstrated success with the simpler ones, they were working their way down the list to more complex ones. The idea behind this innovation is really quite clever. It is easier to equip a PC with a range of communications packages and have it interrogate mainframe systems one by one than it is to integrate the different mainframe systems with each other. The designers of ATPS programmed the PCs to perform all the mainframe inquiries and built in the decision logic that human examiners would have followed. The cost of resolving a suspended claim dropped from $3.85 per claim (the cost when using human examiners and reviewers) to 5.5 cents per claim. Meanwhile *accuracy,* as established by quality-control procedures, rose to 100 percent. The ATPS demonstrated ingenious use of modern technology and a highly innovative way of processing inquiries that demanded access to a range of incompatible mainframe systems.

The system also clarifies the nature of claims-examination medical review function. Three key observations should be made: First, none of the PCs in that room ever telephoned a beneficiary or provider. Second, all the information the PCs used in claim resolution was internal to the claim or to the payment system (including central Medicare databases). Third, none of those PCs ever made a fraud referral, even after resolving hundreds of thousands of suspended claims; "fraud referral" or "forming of suspicions" appeared nowhere on the list of possible outcomes.

Surprising Lack of Fraud Awareness

Some examination and review procedures ignore the possibility of fraud altogether. For example, when claims are suspended for medical review, claimants are frequently asked to provide medical records in support of the claims. What happens if providers do not supply the requested documentation within the time allowed (typically sixty days)? What if they never respond?

Of course that particular claim will be denied; from the point of view of claims examiners or reviewers, that would usually be the end of the matter. Their job would be finished because the unit of work for the entire claims-processing system is the *claim*. Examiners and reviewers have no reason to be curious about providers who allow their claims to drop, rather than simply providing a copy of supporting documentation.

By contrast, the units of work for fraud control are fraud schemes, fraud problems, fraudulent providers, or fraud patterns or methods. In the control business, intelligence about these is a most valuable asset. Fraud investigators would have every reason to be curious, to follow up, and to find out why a provider so casually allowed an account receivable to slip away.

Fraud investigators would be especially interested, given the surprising volume of responses that never come back. One state Medicaid agency reported that between 40 percent and 50 percent of the requests for supporting documentation went unanswered. In each case, the claim was dropped from the system and no follow-up inquiries were made. That was the end of the matter. So, for some strange reason, these providers would apparently rather lose a claim payment (which might be for several hundred, or even thousands of dollars) than spend $2 to photocopy the necessary documents and mail them in to justify the claim.

In stark contrast, examiners at one small private insurer—who displayed a much greater level of fraud awareness—asserted, "We never let one of those drop . . . if they don't respond, we want to know *why*." These examiners would first mail the provider a reminder. After that they would call. If the provider still didn't respond, they would visit the provider's office to discuss the claim.

At one major Medicare contractor, medical review procedures revealed an astonishing lack of fraud awareness. The medical reviewers were fraud-aware and made occasional referrals; the medical review procedures, though, seemed to institutionalize a lack of curiosity. This contractor's medical review was focused on particularly troublesome segments of the industry and upon known or suspected patterns of abuse and overuse. (For example, one project focused on the problem of home health care agencies who billed for two-person visits when the service provided called for one-person visits.) Having picked a segment or practice for attention, the medical review section would introduce screens (selection criteria) into the claims-processing system to pick out a random sample of around sixty pertinent claims. With respect to those claims, the medical review team would mail out (or have the system generate) a standard letter requesting a variety of supporting documentation. When the responses came back, they were examined by medical review nurses; the aggregate results were then examined. If this process confirmed a billing or utilization problem, the team would try to correct the problem, using education as their tool of choice—which, they said, "mostly fixes the problem."

At first sight, a detailed examination of a random sample of claims within a high-risk segment looks promising as a fraud-detection tool; however, this unit scarcely ever made fraud referrals. Under what conditions would they refer a provider for investigation? According to the head of the unit, "We would refer a case for investigation if, from the documents sent in, there was clear evidence of fraud." But who would be stupid enough to mail in "clear evidence of fraud"?

What happened if no documentation was received, or if a provider failed to respond at all? Next to nothing. If the provider did not respond within sixty days, the review procedures would "delete" the claim from the system; this means the system rejects the claim and erases all record of its existence.

Such procedures accomplish nothing with respect to fraud control. Fraud perpetrators remain perfectly safe in the face of these kinds of reviews. If they are unlucky enough to receive a request for supporting documentation, they can simply ignore it, and they do so with impunity. Or, if they prefer, they can take the trouble (and up to sixty days) to send in suitably fabricated documents.

The director of this same medical review unit—which virtually never makes a fraud referral—was aware of fraud and commented that "sixty to seventy percent of all our providers are crooked." The procedures the unit uses were nevertheless designed and operated as if the fraud problem did not exist.

Does that mean these procedures are useless? No, absolutely not. They accomplish their design purpose. They help to control billing that pushes the limits or breaches the rules. They also help to identify erroneous billing or utilization practices by honest providers who did not know they had strayed outside the limits of policy coverage and who are happy to have their errors pointed out. Fraud perpetrators, however, represent a different audience; they know exactly what they are doing wrong and deliberately stay within the confines of policy coverage and medical orthodoxy.

Postutilization Review

Some time after the claims have been paid (usually several months), the postpayment-utilization review function takes the opportunity, outside the pressure of payment cycles, to examine aggregate statistical profiles of providers and recipients. Those that stand out in a statistical sense will have their medical utilization and claims patterns scrutinized more closely.

The Medicaid program calls their postutilization review system "SURS" (Surveillance and Utilization Review Subsystem). The origins of SURS date back to 1970 within the Department of Health, Education, and Welfare, where the objective was to perform comprehensive statistical profiling of providers and recipients.[3] By 1995, the emphasis in most SURS units, and in most other postutilization review units, had shifted almost exclusively to provider profiling.

Various commercial companies now sell profiling systems to assist in utilization review, and many health insurers build their own versions in-house. These profiling systems all operate essentially upon the same philosophy and differ only in the number and types of variables they use to characterize providers' behavior and the degree of sophistication with which they use statistical methods.

The general philosophy is straightforward. First the system divides providers into groups by specialty and by geographic area. Then it chooses a series of variables through which one might characterize providers' behavior. These can be general variables (e.g., the number of procedures per patient visit, the average number of times each patient is seen per month) or variables specific to specialty (e.g., for obstetricians, the percentage of births by caesarean section; or, for home health care agencies, the proportion of home visits requiring two staff members rather than one).

For each variable, the system calculates the distribution for the particular specialty and geographic area. Using that distribution, the system assigns each provider a score that indicates how far the provider's behavior deviates from the mean. The system picks off the few providers that lie at the extreme tails of the distribution (paying attention to whichever of the two tails seems to be more suspicious—usually the one that represents more expensive behavior). Some of the more sophisticated systems assign scores for each variable and combine them into composite scores for each provider. The composite scores are used to rank-order providers within a specialty and bring to the top of the list those whose behavioral profiles appear most unusual.

One of the Medicare contractors I visited had an unusually effective utilization review (UR) unit on the private (commercial) side of their business that seemed to offer tangible results in terms of cost control. It is worth examining how they operated as an example of best practice.

The director of this UR unit was one of a rare and valuable breed in the health care control business—a *suspicious nurse*—combining broad medical knowledge with a deep skepticism about providers' integrity. She commented, "The best thing that has happened in this business is that in the last four years the public's trust in the medical profession has been eroded."

Her unit thought in terms of *projects*: They deliberately identified areas where problems emerged and evaluated their own interventions by subsequent declines in billing levels. The units' projects under way at the time of my visit included examination of the following issues:

- Mammograms reported as "medically necessary" (rather than "routine") to receive higher reimbursement rates.
- Nuclear cardiology scans of questionable medical necessity and accompanied by code manipulation, specifically unbundling.
- Overuse of EEGs (electroencephalograms) and nerve conduction studies.
- Quality of X-ray film: Some providers were using such poor-quality supplies that the results were of no medical value. The insurer was prepared to pay only for good-quality film.
- Overuse of ear tests (tympanometry and acoustic reflex tests) without medical justification.

Problem areas were often identified through statistical trend analysis on the aggregate utilization rates; these showed which procedures' or specialties' average billing rates had accelerated sharply. When a problem area had been identified, analysts would pick out the extreme providers, usually those who lay more than two standard deviations above the mean, and perform a random record review. For each project undertaken, between 15 and 200 doctors would be selected; they would each be asked to provide supporting documentation for between 10 and 50 claims. The unit performed some four hundred such provider audits each year.

If physicians failed to respond to requests for records, the unit would enter a provider flag into the claims-payment system, suspending payment on all of that physician's future claims until they complied. That "usually gets their attention." The unit director described how, when they began to put pressure on a particular problem area, articles would appear in the local medical press discussing the issue and seeking to clarify the rules.

Because physicians' audits took a lot of time, the unit used a variety of other methods also. With some problem areas they would just pick off the top few providers and send them a letter saying, in effect, "We are watching you: Desist, or else." The unit sends out between 6,000 and 7,000 such letters each year, using an automatic letter-generating facility built into their profiling system (which was designed in-house). Roughly one-third of providers receiving such letters call back to discuss the issue; billing rates usually drop off or flatten out immediately.

This unit has the power to formally exclude participating physicians for repeated violations, but the unit's director says the procedure is bureaucratic, difficult, and expensive. She has more effective methods. She refers some cases for fraud investigation to the SIU, and the two units work unusually closely together. She could also ask providers for money back, extrapolating from the audit sample to their entire claims volume. Once they have been found out, she says, it is amazing just how easily they pay up.

Most potent of all, she could suspend a provider's incoming claims by inserting a flag into the claims-processing system; such an action amounts to informal exclusion from the payment system until the provider supplies information or explanations—an unusually tough approach to controlling costs.

In general, postpayment utilization review focuses much more on unusual medical practice than on patterns of criminal deception. Some fraud schemes may produce unusual utilization patterns. Any specialty or provider group that becomes riddled with fraud might show up, in aggregate, through trend analysis. But what of fraud in general, hiding among the mass of legitimate activity? What must a fraud perpetrator do to avoid detection by postutilization review?

To avoid detection, fraud perpetrators need only avoid excessive greed and make sure that their provider profiles are reasonably typical for their segment of the industry. In particular, they should avoid extremes of utilization behavior. The cutoffs used most often are two standard deviations from the mean, which—assuming something like a normal distribution—means that only the top 2.3 percent of providers in a category are likely to face scrutiny.

Fraud perpetrators may also choose specialties that are high volume (so that significant fraud losses do not shift aggregate costs noticeably), or where fraud, abuse, or overutilization are already rampant (so that newcomers are less likely to be among the outliers).

No matter which services are or are not provided, a fraud perpetrator can avoid vulnerability to postutilization review altogether by mimicking, claim for claim, the billing patterns of a legitimate, honest provider. The honest provider delivers the service; the dishonest one does not. Postpayment utilization review cannot tell the difference.

The degree to which postutilization review turns out to be a useful device for fraud control depends upon the degree to which fraud perpetrators create anomalous billing patterns. Of course, the smart ones do not. So only the excessively greedy or stupid fraud perpetrators get caught this way. Once again, this is not a criticism of postutilization review procedures. The principal purpose of utilization review is to review medical utilization patterns, both on an aggregate basis (to help formulate policy changes or provide necessary provider and recipient education) and on an individual provider basis (to eliminate medically inappropriate or unreasonably expensive treatment patterns).

As a fraud-detection methodology, however, postutilization review procedures, with their strong emphasis on profiling providers, have certain limitations that must be understood:

- First, they detect fraud only where it produces anomalous billing patterns, as discussed already. They are much better suited to detecting waste and abuse, which do not amount to criminal fraud.
- Second, utilization review generally leads to scrutiny of only a few extreme outliers within each provider category, leaving the bulk quite safe from detection, even if the bulk is rotten.
- Third, most utilization-review units prefer to inform and educate providers when they detect anomalous billing patterns, rather than investigate. So, as with prepayment medical review, fraudulent providers remain safe from investigation, provided they change tactics when warned.

- Fourth, utilization-review procedures come long after the fact and are useful only in the context of a continuing relationship between payer and provider. Utilization-review systems operate in batch mode, periodically processing three to six months of claims data at a time. Due to processing constraints, the resulting profiles may not be available for some time after the period in question and may not be updated in a timely manner. The claims data forming the basis for provider profiles is usually at least three months old; in some cases, it is much older. Postpayment utilization review therefore comes too late to be useful in combating the increasing number of fraud schemes run by fly-by-night operators. Storefront businesses, which fraud investigators say are increasingly prevalent, bill fast and furious, creating extremely anomalous billing patterns; they disappear with the money long before postutilization review catches up with them.

To counter the threat of quick, high-volume "hit and run" schemes, the only sure defense is *prepayment* provider profiling—which would monitor each provider's aggregate billing patterns and acceleration rates before claims are paid. None of the sites I visited had prepayment provider profiling or a (prepayment) method of watching for sudden surges in billing from individual providers.

Analogous defenses in the credit card and banking industries are commonplace; they consist of spending-pattern analysis and acceleration-rate monitoring, with preapproval intervention and verification procedures. Consumers experience such control systems when, at the point of sale or at an ATM machine, they are required to speak by phone to a credit card authorization representative before their credit card purchases are accepted. Such systems monitor the transaction patterns of credit card or account holders as well as the selling patterns of merchants, and serve to intervene before payment when the transaction pattern is suspicious.

Audits

Part A of the Medicare program—which covers hospitals, nursing homes, home health agencies, rehabilitation clinics, hospices, and some other providers of institutional care—uses a form of audit called a "Medicare audit" (or "cost report audit"). These audits focus on the cost reports of the institutions upon which the Medicare reimbursement rates for that institution are based. The audits look for a wide range of costs that ought not be included on the Medicare cost report: excessive charges for lunches, cellular phones, cruises, vehicle expenses, or salaries for people who spend most of their time working on something other than Medicare business. All expenses included in the cost reports are supposed to be related directly to health care for Medicare beneficiaries.

How effective are such audits in uncovering fraud? The most important point to realize is that these audits do not examine claims at all; they examine cost reports. The focus is solely on the mechanism through which reimbursement levels are set and not on the subsequent use of those rates when submitting claims.

The head of one audit unit—with forty auditors working for him doing nothing but Medicare audits all year—explained that Medicare audits rarely establish fraud as such and are not designed to do so. They are obliged to give four weeks' notice in advance of the audit. Even so, he said, many providers refuse to provide documentation or pretend they can't find it.

If auditors find misreporting, they make adjustments in the cost reports. If the same thing happens three years in succession, they can refer the case to the Office of Inspector General (OIG) for investigation! So all the providers have to do is change the *nature* of their misreporting from year to year.

Half the auditors in his unit focused exclusively on home health care agencies. These auditors each recovered an average of $1.8 million per year in overpayments. Nevertheless, these audits hardly ever established fraud or referred suspected fraud for investigation, in part—as the head of the unit explained—because they did not really expect juries to be able to deal with financial statements and accounting conventions.

Another type of audit under Medicare involves managed care organizations. Audits of the MCOs (managed care organizations) seek to establish the financial security of the company to minimize the danger of its going out of business or of being unable to deliver adequate care once the managed care contracts have been signed. Once again, the purpose of such audits is not to find fraud.

One senior auditor at HCFA, commenting on the various purposes of the different audits, explained:

> We would comment that this is the job the CPA firms who do audits for managed care companies are hired to do. They do a *financial* audit. For Medicare purposes, CPAs or other auditors do a *Medicare* audit. The prime purpose of neither type of audit is to detect fraud. A Medicare audit is per-

formed primarily to verify that costs claimed on the cost report are related to patient care, necessary, prudent, reasonable and properly allocated to the Medicare program.[4]

If fraud is discovered during an audit, it will be referred to the proper authorities. The purpose of the audits, though, is not to find fraud but to focus on other issues.

Private sector insurers use audits for a variety of purposes. They perform random *claims audits* to check the accuracy of the claims examination process (as discussed in Chapter 6); however, because these audits are focused on procedural correctness (quality control) and do not include external validation, they are unlikely to detect fraud. Private sector insurers also perform *internal* audits, which are designed to protect the company against employee corruption by guaranteeing separation of duties and adherence to security policies. They also perform *external* audits, designed to establish the financial viability of business partners.

In general, in both the public and private sectors, audits are not designed to find fraud, and they seldom do. Just as with claims examination and medical review, audits may reveal fraud occasionally, but that is not their purpose.

Special Investigative Units

The investigative units sit at the end of the referral pipeline, their cases coming from beneficiary complaints stimulated by explanation of medical benefits forms (EOMBs), from data entry clerks or claims examiners, from prepayment medical review, from postpayment utilization review, or from auditors. A small number of tip-offs from other insurers, from law-enforcement agencies, or from anonymous telephone calls augments the total referral volume.

Any reasonably astute fraud perpetrator avoids all of these standard detection methods by billing correctly, by using orthodox treatment/diagnosis combinations, and by avoiding excessive greed (which might put their billing profiles at the statistical extremes for their specialty). As Joe Ford, one of the FBI's pioneers into the field of health care fraud investigation, pointed out as early as 1992: "For the most part, the audit systems established by the various Federal and State regulatory agencies do not detect this type of criminal activity." [5] Ford's statement was right then and is right now. His point helps explain the assessment, made by an experienced special investigative unit (SIU) investigator, that the referrals SIUs receive are, on the whole, just "dumb junk." Existing referral mechanisms detect only the stupid, careless, or excessively greedy fraud perpetrators. The SIUs' incoming workloads represent only the tiniest fraction of the total fraud volume; this explains why these units, so ridiculously underresourced, are not generally overwhelmed by their caseloads.

Most investigative units work predominantly in reactive mode and just about keep up with the work that comes to them. No matter which mechanism produced the referrals, the investigators' job is the same: to investigate and to make cases. Following a traditional enforcement model, most of these units count their workload in terms of the number of incoming complaints or referrals and count their successes according to the number of cases made, settlements reached, aggregate dollars recovered, and convictions obtained.

Investigators in these units may work extremely hard and be quite expert at what they do. However, whenever investigative units fall into a case-disposition mode, they lose most of their value for fraud control. If they also develop an appetite for monetary recoveries (which is the safest way to preserve the unit's budget), they can often end up doing little more than recovering monies paid to fraud perpetrators.

Surely recovering money paid to criminals is a valuable objective? Yes, indeed it is. If that becomes the primary accomplishment of a fraud investigative unit, however, their contribution to effective fraud control has dropped virtually to zero. Fraudulent providers are notoriously eager to repay money when they have been caught cheating. Such a small proportion of their fraudulent activities are ever detected that quick repayment accompanied by a profuse apology for the "mistake" is a small price to pay for the ensuing peace and quiet that enables them to continue their fraudulent activities.

One fraud investigator told me how she happened to be at a dialysis clinic one day when an ambulance pulled up outside. Three patients climbed out and walked into the clinic under their own steam. She asked for, and obtained, their names. Checking the claims histories later, she found that the transportation company had billed more than $70,000 over several months for services to these three patients on the basis that they were wheelchair-bound (which they visibly were not). The investigator called the OIG, who declined to pursue the case (too busy). Subsequently, an overpayment of $75,000 was requested from the transportation company. The transportation company delivered a check the *very next day,* without argument, "Just like that!" They stayed in business.

The ease and rapidity with which some providers pay back seems disconcerting. It suggests that the fraud-control apparatus finds only a thin sliver of the cake; providers would much rather give up the sliver than have anyone go looking for the whole cake. Fraud perpetrators, both individuals and major corporations, always prefer to settle the case, quickly and amicably, than to have investigators delve into their general business practices.

What of effective fraud control—and the child playing the whack-a-mole game? How can SIUs help their organizations see more clearly and respond more effectively to emerging fraud threats? If the SIUs remain in reactive mode, fed by ineffective referral pipelines, they will see the truth dimly, partially, and probably very late. The extent to which they gain a better understanding of fraud depends on the extent to which they deliberately engage in proactive outreach and intelligence gathering. Many of them, sadly, do not regard that as their business; and so many of them spend an inordinate amount of time complaining about the lack of referrals.

However deep the reservoir of fraud may be, many of these SIUs sit passively on the end of the detection and referral pipeline, locked in a reactive casemaking mode. Their referrals, when measured against the underlying volume of the reservoir, are no more than a mere trickle. The simple reason: The detection and referral pipeline doesn't work properly because none of its components were designed with fraud in mind.

Lack of Coordinated Control Strategy

When the control apparatus is examined piece by piece, it becomes clear why effective control remains elusive. The fraud units, however dedicated and competent, are incredibly small when compared with the size of the problem; they work largely or exclusively in reactive mode, generally managing to keep up with the few cases produced by a collection of highly ineffective and vastly overrated referral mechanisms. Add to this situation the lack of functional coordination and the absence of a coordinating strategy tying together the efforts of the various functional units, and the reason for the persistence of the health care fraud problem becomes clearer still.

The question "Who here is responsible for fraud control?" is a revealing one to ask an insurer, and it is usually met with bemusement and bafflement. The standard answers are either "No one" or "Everyone." As Senator Donald Halperin pointed out in testimony about New York State's Medicaid program: "Overall, there is no single individual or agency in New York State with overall control to ensure that programs work, money is not wasted, and dollars are not stolen." [6]

The bigger the claims-processing operation, the worse communication and coordination across functional lines tend to be. Larger organizations have more clearly drawn functional boundaries and less frequent communications across those boundaries. Opportunities for coordinated intervention using the entire range of available tools—investigation, administrative action, prepayment and postpayment review, adjustment of edits and audits, education—are particularly difficult within the Medicaid program, where investigative units (for all kinds of good reasons) are organizationally separate from the claims-processing operation.

There has to be a brain, or a team of brains, playing the fraud-control game. Most often that will not be one person, but a group drawn from multiple functions and multiple agencies, organized around the purposes of fraud control. In several programs around the country, cooperative relationships supported by regular meetings are emerging to form a basis for integration and coordination. In many more programs around the country, though, such meetings never happen; the fraud-control agenda is never laid out.

Whoever is responsible for fraud control must see the big picture; this means collecting and collating intelligence from different sources and systematically measuring and monitoring the shifting patterns of fraudulent behavior. Like a chess player, that person or team must to be able to coordinate the various functional pieces of apparatus like chess pieces on a board, to defend against each attack, and to wear the opponents down.

8

The Antithesis of
Modern Claims Processing

Fraud investigators throughout the industry readily acknowledge that they only see a fraction of the fraudulent claims running through their claims-processing systems. They realize the fragility of detection and referral mechanisms; they bemoan the primacy of efficiency as the goal for the claims-processing system; and they see staff in other functions as oblivious of the fraud problem. The investigators, closest to the realities of the streets, know full well that their fraud-control apparatus—fragmented and understaffed—barely scratches the surface.

Against that depressing backdrop, the confident claims of managers at one particular insurer came as a stunning surprise. I shall refer to the insurer as Company X because the anonymity of the sites was a condition under which I visited them to conduct my fieldwork. Managers at Company X claimed that their fraud-control systems detected around 80 percent of the fraudulent claims submitted to them. They felt they had fraud under control; no other company I visited came anywhere near making such claims. Could such confidence be justified? Perhaps they were deluding themselves. Or perhaps they had such terrible detection apparatus that they really had no sense of the magnitude of the fraud problem. Or perhaps, conscious of the company's reputation, they were merely putting forward the "official position." They could not prove that they stopped 80 percent of the fraudulent claims because they, like everyone else, had no systematic method of measuring the overall level of fraud losses. They saw only what their detection systems showed them. However, company X differed from all the other insurers in several ways, not just in its confidence about fraud control. Its entire claims-processing apparatus was unique and, in many respects, represents the antithesis of modern claims processing.

Background

Company X's business, at the time I visited them, was confined to one state, and they had just one policyholder—a labor organization—with around 17,000 certificate holders under that policy. The health benefits were the same for each certificate holder, but each family could choose between 4 or 5 options with respect to deductibles. Certificate holders obtained coverage for their families, with an average of 2.25 people covered for each certificate. The average age of those covered was 56 years. Any resident of the state could join the health insurance program, but first had to become a member of the labor organization holding the policy. (The organization's rules permitted anyone to join as a nonvoting member, although voting membership was reserved for particular categories of workers.)

The company also ran 4,600 Medicare Supplemental Policies (privately issued policies that cover deductibles and copayments not normally covered by the Medicare program). The company received $46 million in health insurance premiums and paid out $36 million annually through the issue of 90,000 checks. The company's corporate parent and affiliates offered a range of other insurance products, but the health insurance operation was self-contained and employed about 30 people. The employees worked in one open-plan office, and they all knew each other personally. This, as modern health insurance systems go, was a tiny operation.

Evidence of Success

In the absence of formal measurement, how could anyone be sure that this company did better at controlling fraud than anyone else? What signs or indicators could be taken as evidence of more effective control? Between them, the managers at Company X came up with the following list of indicators:

- *Company X often catches people the first time around:* When the company discovers someone trying to defraud them, they write the suspect a letter outlining the facts as the company sees them and warning the perpetrator to desist; the company also reviews the relevant claims history to check for previous occurrences of fraudulent behavior. In the majority of cases, the review of previous history finds no past pattern of fraud; this suggests the fraud was detected at the first attempt. In other words, Company X seems able to catch emerging fraudulent practices early. By contrast, other insurers digging into false claims usually find established patterns of fraud; indeed, most fraud investigators relish what they call "tip of the iceberg" cases where investigation of an apparently isolated false claim leads to the discovery of multimillion-dollar patterns of cheating. Such cases reveal the diligence and persistence of investigators, but they also show late detection of a pattern of fraud.

- *Tips received from outside rarely reveal anything new:* Of the tips the company receives from other insurers, from law enforcement, or from informants, only one in ten tells them of a vulnerability or fraudulent practice of which they were unaware. In six out of ten cases, the tip involves a provider who does not do business with them. In three out of the remaining four cases, Company X already has the provider flagged as problematic and under scrutiny; this means that when someone outside the company tells them of a provider who cheats, they are already aware roughly 75 percent of the time.

- *Company X often tips off other, bigger, companies:* The converse is not true. Staff recalled seven instances where their own methods had uncovered fraudulent providers and where they had been able to tip off larger companies facing much greater exposures. In each case, the other (larger) company had not previously identified the problem.

- *Company X is highly active in flagging problematic providers:* Company X, despite its comparatively small size, is one of the most active participants in flagging troublesome providers for the sake of warning other insurers. The company flags the problematic providers on national databases set up by industry groups to facilitate information sharing between insurers about fraud cases and investigations.[1]

- *Feedback from chiropractic community:* Company X uses some chiropractors as consultants to help with medical review of chiropractic claims. These consultants report back that the word within the chiropractic community is "Don't bother trying to cheat company X. It's too hard."

- *Feedback from law enforcement:* Feedback from the law-enforcement community confirms that Company X has earned the reputation of being a hard target. Lists obtained from fraudulent telemarketing operations always show the company on the "difficult" side.

- *Limited losses to major fraud schemes:* Company X, like many other insurers, was defrauded by the Smushkevitch brothers' rolling labs scheme and also by National Health Laboratories (NHL). In both cases, the company spotted the problems and cut off payment before accruing heavy losses. In the "rolling labs" case, Company X paid out around $5,000, which represented only 1 percent of the claims they received. A claims examiner caught the problem early and flagged the providers. Company X had therefore been independently denying claims for several years before they learned from the rest of the industry just how much damage had been done elsewhere. With NHL, Company X had paid only $1,000 for the unnecessary ferritin tests when they noticed the pattern; they immediately wrote to NHL and explained that the extra tests were neither requested nor necessary and asked for their money back: "NHL paid it back, just like that." Whereas other insurers lost millions to NHL, this company lost nothing at all.

- *Stable premium rates:* Perhaps the most encouraging indicator of Company X's fraud-control success is that the company was able to keep premium increases below industry averages, an accomplishment the employees are extremely proud of. Although other factors could contribute to Company X's cost-control success, such success in recent years is nonetheless rare indeed.

What Company X Does Differently

What accounts for Company X's apparent success? How do the assumptions, policies, and systems used at Company X differ from industry norms?

Integrated, Professional Claims Examination

First of all, Company X had developed a professional role for its claims examiners that incorporated and integrated the normally separate functions of medical review and fraud detection. At Company X, there were no functional divisions, no formal organizational chart, and no formal budget for claims processing. They spent whatever they needed to spend to ensure accuracy of claims payments and regarded accurate claims payment—not processing efficiencies—as the key to effective cost control. The company rigorously measured payment accuracy (through quality-control procedures), but did not measure or seek to minimize processing costs.

The examiners had, on average, ten years experience in medical claims examination and over five years with this company. Very little staff turnover meant little cost in retraining; the company invested, instead, in continuous training and "upskilling" for staff by encouraging them to obtain additional qualifications. A specified sequence of training experiences, spread over two years, acted as a minimum qualification for the title *senior examiner*, and the company promoted only from within. Company X rejected the typical union-shop environment and regarded claims examination not as a clerical job but as a profession.

All the claims examiners met for half an hour every Wednesday morning to discuss fraud trends and changes in payment policy, or to talk about each other's suggestions. Often, a visiting speaker would attend these meetings to teach the claims examiners about developments in medical practice or medical research, to discuss new methods used by fraud perpetrators, or to look at new methods for fraud detection. Examiners were encouraged to nominate items for the agenda; often they would bring in advertisements for medical services they had clipped from newspapers or magazines (e.g., for cataract surgery) and figure out together what the provider in question was doing. They were particularly curious about advertisements that offered free medical services because providers often try to bill insurers for such services or use the offer as a way of obtaining patient information. Different teams of claims examiners actually competed to see who could find the greatest number of suspicious newspaper and magazine advertisements—with a nominal prize like a box of doughnuts at coffee time.

The examiners' mission statement—which they formulated themselves through another internal competition—read, "Our mission is to provide quality claims service through the process of prompt, fair, and accurate evaluation of our insureds' claims." That sense of purpose, managers explained, made for a much more interesting job than the typical production-line environment obsessed with efficiency. Managers emphasized that although the goal was to pay accurately and to establish that as a norm, *paying accurately* was quite different from *cost control*. Company X wanted to pay the right amount, not too much, not too little. When they measured payment accuracy, they made no distinction between overpaying and underpaying. When circumstances warranted, Company X did not feel bound by "usual and customary" rates and often found a way to pay *more*. Also, to avoid unnecessarily inconveniencing providers, a senior examiner would review all claim adjustments that would reduce the amount paid by more than 20 percent or more than $500. Other insurers, they said, were much quicker to shift the burden of proof to the provider and wait for them to appeal before reviewing such decisions.

The claims examiners reviewed every single claim that came in, not just those selected by an automated system and not just 7 percent of the total volume. Every one. What about the ones that came in electronically? At the time of my visit, there were none; Company X took only paper claims. The work was divided among sixteen claims examiners and four senior examiners. When examiners received claims, they were responsible for handling and payment from start to finish. The examiner's role included data entry, medical review, fraud detection, and claim disposition. Claims examiners took responsibility for a zip code or combination of zip codes (usually specifying an area by the first three digits of the zip code) and handled all claims from customers (patients) living within that area. Focusing on a small geographic area allowed the examiners to get to know their clients and to spot unusual localized patterns of activity.

For example, one examiner noticed claims relating to three auto accidents within her area, all of which bore the same provider's name and showed that the policies had been sold by the same insurance agent. A little investigation revealed the beginnings of a fraud scheme coordinated and executed by the agent and involving colluding physicians.

The claims examiners rotated for three-month periods through a small *technical claims* section, where they performed major case reviews, third-party recoveries, and generally exercised their hypercritical skills on more serious cases of fraud and abuse. (These attachments enhanced examiners' investigative skills.) After their rotations, examiners returned to their regular claims-examination tasks better prepared to recognize the early signs of cases that could grow big and expensive if left unattended.

Investigative training for the examiners was encouraged and formally recognized. Managers recognized that some examiners had better investigative skills and instincts than others and deliberately allocated the better ones to the fraud-rich zip codes. Examiners were encouraged to take responsibility for medical review as well as fraud detection. On medical questions, as on anything else, they could always ask the senior examiners for help. If the senior examiner could not make the determination, he or she referred the issue to an outside consultant—one of a panel of physicians retained to offer advice as needed. One physician came in routinely once a week to go through unresolved issues that required review of medical records. Consultants were available to the senior examiners by telephone at any time.

According to their manager, the claims examiners relished the business of fraud control and would get excited when they unearthed a scam. Reflecting on their success in shutting off NHL's unwarranted ferritin tests, she said, "That was a big thing for the staff [when they discovered how hard others had been hit]. It really encouraged them to go after other labs that might be doing the same, or similar, things." The idea that claims examiners would identify with an opportunity, as a group, to go after a particular fraud problem and that they would be capable, as a group, of delivering concerted action on such an issue across the entire population of claims seems highly unusual.

As an instrument for fraud control, this claims-examination function was clearly exceptional. They reviewed every single claim. They had a formal meeting every week to discuss new trends or problems they had observed and to formulate appropriate intervention strategies. Just by turning their chairs around to face each other, they could pool their knowledge and experience informally, anytime they chose. The examiners prided themselves on their abilities to detect fraud and, once they had detected it, to shut it down completely.

Single Point-of-Contact Service for Customers

Company X's second major departure from customary practice concerns customer service: how they conceived it, how seriously they took it, and its practical outworkings. Company X's "customers" were the certificate holders, or insureds, not the providers. Claims examiners were careful to treat providers respectfully and properly, but that was not their primary concern. The primary concern was to look after the insureds and to make sure they felt looked after. By contrast, many other insurers—especially in public programs—focus more on maintaining their provider network and spend much more time keeping the providers happy than keeping the patients happy.

High-quality service to the customer was the basis of Company X's marketing strategy. Their rates were reasonably competitive, but their distinctive mark was the focus on customer satisfaction. Most of their customers were self-employed and paid their own premiums, so they had options when it came to choosing a health care plan. High-quality service attracted customers to Company X, and it kept them. With the allocation of claims to examiners by zip code, the examiners acted as service representatives for each of their customers, providing a single point of contact. They gave their own names and telephone extension numbers to their customers, and they would always interrupt routine claims-processing tasks to take telephone calls from their clients. (Each examiner had a backup partnership with another; if one became overloaded, the second—who would also develop some knowledge of the area—could help out.) If a patient became really sick or was hospitalized, the examiners had the authority and discretion to send flowers or a teddy bear with a get-well-soon card.

The examiners at Company X deplored physicians' use of software packages that systematically tested the upper price tolerances for each procedure, and they knew exactly which providers were using them. These packages bill high so that the claim is rejected, then resubmit the bills, gradually lowering the price until the claim is paid. The software packages then record the optimum billing level for future use. As the examiners put it, "We try to pay the *right* amount. Why shouldn't they just bill the right amount?" The use of such software packages is perfectly legal, but the examiners thought it showed that many physicians did not share the examiners' sense of service. It certainly helped the cause of fraud control to have examiners in close contact with their customers. Examiners said they talked to their customers "all the time." If there was anything at all suspicious or unusual about a claim, the examiner would call the patient immediately to check the facts. If a new diagnosis appeared for a particular patient, the examiner might call to discuss which types of future treatment would be covered by the policy and which would not.

One examiner caught a fraudulent claim for services not rendered because the patient's weight was incorrectly recorded on the claim form. The examiner knew the patient was pregnant and had been watching her weight rise (on various claims) over the previous few weeks. A fraudulent claim, submitted by a physician who had never seen the patient, listed her weight incorrectly.

Examiners had no qualms about checking up on hospitals, either. They knew that hospitals solicited business on the basis of waived copayments. Company X's view of this practice was that Company X should pay exactly 80 percent of the aggregate liability; if a hospital waived a copayment, Company X wanted to pay exactly 80 percent (not 100 percent) of what was left. When Company X suspected a hospital of waiving copayments, they routinely called *all* their members who use that hospital to establish the precise nature of the agreements the hospital staff had made up front.

Examiners had no compunction at all about contacting their members, and nobody ever complained about it. Quite the opposite: Friendly, high-quality service was Company X's major selling point.

Fraud-Control Philosophy

Company X had no separate budget for fraud control. A recently enacted state law required every health insurer to have a special investigative unit, so Company X employed one woman as director of the special investigative unit (SIU); but she had no staff. Rather she worked with, and among, the claims examiners, who did the bulk of the fraud-detection work. Once a fraud case was opened, however, the SIU director took it over and saw it through to disposition.

Company X did not employ specialist investigators. The company valued investigative skills a great deal, but preferred to employ medical-claims specialists and teach the necessary investigative skills. The director of the SIU rarely went out on inquiries. When she needed some footwork done she used private investigators retained under contract. The company placed no budgetary constraints on the use of outside investigators; the SIU director used them when she saw fit, and the vice president for operations occasionally reviewed the expenditures.

Company X did not put much effort into the traditional casemaking form of fraud investigation, and they had not yet brought a case to court, either civil or criminal. Company X generally did not consider civil actions worth their while because the legal expenses normally outweighed the potential dollar recovery (they lost so little). They did believe in criminal prosecution for fraudulent providers and had two cases pending, but brought few cases to court themselves. They found prosecutors generally disinterested in their small-dollar losses, which usually fell well below prosecutorial thresholds. Their dollar losses remained small partly because Company X is such a small company and partly because they usually detected fraud schemes long before significant losses had accrued. Often Company X detected fraudulent providers and warned other, bigger companies, who then developed significant cases based upon their own, much greater, losses.

In the absence of significant casemaking, investigative work served predominantly as an intelligence-gathering exercise. Company X used private investigators not to make cases but to find out what was happening and to confirm the examiners' suspicions. The claims examiners and the

SIU director focused on early detection and prevention. They used the following tools to procure compliance:

1. Sending letters to providers demanding money back once claims have been established as illegitimate
2. Putting providers on review so that all their claims get flagged and scrutinized even more carefully
3. Requiring second opinions (which they are prepared to pay for) in the case of medical procedures prone to abuse
4. Referring a corrupt provider to the state medical board (although they say they scarcely ever receive feedback or see a follow-up)
5. Making providers substantiate claims by requesting provision of medical records

They used this last tool liberally, requesting supporting documentation of one kind or another for 20 percent of the claims submitted. This held up claims payment, but Company X still managed to keep the average claims payment turnaround time down to four days. If the claim resulted from an accident, the request for additional information went to the certificate holder. Other requests went to the doctors.

All the managers agreed on one central point of their fraud-control philosophy: They "never let a doctor go." They said they became suspicious of doctors who could not produce convincing medical records. Once a claims examiner had requested records or other supporting documentation, he or she would keep reminding the doctor until the requisite records appeared; some doctors eventually asked examiners to drop the claims and forget it. Examiners persisted, however, until claims were established as either legitimate or illegitimate.

When a claim turned out to be illegitimate, the physician or provider responsible would be put "on review," a status under which every claim filed must have supporting documentation. Any provider caught cheating even once would remain on review until the examiners decided the provider could be trusted once again.

Doesn't giving examiners almost complete control over a particular geographical area open the door to employee corruption? What of prudent separation of duties, for the sake of corruption control? The management at Company X was well aware of that possibility, but felt the risk was adequately controlled. The director of the SIU considered it her job to monitor for signs of corruption. Throughout the day, she moved around the claims examiners' area, helping out, answering queries, and updating the examiners' *fraud watch files* (a compendium of current fraud concerns). Even so, she deliberately maintained a little professional distance in case she ever had to investigate one of her own examiners. From time to time, she performed various other precautionary audits such as running the file of payment destination addresses against personnel records to make sure payments were not being diverted. Examiners did not have complete control over their areas. Several days a month, one examiner's claims would be handled by the backup. The backup arrangement kicked in if an examiner was too busy or went away for vacation or training. To avoid corruption, managers counted on the professionalism and integrity of the claims examiners; the company paid examiners as professionals and treated them as such, not as clerical workers. Company X had never had (at least, had never discovered) internal corruption. The open-plan everyone-knows-everyone environment, coupled with the professional culture, made Company X a tough place in which to operate internal schemes unnoticed.

Attitudes Toward Technology

Company X regarded claims examination as an essentially human business. Although they used a variety of software packages to assist in claims examination, they emphatically rejected the idea that claims examination could or should be done by computers. They refused to contemplate electronic claims submission, concerned that the loss of experienced human scrutiny would tear the heart out of their approach to payment accuracy.

They admitted, reluctantly, that electronic claims processing would inevitably come to them, as to the rest of the industry, but they were holding off for as long as they could. When industry pressures forced them to move to electronic claims submission, they said, they would experiment very cautiously and only in well-protected areas of their business. Even with their Medicare supplemental policies, they resisted further automation. Most Medicare supplemental policy issuers set up electronic systems to pay claims automatically once the base Medicare payment is approved. Not Company X. Because they found Medicare often paid in error, they preferred to review the claims.

Going electronic with Medicare supplemental policies would also have meant "going on-line with eligibility" (creating the facility for billers to query the customer database remotely, without the company's knowledge). On-line eligibility, managers said, might make life just a little simpler for honest billers, but it also opens up huge new opportunities for the dishonest.

Managers were concerned about the possibility of computer-generated fraud schemes involving "perfect claims," where the computer reproduces the same claim time after time but substitutes a different patient each time. Each claim would be correct with the exception of a patient's identifying characteristics such as height, weight, or condition. The diagnosis, the treatment, and the price would all look perfectly normal.

Examiners at Company X said that although these schemes were becoming more frequent, they were easy to detect in their company's environment because the claims would all come in at once, would all go to the same examiner, and would all be far too similar. When that happened, a quick telephone call to one of the patients would confirm the claim as bogus—at which point all the others would be pulled from the claims process for investigation.

Managers at Company X suspected (quite correctly) that there was nothing in most electronic claims-processing systems to detect such schemes. Provided the claims were billed correctly and were medically orthodox, they would all slide straight through auto-adjudication to payment without human intervention. The examination process at Company X naturally provided such monitoring by valuing, nurturing, and unleashing the extraordinary pattern-recognition capabilities of the human brain and by allocating claims to examiners zip code by zip code, giving one examiner the chance to see the whole scheme (assuming all the claims came from one locality). Even when fraud perpetrators deliberately spread their "patients" across several zip codes, they would get caught at break time when the examiners met around the coffee machine.

Managers at Company X showed no interest in electronic claims processing as a cost saver, or as a way of keeping premiums low. They regarded their fraud-control capabilities as the best method for accomplishing those objectives. In fact, they regarded effective fraud control as one major source of Company X's competitive advantage. The company recently considered a proposal to install a document-imaging system with OCR capability. When the vendor suggested the company could get along with three claims examiners instead of twenty, one manager responded, "Now why would we want to do that? May as well shoot yourself in the foot." The proposal was soundly rejected.

The company, nevertheless, was not against technology. Examiners used technology for processing claims. While they visually reviewed the claims, they entered the fields required to process a payment into their own computerized payment system. The system incorporated a commercial rebundling package, which checks for various standard forms of code manipulation. Another commercial package checks the procedure code against the diagnosis and the diagnosis against the age and sex of the patient. Finally, examiners used a commercial pricing package to check the price of the procedure against a table of prevailing rates. Whatever help these software modules offered, they offered it *to the examiner*. There was no automatic claims rejection, or correction. The examiner took the information provided and used it as he or she saw fit.

The director of the SIU also used modern data-analysis tools to help her spot fraud problems. One of the natural forms of analysis, given the way Company X was set up, was by zip code. A pattern of abuse by a particular specialty often starts off on a highly localized basis and then spreads. Monitoring specialties by zip code gave Company X one useful way of spotting such trends early.

For example, data analysis revealed two zip codes in which the frequency of septoplasties suddenly shot up. Septoplasties involve repair to the cartilage structure of the nose, usually following an accident. Providers were selecting the procedure code for septoplasties as a way of disguising cosmetic nose surgery as medically necessary operations. The patients were newly established certificate holders, who, within the first month or two of coverage, would report an accident (like walking into a door) that damaged the nose but no other part of the body.

The director of the SIU also valued technological assistance when investigating providers suspected of fraud. Once interested in a particular provider, she would normally take an extract of the last three years' claims from the processing system and download them onto a workstation for manipulation by a variety of modern database query tools. She also used, and encouraged the examiners to use, on-line access to various national databases such as National Health Care Anti-Fraud Association's (NHCAA) provider database, the INDEX (ACE) system for information about road accidents, and INFOTECH for background inquiries about individuals or businesses.

Lessons for the Industry

Without systematic measurement, nobody can be sure that Company X did a better job of fraud control than anyone else. The evidence is compelling, however. Company X routinely detected schemes that other sytems would never notice. They suffered minimal losses in major cases and frequently acted as the early warning system for other larger corporations.

In trying to draw useful lessons from Company X's unusual approach, however, it would be foolish to conclude only that small is beautiful, and to recommend fragmentation of the massive systems that now dominate the industry. Much of the health insurance industry continues to move toward consolidated, high-speed processing, and could not possibly contemplate breaking up highly efficient claims-processing operations into multitudes of small, friendly, personable claims-examination units. Any such recommendation would (and should) be rejected as an absurd irrelevancy for the bulk of high-volume claims processors.

No antitechnology lessons should be drawn from Company X's experience, either. For one thing, the company used technology extensively, even though they eschewed electronic claims submission. Moreover, electronic claims submission is undoubtedly here to stay. Returning to paper-based and manual claims-processing operations is not an option for most companies.

If the lessons drawn from Company X are to be genuinely useful to the industry, they have to be as relevant to large, automated processing systems as they are to small, paper-based ones. Smallness, or rejection of EDI (Electronic Data Interchange), are not the important issues here. Being small is only one of many ways in which Company X runs against the grain. Some of the *other* ways in which they deviate from industry norms present serious challenges to the predominant practices and policies of insurers—large or small, automated or manual.

Primary Focus Should Be Payment Accuracy

Perhaps the most fundamental challenge to industry norms is Company X's focus on payment accuracy as the principal source of effective cost control. Because most other claims-processing environments are obsessed with administrative cost control, they strip resources away from prudent payment controls. The management at Company X is convinced that the rest of the industry has focused on the wrong thing, and they believe that rapidly rising costs throughout the industry result, in part, from that error of judgment. If a $500 claim comes in, which matters more? That it costs $0.87 to process rather than $7.00, or that the item actually delivered might have been the version that costs $150 rather than the one that costs $500? Or that the service might never have been delivered at all? Or that the diagnosis might be fictitious and the service might have been unnecessary?

Management at Company X took the view that it was worth spending whatever it took to validate claims. For them, it was always money well spent. Company X deliberately avoided calculating how much they spent on processing claims because they did not want anyone's attention focused on that issue. As purchasers of services, they felt they should use their common sense on behalf of their customers. Common sense, for them, meant checking to see that they got what they paid for and that the patient needed the service. If that took a couple of well-placed telephone calls and the inconvenience of record review, so be it. That's what they thought sensible purchasers ought to do.

Every insurer in the industry, whatever their budgetary arrangements, can usefully reconsider the degree of emphasis they place on processing efficiency versus the degree of emphasis they place on claims verification and fraud control. Company X positioned itself at one end of this spectrum, placing their emphasis fairly and squarely on payment accuracy. They took care to organize their operations efficiently, too, but would never allow processing efficiencies to limit or restrict the level of payment reviews. Most of the industry lies at the opposite extreme and appears to have forsaken many prudent payment controls in a headlong rush for processing efficiencies. It is time to reconsider that balance.

Humans Analyze; Systems Support

Most high-volume claims-processing operations use automated systems as their central backbone. Electronic claims feed directly into the system; data entry clerks feed paper claims into the system as well. The system rejects some claims automatically, amends others, accepts most, and kicks some out for human inspection. The system's edits and audits decide which claims need to be examined by humans and for what reasons. The general model for claims review is *systems select; humans inspect*. Humans inspect only when the system selects.

Chapter 7's review of the industry's standard control systems confirms what Company X also believed: that systems currently in use cannot generally detect fraud. They do not spot interesting or unusual patterns. They never get suspicious. They never make telephone calls just to check the facts.

At Company X, the model for the interaction between examiner and technology was *humans inspect; systems support*. Company X still used technology, but the automated systems served the examiners, not vice versa. The examiners were responsible for keeping abreast of emerging fraud patterns and trends, and then using the systems to pick out claims for more detailed review. Examiners also used a variety of other technological tools to support their investigation of those claims.

By contrast, under the *systems select: humans inspect* model, the *system* is effectively in charge, and routine edits and audits remain unchanged for months or years, unresponsive to emerging trends; the humans who do the claims inspection have little or no control over claims-selection criteria. Effective fraud control requires the alternative model, with human beings playing the fraud-control game, intelligently and adaptively, using technological tools in support. (Chapters 9 and 10 develop this concept in considerable detail.)

Fraud Detection Demands Routine External Validation

The customer service orientation at Company X made it natural and easy for examiners to call patients, agents, and providers. By so doing, they introduced information for use in claims determination beyond that contained in the claims themselves.

Some provider groups make an enormous fuss when insurers start contacting their patients to verify treatments and services. They may have grounds for complaint if they really feel that such inquiries breach their notion of patient/physician confidentiality. However, unless the claims were properly verified, Company X would simply refuse to pay them.

None of Company X's providers objected to the company's claims-examination practices because providers were treated well and promptly and properly reimbursed. That is exactly what honest providers want. None of the patients ever complained, either; they *loved* the personal service and the cost control.

That Company X is small offered some additional benefits; for example, the thorough integration of fraud control, customer service, and medical review into the claims-examination process. These additional benefits may not be so readily realizable within larger systems.

However, three basic principles seem central to this operation and critical for effective fraud control; they apply equally well across different claims-processing environments:

1. Payment integrity should never be sacrificed to processing efficiencies.

2. The role of human inspection in fraud detection should never be underestimated or displaced.

3. Effective fraud control requires routine external validation of claims information.

Although these three points seem sensible, maybe even obvious, they separate Company X from most of the rest of the industry. As does Company X's clear conviction that their primary customers were the patients, not the providers.

PART FOUR

Prescription for Progress

9

A Model
Fraud-Control Strategy

The preceding chapters have focused on diagnosis of the problems and assessment of current conditions rather than on prescriptions for improved controls. If the book were to end here, the parting picture would be gloomy indeed: criminals feeding off the health care system, largely with impunity; criminal fraud in the system essentially uncontrolled; control systems offering little protection to the public or insurers who place their faith in them; theft on a massive scale and at the speed of light through electronic claims processing; managed care producing forms of fraud potentially much more dangerous to human health; and the scale of government's interventions to date insufficient to make a serious dent in the problem.

The goal of earlier chapters was to produce a clear understanding of the challenge and complexity of fraud control and to provide an honest and realistic evaluation of existing control systems. Nevertheless, many prescriptive observations emerged along the way, and it is time now to pull these together and present them as a coherent whole. The task for this chapter, however, is more ambitious than merely compiling and presenting miscellaneous prescriptive recommendations. The task here is to define a model fraud-control strategy. To be of use, the strategy must offer the promise of effective fraud control and be suitable for broad use throughout the health care industry.

Almost all the elements of this model strategy exist somewhere in private insurance companies or government programs; the strategy as a whole, however, can be found nowhere. It does not yet exist. This control strategy is new, and adopting it will require managerial courage, commitment, and persistence. For most insurers, adopting this kind of fraud-control strategy would involve radical changes in the way they approach the entire business of fraud control.

The strategy described here is most relevant under fee-for-service systems, where payment systems are driven by incoming claims, and where fraud schemes involve the submission of bogus or inflated claims. Why the focus on claims-based payment systems, when managed care continues to grow?

First, despite the growth of managed care, for the time being the majority of payments to providers are still made under fee-for-service systems, and that will probably remain true at least for the next few years.

Second, most managed care plans are only partly capitated, with major components of the total care package (called "carve-outs") remaining under fee-for-service arrangements. Many managed care plans take the form of fee-for-service systems, with patients directed to a more restricted network of providers. (These are "managed" fee-for-service systems.) For a variety of reasons, then, managed care is unlikely to eliminate claims-based payment systems.

Third, claims-based payment systems are a familiar and attractive target for fraud perpetrators, and the perpetrators have developed a host of methods for attacking them. Present defenses are woefully inadequate. Claims-based payment systems are the principal mechanism through which criminal fraud currently bleeds the health care system. The job of stanching that flow is urgent and cannot be put off in the vague hope that managed care will one day solve the problem.

In any case, most of the more general aspects of this fraud-control strategy apply equally well within the context of capitated systems. When all the elements of the strategy have been laid out, a later part of the chapter will identify those pieces that apply to capitated systems.

The individual elements of this strategy are not arbitrarily selected. Each one arises as a direct consequence of the nature of the fraud-control business and from an understanding of the way fraud perpetrators think and behave. In trying to design defenses, it may be worth taking a moment—as a serious chess player would—to put oneself in the opponent's shoes and to work out what the opponent is trying to achieve, and how. With that strategy in mind, ponder for a moment the intentions and tactics of criminal fraud perpetrators.

It might be useful to remember two particular categories of fraud perpetrators so that our control strategy can be tested against each of them. In some ways, these two categories represent opposite extremes of the fraud spectrum; considering them both helps produce a control strategy of sufficient breadth and versatility.

One of these categories represents a comparatively modern phenomenon: the "hit-and-run" scheme, where quick, high-dollar-value hits are the goal. The idea is to "get in quick and get out with the money," then vanish from sight before anyone realizes what has happened. These so-called "fly-by-night" operations are not interested in providing medical services; they simply want to maneuver themselves into a position to bill insurers, public or private, and to be paid. They may present themselves as durable medical equipment (DME) suppliers, home health care suppliers, physicians, laboratories, pharmacies, transportation companies, radiological services, or as any other provider who fits a small-business model.

Hit-and-run operations bill fast and furious, knowing their time is limited. Postpayment utilization review will eventually show them up, even though it may take several months to do so. If they receive system-generated requests for supporting documentation, they do not respond (knowing that those claims will be disallowed). They watch closely for any signs that an insurer has discovered their fraudulent activity; if they see signs of human investigation into their activities, they leave. By the time investigators come calling, the office has been vacated, the money is untraceable, and the principals are in business somewhere else under a different name.

At the opposite extreme lies a more traditional kind of villain: the white-collar criminal who lives by the maxim that the way to get rich is to "steal a little, all the time." These are providers who run legitimate businesses and provide genuine services, but they use the bulk of their legitimate business transactions to hide their stealing. When they steal, they use such familiar methods as billing for services not provided, billing for more expensive services or products than those actually provided, and falsifying diagnoses to support more expensive claims. Mindful of postutilization review, they moderate the volume of fraudulent claims to avoid the statistical extremes under provider profiling. They prefer to cheat, if possible, in the same ways that others in their specialty cheat because such methods make their own behavior less likely to appear abnormal.

When their bogus or inflated claims are challenged, these white-collar criminals have the choice of two tacks: (1) if challenged on something as blatant as services not provided, they confess their mistakes immediately, offer repayment or restitution, and blame clerical error; (2) they deny culpability, bemoan the complexity of the regulations, feign ignorance of the particular point in question, and eventually acknowledge the "education" they have just received. In each case, they then abandon that method of stealing and replace it with others. They figure out the detection mechanism that caught their last scheme and devise a way to circumnavigate it in the future.

The white-collar criminal's strategy is to exploit to the full the respectability of the medical profession, acting at all times and responding to queries as if, utterly trustworthy and well-intentioned, they made administrative mistakes just because they were too busy caring for patients; at the same time they abuse that trust—constantly, deliberately, and systematically. This strategy is used by individual providers and (as the introduction showed) by a range of major corporations.

These represent just two of the opponents' possible strategies. Although there are many others and many variations on these themes, these two— the "quick-hit" and the "steal-a-little-all-the-time" strategies—are major classes of fraud not adequately controlled by existing systems. It is useful, therefore, to hold at least these two in the back of one's mind in reviewing fraud-control proposals. If a new strategy does not work for these two major types of fraud, then it cannot be the right answer.

Components of a Model Fraud-Control Strategy

A model fraud-control strategy would comprise the following characteristics:

1. Commitment to routine, systematic measurement
2. Resource allocation for controls based upon an assessment of the seriousness (i.e., measurement) of the problem
3. Clear designation of responsibility for fraud control
4. Adoption of a problem-solving approach to fraud control
5. Deliberate focus on early detection of new types of fraud
6. Prepayment, fraud-specific controls
7. Every claim faces some risk of review

Commitment to Routine, Systematic Measurement

To control fraud, you must be able to see clearly. Without systematic measurement, a fraud-control operation flies blind. Without measurement, no one can tell whether an increased detection rate represents good or bad news. No one can tell whether the time and expense devoted to investigating and prosecuting cases is producing a real deterrent effect. No one can tell whether one health care insurer or program is more or less vulnerable than another, whether payment safeguards are better or worse than they were last year, or how the patterns of abuse in one part of the country differ from those in another. In the absence of measurement, the debate about fraud rattles loosely and uselessly around the extent of the problem rather than proceeding to the design of appropriate solutions.

Thus the importance of measurement—already discussed in Chapter 6. A commitment to routine and systematic measurement is the cornerstone of a fraud-control operation; without it, officials cannot see what they are working on, nor can they tell whether they are making progress. Without measurement, no one can make the case for adequate fraud-control resources.

The mechanism for measurement, using random audits, is well understood and has parallels in other environments. For health care fraud, measurement would require

1. the selection of a statistically valid random sample of claims with
2. a thorough audit of each one; this audit would involve
3. external validation of the information within the claim rigorous enough to identify fraudulent claims.

The sampling should be done soon after the routine operation of control systems. This means that edits and audits and other claim-suspension systems (including medical review) should complete their own review procedures before the random sample is taken. After all, fraudulent claims that the system already detects and rejects are not part of the problem to be measured. The important measure is the volume of fraudulent claims *paid* as a proportion of total claims paid—which represents the proportion of program costs lost to fraud.

Only by allowing detection systems to operate first, before taking the sample, can one determine what those systems miss. For precisely this reason, the U.S. Customs Service's Compliance Measurement Program sets up random inspection programs that operate behind all normal inspectional procedures. When the Customs Service wants to know, for example, what kinds of contraband their inspectional processes along the Mexican border miss and with what frequency, they establish an inspection program half a mile down the road from the inspection booths at the border. They do it out of sight of the primary inspectors and without notifying them. (If alerted, inspectors might change their behavior, invalidating the measurement.) At the secondary site, cars and trucks are pulled over at random and searched thoroughly—not because it is an efficient way of finding contraband (it is not), but because it is the only way to measure the level of compliance and to assess the value of inspection procedures.

Just as it would be a mistake to take the samples too early, it would also be a mistake to take them too late. Retrospective studies, where a sample of last year's paid claims are picked out for review, suffer greatly from the effects of elapsed time. Fraud perpetrators may have moved on. Patients may have died, moved away, or simply forgotten what happened. In some circumstances, a measurement study might contact claimants (the providers) when they are still waiting to be paid. They remain uncommonly available during that time.

Some officials hold the position that such measurement is not technically feasible because of the ambiguity of the distinctions between fraud and abuse. They say it is impossible to classify a claim as fraudulent or merely abusive because the intentions of the claimant cannot be reliably determined. The IRS successfully dealt with that issue when measuring the refund fraud problem (based on false claims for the earned income tax credit [EITC]). They picked their random sample, sent a criminal investigator to each taxpayer's home address to investigate, and allowed investigators to use their professional judgment in categorizing the outcome. Investigators were not asked to make cases or to prove them in court; they were asked to determine whether the children claimed as dependents actually lived with the claimant, whether the employment could be verified with the employer, and whether the reported income was correct. Each claim not clearly valid also underwent full examination by a tax examiner, who subsequently validated or adjusted the investigator's original opinion, using the traditional outcome classifications for IRS examinations.

In designing the classifications, it is important to be clear about the goal. The goal is not to prove criminal intent beyond a reasonable doubt, as in a court of law. Rather, the goal is to see how bad things are and to determine whether they are getting better or worse. The professional judgment of experienced auditors or investigators provides an adequate basis for such measurement. Not only are these officials best placed to classify claims reliably but they are also best placed to design classification systems that make practical sense. They know which distinctions can be drawn in an operational environment and which cannot. The kinds of judgments that auditors and investigators can make perfectly well after a rigorous claim review (judgments they routinely make in the course of their regular duties) address objective realities:

- Does the service or product appear to have been supplied as claimed?
- Did the patient suffer from the condition corresponding to the diagnosis entered on the claim form?
- Can the referring physician confirm his or her referral?
- Would the claim, if all these surrounding facts had been known when the claim was processed, have been paid?

The IRS, in their first study of refund fraud in 1994, randomly selected just over 1,000 tax returns, resulting in answers (to these kinds of binary questions) with a 3 percent margin of error. In subsequent years, the IRS enlarged the sample to give greater accuracy and to support more detailed (segmented) analysis of the results.

Even with technical issues of measurement clarified, no one should imagine that measurement of health care fraud will ever be straightforward. The technical problems may be more easily overcome than the political. Many managers will remain nervous about the prospects of having to reveal the results of such measurement. Many managers would worry that, even if they discovered the true extent of fraud, they would be unable to bring it under control. Some would prefer not to know. Some, preserving their own interests, will do whatever they can to sabotage measurement studies that might reveal bad news.

The model fraud-control strategy, however, begins with an emphasis on seeing clearly, which requires a commitment to systematic measurement—painful and difficult as that may be.

Resource Allocation for Controls Based upon the Seriousness of the Problem

In the absence of systematic measurement, the level of resources allocated for fraud controls is normally based on the volume of the reactive workload, sufficient investigative capacity being established to keep pace with the caseload generated by fraud-detection and referral systems. That caseload is tiny, however, when compared with the size of the problem; the detection and referral systems do not work well, and they typically uncover only a small proportion of the fraud schemes. If the referral volume remains the basis for investigative resource allocation, massive underinvestment in controls will persist.

Under a model fraud-control strategy, investment in control systems (people and technology) would be related in some direct and obvious way to the size of the problem as determined by measurement. If the proportion of fraudulent claims within a program was confirmed to be 10 percent, it would make no sense to maintain investment in controls at a level of 0.1 percent of program costs (or thereabouts), especially when the ratio of return on marginal investments in controls exceeded three to one.

There is no substitute for rational resource-allocation decisions based fairly and squarely on the size of the problem. In the short term, it may be tempting to address fraud detection and overpayment recovery on a commission or contingency basis, with contracts let to commercial companies to detect and recover overpayments. Such arrangements can help to kick-start fraud control in programs where resources would otherwise be tightly constrained. They take advantage of some private sector companies' willingness to make the necessary capital investments, up front, in exchange for a portion of the recoveries (which can be huge). Sometimes, the structure of these contracts feeds a portion of the recoveries back into the control apparatus, expanding the capacity for future work.

Wherever such arrangements are used, officials should bear in mind that the incentives associated with schemes may produce some rather odd dynamics—which they will have to manage over the long term. For example, the rate at which resources available for control grows would be directly proportional to the volume of monetary recoveries. In other words, when control systems are small and feeble (when rapid growth is most urgent), the rate of growth would be slow; whereas control operations that came anywhere near optimal size would be flooded with additional resources because of the larger caseload during that phase.

Also, having a budget that depends to a significant extent upon reactive successes provides a disincentive for preventive work. Any desire to maximize the budget by focusing on the production of recoveries and penalties after the fact might produce the temptation to leave room for fraud to occur. Such a system offers no reward for preventive work. Also to be recognized and carefully managed is the impression that an enforcement bureaucracy feeds on its own success and operates on a bounty hunter basis, raising the question of whether "enforcers will be motivated by a desire to protect the integrity of the health care system, or will they be encouraged to prey upon the unwary and unconventional as a means of increasing their coffers." [1]

Despite these potential objections, more resources for fraud control are still better than fewer resources. The use of contingency structures can represent a major step toward the situation where returns on investment can be considered more seriously as a basis for resource allocation. It would still be an enormous mistake, however, for lawmakers or policy-makers to assume that establishing these kinds of arrangements (which essentially cost them nothing) relieves them of their obligation to provide controls commensurate with the seriousness of the problem. The requisite level of control will never be established without substantial increases in the relevant pieces of the administrative budget. Within public programs, both at the federal and state levels, the current budget climate makes significant increases unlikely for now. Increases will remain out of the question until the fraud problem is measured—so that the true costs of fraud can be laid out plainly for all to see.

Clear Designation of
Responsibility for Fraud Control

Somebody has to be responsible for fraud control. A collection of loosely connected functional components cannot constitute a coherent fraud-control strategy. Someone, or a team of people, has to be in charge. Someone has to be responsible for playing the fraud-control game, for grappling with its complexity, and for coordinating the contributions of the various functional tools.

A common mistake is to equate fraud investigation with fraud control. Investigation, and the business of preparing cases, is one valuable tool in the control toolbox. It is not the whole toolbox, however. The performance of an investigative unit tends to be measured by the number and seriousness of the cases it makes. The performance of a fraud-control unit should be measured by its success in lowering or suppressing the level of fraudulent claims the system pays, which would be measured periodically. Target levels would be set; these could be lowered year after year as the control operation matured until the fraud level was low enough to be regarded as "an acceptable price of doing business." For the credit card industry, that level is roughly 0.1 percent of transaction volume, and fraud volume is generally kept close to that mark.

When the IRS realized how serious the refund fraud problem was, one of their first actions was to create a new position, which they called the fraud-control executive.[2] They already had executives in charge of each of the relevant functional branches—criminal investigation, examination, audit, information systems, and so on. But it was the fraud-control executive's job to focus on the fraud rather than on the internal functions. The fraud-control executive was given overall responsibility for all aspects of fraud control, with freedom to design new policies and procedures, to target investigations and examinations on particular aspects of the problem, and to propose changes in regulations.

The simple test is to ask, "Who here is responsible for fraud control?" In most organizations, nobody has that responsibility, in which case the fraud perpetrator, in designing scams, has only to chart a course around each isolated function; then nobody will be left to oppose them.

A Problem-Solving Approach to Fraud Control

Many officials, both within private and public programs, were keen to explain how they were deliberately shifting away from a predominantly reactive stance and putting greater emphasis on prevention. Medicare contractors, for instance, often quote the Health Care Financing Administration's (HCFA) maxim "Stop the bleeding," borne from a realization that "pay and chase" (trying to recover the money after it had been paid out) was a losing strategy.

On occasions, the preventive and reactive philosophies come sharply into conflict. When a major fraud scheme is discovered, investigators confront a dilemma: Should they stop the bleeding immediately, cutting the perpetrators out of the payment system to minimize further losses, or should they allow the scam to run on for a while, under their surveillance, so they can collect evidence and make a compelling case? A traditional law-enforcement approach would favor the second action and would ask managers to continue paying out for the sake of the opportunity to build a high-quality case. A purely preventive approach would favor the first action so that losses can be cut immediately, even at peril of alerting the fraud perpetrators and ruining the prospects of a successful prosecution.

Much is to be said on both sides. On the face of it, the reactive strategy better serves the goals of justice, and prevention appears to serve cost control better.

Defining a control strategy is more complex than simply choosing between reactive and preventive philosophies. Switching from a traditional enforcement approach to prevention as the guiding maxim would be quite dangerous—and could be viewed as leaping straight from one ineffective extreme to the other by jumping right over much more promising middle ground. Before trying to define a better position, it may help to lay out the two extremes and to show why neither can produce effective control.[3]

The Reactive, or Enforcement, Approach. At one extreme lies the purely reactive approach. This incorporates a classic enforcement mentality, based on the fundamental assumption that a ruthless and efficient investigative and enforcement capability will ultimately produce broad compliance through the mechanism of deterrence. The way to get people to obey the rules is to pick some offenders, prosecute them vigorously, publicize their convictions, and then rely upon the resulting publicity to bring everyone else into line. The reactive approach waits for the fraud to occur, then steps in to repair the damage. It deals with control failures, case by case, after the fact. It seeks justice, case by case, but places little emphasis on control.

Defenders of the reactive approach, if asked why vigorous case making has so clearly failed to control fraud, point to inadequate resources, the failure of the courts to keep up their end of the bargain, and the shortage of jail space. What is needed, they say, is more of the same: more investigations, more cases, more convictions, more jail terms.

In the context of fraud control, the flaws in a purely reactive or enforcement strategy have become apparent. There are too many violations, too many violators. Making cases is laborious, difficult, and expensive. Due to the limited capacity of the criminal and civil court systems and the reluctance of many prosecutors to take on any but the most straightforward of health care fraud cases, only a small minority of cases prepared by investigators ever go to court. The resulting deterrent effect, based largely on the probability of being caught and convicted, turns out to be minimal.

A strategy that relies on the capacity of the justice system is necessarily a limited one. Some particular types of fraud are better controlled by instituting new eligibility criteria, by operating additional edits and audits in processing systems, by running education and information campaigns, by instituting requirements for supporting documentation, or by other procedural or administrative changes. In other words, a variety of tools turns out to be useful in a variety of fraud-control contexts. Many fraud problems can be eliminated most efficiently by using methods other than enforcement post factum.

Those who emphasize the goal of cost control also criticize the enforcement approach because of its failure to recover funds. Even in the relatively few cases that make it to the civil or criminal courts, stolen funds remain notoriously hard to recapture. Often the proceeds of fraud have already been squandered on the high life, secreted into offshore accounts, or invested in foreign assets. For small insurers, pursuing civil or criminal cases makes poor economic sense. The costs of bringing the cases often outweigh the insurer's losses and nearly always exceed likely recoveries.

The most critical deficiency of a reactive approach to fraud control—in the context of health care fraud—is its reliance on detection systems. A reactive strategy can only deal with those instances of fraud that detection and referral systems uncover. Anything that detection systems miss, a reactive strategy does not address. Investigative units only investigate what they are fed. Given the ineffectiveness of detection and referral systems, the investigative caseload therefore represents only the tiniest sliver, and a very biased sample, of the whole fraud universe.

If detection systems only scratch the surface, a reactive strategy can only scratch the surface. Given the painstaking nature of case preparation and the constraints of the justice system, a purely or predominantly reactive strategy not only merely scratches the surface, but does it slowly and in a very limited number of places. It accomplishes too little, too late.

The Pure-Prevention Approach.   At the opposite extreme lies a philosophy of pure prevention. The preventive strategy focuses on the construction of systems that prevent losses up front: comprehensive batteries of automated edits and audits designed to keep fraudulent claims out of the system altogether, significantly diminishing the subsequent need for claims review, audits, and investigation.

At its most extreme (and most dangerous), a philosophy of prevention can undermine the investigative and enforcement capabilities. By stressing other tools and remedies, it diminishes the importance of the investigative and enforcement apparatus and may transfer resources away from them. Often investigators perceive the shift to prevention as an assault on their status and the importance of their work. They see their evidence gathering sabotaged through premature termination of providers or other administrative actions that warn perpetrators off. They see investments being made in claims-processing systems in preference to their own units and sometimes at the expense of their existing budgets. They hear only the language of prevention, which seems to hold no place for investigation or prosecution.

A Familiar Dichotomy.   The tension between enforcement and prevention appears in many contexts other than fraud control. In a range of regulatory and enforcement professions—including policing, environmental protection, tax administration, customs, and occupational safety and health—the traditional enforcement approach has come under considerable stress. These professions have each recognized that the enforcement strategy waits until the damage has been done and then reacts, case by case, violation by violation, failure by failure. They have begun to recognize the foolishness of organizing their work around failures rather than around opportunities for intervention.[4]

In response to the perceived deficiencies of a purely or predominantly reactive strategy, many of these regulatory professions have begun exploring alternative strategies, many of them emphasizing voluntary compliance and using a broader range of tools including education, outreach, and voluntary programs. They seek to influence compliance more broadly, stressing prevention rather than counting their success solely in terms of specific outputs (such as inspections, audits, prosecutions, convictions, or jail sentences—the traditional measurements of an enforcement operation).

Certain predictable dangers beset regulatory agencies that attempt to make this strategic shift. Experienced investigators and enforcement officers perceive the new emphasis on prevention as an attack on their own role and status. Moreover, mindful of the egregious bad actors with whom they have traditionally dealt, investigators express skepticism about the usefulness of tools such as persuasion, education, and the new machinery of "voluntary compliance." Many members of the regulated industry will comply, they say, only if made to do so; take away the threat of enforcement, or diminish the capacity of the investigative unit, and law breaking will run rampant.

Enforcement officers also point out, correctly, that no preventive operation can be successful enough to make a reactive capacity unnecessary. No matter how much effort goes into making the highways safe, accidents still happen. No matter how sophisticated pollution-prevention technology is, some industries still pollute. No matter how diligent the IRS's taxpayer education programs are, some people still cheat. Investing everything in prevention is as foolish as investing everything in enforcement.

What follows, unfortunately, can be a bitter and destructive internal battle. People divide into camps—joining the enforcement camp or the prevention camp—depending on their experience and functional loyalties.

Problem Solving or Compliance Management.   Many regulatory professions are now finding their way out of this uncomfortable predicament,
exploring a new strategy that is broadly labeled either *problem solving* or
compliance management.

Regulatory professions discover, eventually, that the internal battle between enforcement and prevention is a battle over tools, not goals. The
enforcement and prevention camps can both be persuaded that the goal is
broad compliance and that the remaining argument is about the comparative effectiveness of the tools. They realize the argument turned bitter
when it turned into a competition between the functions for resources.
The issue then became how much to invest in investigative units, how
much in education programs, and how much in the development of preventive systems. What started out as a philosophical or strategic debate
over the best way to procure compliance had quickly degenerated into a
functional fight over money, status, and jobs.

The problem-solving approach rescues regulatory agencies from these
destructive tensions and provides a constructive way forward. It dismisses
the inward-looking focus on tools and replaces it with an outward-look-
ing focus on important areas of noncompliance. The problem-solving approach was first laid out explicitly by Herman Goldstein, a professor of
law at the University of Wisconsin, widely acknowledged as the father of
problem solving within the policing profession.[5] Goldstein argued that
policing becomes more effective when it pays attention to the problems or
patterns that underlie individual incidents rather than by dealing with the
incidents one by one and in isolation.

Goldstein suggested some useful definitions of problems: "clusters of
similar, related, or recurring incidents rather than a single incident"; "substantive community concerns"; and "the unit of police business."[6] He also
explained that problems come in many shapes and sizes and can be defined in a variety of dimensions. For example, some policing problems are
concentrated in particular locations and at particular times of day or
night (known as "hot spots"). Others might concern common patterns of
behavior, or involve a particular class of offender, a particular type of victim, a repeat offender, a repeat victim, or a particular type of weapon.

The problem-solving approach turns out to be relevant to many more
professions than policing. Just as it allows policing to get to the heart of
important, persistent, or recurring problems (which therefore generate
multiple 911 calls), so it also allows environmental agencies to identify
and focus upon important environmental problems. The problem-solving approach allows tax and customs agencies to identify and concentrate

on important patterns of noncompliance, and it allows occupational safety and health professionals to identify and focus upon significant workplace hazards.

In each case, the goal of problem solving is to identify important problems early and fix them. The strategy permits the range of available tools to be considered with respect to each problem and demands the use of creativity and innovation in fashioning tailor-made responses to each identified problem. With respect to each problem nominated for attention, the object is to design an intervention that fixes the problem, preferably for good, thus diminishing the reactive workload and enabling the agency to shift its attention to the next set of problems.

In fashioning a solution for any particular problem, the enforcement tool (making cases) is always available, but it is never assumed to be the most effective or the most resource-efficient approach. For some problems, the most effective intervention may well include a campaign of vigorous and well-publicized enforcement. For others, the solution might be a procedural or policy change, or the requirement for additional information, or a second opinion. Problem solving, recognizing the scarcity of the resource, uses enforcement surgically, incisively, and in the context of a coherent control strategy.

Problem solving quiets the functional, tool-centered arguments. The foolishness of those arguments becomes immediately apparent once an organization develops a clear focus on its work. No one would dream of telling a furniture maker to use the lathe a little less and the hammer more. How much a craftsman uses a lathe depends on what he is making, and the essence of craftsmanship includes knowing when to use which tool. A problem-solving strategy picks the most important tasks and then selects appropriate tools in each case; it does not decide first which are the important tools and then pick the tasks to fit. A problem-solving operation organizes the tools around the work, not the work around the tools.

Applying Problem Solving to Fraud Control.   Adopting a problem-solving approach to fraud control accomplishes a number of things. It places the emphasis on fraud control rather than on functionally specific goals such as fraud investigation, fraud detection, or fraud prevention. It also provides a rational framework so that the different methods and tools can take their proper places within it. It also makes more efficient use of available control resources and accomplishes this partly by providing a formal system for focusing attention and resources on the most critical problems; partly by changing the unit of work from cases to problems, giving staff the opportunity to design lasting solutions rather than plodding through their caseloads; and partly by bringing the whole toolbox to every problem.

Stages of Problem Solving.   Herman Goldstein has laid out the problem-solving process in great detail in his *Problem-Oriented Policing*. Goldstein's ideas were subsequently adapted for use within other professions. The following summary framework divides the problem-solving procedure into discrete phases:[7]

Stage 1:	Nominate Potential Problem for Attention
Stage 2:	Define the Problem Precisely
Stage 3:	Determine How to Measure Impact
Stage 4:	Develop Solutions/Interventions
Stage 5(a):	Implement the Plan
Stage 5(b):	Periodic Monitoring/Review/Adjustment
Stage 6:	Project Closure, and Long-Term Monitoring/ Maintenance

All this sounds like common sense. Health care insurers might be tempted to assume that the process to be followed, once a problem has been appropriately identified, is obvious; but experience within policing and a variety of other regulatory agencies suggests that the process, while intellectually logical and straightforward, is foreign to traditional bureaucratic behavior. Adopting a problem-solving approach is far from easy.

Stage 1 involves nominating fraud problems for attention. Problems can be defined in many ways. Some problems may be defined in terms of repeat offenders: providers, patients, or corporations who persist in their attempts to cheat. Sometimes persistent offenders can be detected initially through aberrant utilization patterns. Often they cannot.

Some problems may be defined in terms of particular fraudulent practices within specific industry segments. For example: home health care agencies billing for two-person home visits when only single-person visits were conducted; durable medical equipment suppliers billing for motorized wheelchairs when a cheaper version was supplied; pharmacy chains deliberately billing for prescriptions even when patients fail to pick them up; or cosmetic nose jobs (not usually covered by insurance) billed as septoplasties (medically necessary repairs), which are covered.

Some problems may be defined in terms of improper use of particular diagnoses or procedure codes. For example, the diagnosis *dysphagia* (difficulty swallowing) appears in connection with one of hottest forms of DME scam, involving provision of equipment and supplies for feeding patients through tubes—either *enteral feeding* (through the gastrointestinal system) or *perenteral feeding* (directly into a blood vessel).

Thus there are many ways—or dimensions—in which problems can be defined. A mature problem-solving approach can recognize any of them and organize around them.

The health insurance industry is no stranger to the idea of grouping claims together so that attention can be focused upon particular problems. Focused medical review, which is widely practiced, does exactly that: defining the units of work as patterns of abuse. However, focused medical review teams—like medical review more generally—pay attention to medical necessity, treatment orthodoxy, and policy coverage, not fraud. Their audit procedures normally assume the truthfulness of the claim content and lack the rigorous external verification processes required to uncover fraud. Nevertheless, the project approach to identified issues, as practiced by Focused Medical Review teams, is exactly what needs to be produced with respect to the control of criminal fraud.

Stage 2 of the process—problem definition—involves disaggregating and accurately labeling problems; this seems, at first glance, to run counter to the initial stage of grouping them meaningfully together. The object of including this second stage is to make sure that the level of aggregation is not only high enough but is the *right* one.

Whenever agencies begin learning the art of problem solving, they often give in to the temptation of defining problems in excessively broad terms. In health care fraud, examples of such broad categorizations might be "chiropractic fraud," "DME fraud," "medical transportation fraud," or "pharmacy fraud." Such problem definitions are too broad to permit the construction of a sensible plan of attack and too vague to permit rigorous assessment of whether the problem has been controlled.

This second stage also involves analyzing the views of other parties with respect to the problem—making sure that all other parties who have a legitimate interest in the area or practice under scrutiny have their perspectives properly considered before a plan of action is finally agreed upon. Failure to consider such legitimate interests early in the process can lead to frustration and failure later on.

Stage 3—picking the measures by which you would be able to measure progress—often requires as much imagination and insight into the problem as designing a plan of action. Establishing proper mechanisms for measurement also runs contrary to traditional practices in the industry.

The norm—in the absence of systematic measurement—has been to adopt new controls from time to time and then leave them in place for ever. In the absence of contrary indication, everyone assumes they are having their intended effect and that they should continue to operate exactly as they did on day one. The problem-solving process demands that problem-solvers decide, before implementing any solutions, how impact is to be measured. In some cases, the impact may produce a decrease in the number of claims of a particular type, or a decrease in the frequency of beneficiary complaints in a particular category. In other cases, intelligence reports or undercover operations might report that, from the perpetrators' point of view, a particular modus operandi has become too difficult and has therefore been abandoned. In some cases, randomized programs of audits targeted on the particular problem area may be the only method of getting reliable information about practices that cannot be detected without external validation.

With respect to each fraud problem, the fraud-control team needs to decide what to measure and how, and they need to obtain some initial baseline measurements so that changes for better or worse can be detected. Finally, there has to be a commitment to measuring the impact of solutions after implementation. False claims of success ultimately backfire, and there is little merit in replacing ineffective responses with different but equally ineffective ones. Measurement needs to be followed by adjustment, and adjustment by measurement, and so on until substantial progress is made. The temptation is always to defend the effectiveness of the policies, systems, and procedures that happen to be in place. Genuine honesty about operational failures is painful and difficult; such honesty, however, is the prerequisite for progress.

During the action plan design stage (stage 4), a truly uninhibited search for tailor-made solutions tends to run afoul of the enforcement mentality. Many investigators feel they already know the solution: Continue to make cases; just "lock 'em up!" They resent further discussion. They believe their traditional tactics would work perfectly well if the courts and the prisons had the necessary capacity and if their own budgets were increased substantially. Truly uninhibited searches demand that officials let go of many firmly entrenched views about what works and what does not. Capturing and critiquing the current response demands a dose of honesty. Which control systems or procedures currently deal with this problem? Do they work? How do we know? Why is the current response structured in this way? Which pieces of the current response appear to have some effect? Exactly what effect do they have?

Some components of the current response might be useful and should not be lightly discarded. Others might simply be based upon tradition, on erroneous assumptions about the nature of fraud control, or on nothing more solid than "this is what we do." In any case, an honest appraisal both of the nature of the responses and their impact lays a firm foundation for the design of better solutions.

Problem-Solving Requirements. The previous description of the problem-solving methodology does not do justice to its complexity. The central idea—picking important fraud problems and suppressing them—seems simple enough. Yet institutionalizing that simple idea presents significant organizational challenges.

With respect to broad national or regional fraud patterns, problem solving also requires major changes in the manner and degree of cooperation between different agencies. Tackling major fraud problems that do not fit neatly within the responsibility of a single organization will require insurers, policymakers, and law-enforcement agencies to work together around the common goal of fraud *control.* They have already demonstrated their capacity to work together on specific high-profile prosecutions. Working together to accomplish effective control will be harder still.

Figuring out the more complex implications for interagency relationships is not necessarily the top priority. For now, the health care industry could learn a great deal about fraud control if one or two major insurers developed models of a problem-solving approach within the confines of their own claims-processing system; others could then examine, imitate, and adapt those models to their own organizations.

At a minimum, successful adoption of a problem-solving approach to fraud control will combine the following features:

- A deliberate and continuing commitment to search for new and emerging patterns of fraud
- A person or team of people clearly designated as responsible for fraud control, with access to and influence over the whole range of functional tools—from the design of eligibility criteria at one end of the process, to investigation and prosecution at the other end
- Conscious recognition of the fraud *problem* as the relevant unit of work, producing a project focus rather than a case-by-case focus
- A focus on effectiveness (as opposed to outputs), with a commitment to monitoring the impact for each problem tackled

Deliberate Focus on Early Detection

The real promise of the problem-solving approach stems not just from the capacity to analyze important fraud problems and tackle them creatively, but also from the opportunity to intervene early before too much damage has been done. Like the child playing whack-a-mole, successful fraud control depends on the ability to see clearly and to react quickly. All too often, as the continuing supply of health care fraud scandals attest, fraud problems become endemic before control systems respond. A model fraud-control strategy must stress early detection of emerging fraud problems rather than remaining in a reactive posture and waiting until the problems, much enlarged, threaten to overwhelm.

Thus scanning for emerging problems becomes a priority. Resources must be set aside for proactive outreach and intelligence-gathering operations, and these resources must be protected from the demands of the reactive workload—otherwise proactive activities will never survive. Proactive outreach requires the use of many tools; here are some of the more familiar ones:

- establishing and maintaining a network of contacts with other insurers and law-enforcement agencies to provide early warning of fraud trends already spotted by others;
- conducting undercover operations, such as "undercover shopping" of newly established storefront clinics (the object being to find out what kinds of services are really being provided, and to whom);
- developing informants who can report on emerging practices within criminal networks;
- interviewing convicted fraud perpetrators who may be willing to describe a variety of fraud methods and who may be able to point out vulnerabilities in payment systems;
- data mining: using a broad range of analytical tools to search for anomalous patterns (Chapter 10 examines the analytical tools currently available and describes the need for a broader range of analytical methods);
- employing focus groups to pick the brains of patients and providers about system vulnerabilities and observed patterns of suspicious behavior;

- educating claims processing staff (those few who retain the opportunity to examine the contents of claims) about indicators of fraud; and

- creating "tiger teams" within the organization (whose job is to come up with creative new ways to cheat the system) as a way of testing and refining defenses.

A collection of such activities constitutes an intelligence operation. These activities may well generate cases, but they are not case-based. The objective is to discover emerging fraudulent practices so that the control operation can find antidotes.

These intelligence-gathering mechanisms have already been used within the health care industry, but they are used sporadically and quickly displaced when the caseload builds up. Investigators report that they uncover more trouble than they can possibly deal with whenever they use these methods. They describe this experience with a mixed metaphor that has become conventional wisdom: "Every rock we look under, we find a whole new can of worms."

The critical need to spot emerging patterns earlier shifts greater emphasis onto these proactive methods and intelligence-gathering tools. Timely and accurate intelligence feeds the problem-solving strategy and ensures that the resources of the defending organization focus on the right things at the right time. In the control business, intelligence counts, even more than cases.

Fraud-Specific Prepayment Controls

The fraud-control team must be able to operate prepayment as well as postpayment; this means they should be able to insert their own fraud-specific edits and audits into the processing system. The team should have their own resources to validate suspended claims instead of relying on medical review teams (already overburdened and focused on different issues) to do it for them; and they should be able to design and operate their own focused reviews, randomly selecting claims within fraud-prone areas and using external validation procedures—telephone calls, visits, on-site audits—to check them out.

In particular, the fraud-control team must be able to prevent rapid, high-dollar-value fraud schemes, characterized as bust-outs; they must have the capacity to operate the types of controls (which are invariably missing) that eliminate this threat. These controls would involve, at a minimum, automatic suspension of high-dollar payments (above some arbitrary threshold) pending human review of the contributing claims; provider-level monitoring (looking for sudden accelerations in aggregate claims levels, or totals in excess of reasonable norms for that specialty); and the routine random selection of a small proportion of claims for validation.

Chapter 10 provides a detailed discussion about the design of detection tools and their operation at different stages of the claims process. Whoever is given responsibility for fraud control needs the freedom to intercept claims prepayment rather than operating entirely postpayment.

Every Claim Faces Risk of Review

Every claim submitted for payment should suffer some risk of review for fraud, no matter what its dollar amount, regardless of its medical orthodoxy, and regardless of the reputation of the claimant. When reviewing claims before payment, the fraud-control team should be responsible for extracting claims for random review and making inquiries to establish the legitimacy of each one. Such a provision would go a long way toward eliminating the vulnerability of payment systems to massive computerized billing schemes—one of the most worrying modern threats. Some risk of random review eliminates this threat. When prepayment inquiries show a claim to be even a little suspicious, and do it reasonably quickly, the fraud-control team can then suspend all claims pending from the same source and subject them to detailed scrutiny.

The industry will raise two objections to such a practice. First, they will say that random selection, with external validation, constitutes an arbitrary and unwarranted intrusion into the affairs of perfectly respectable providers; however, such an intrusion may be part of the price society has to pay for reasonable protection of the health care system. Insurers cannot control costs if they give up the right to verify the truthfulness of claims. Besides, all the insurers will ask the patients to do is to verify what they know already—that is, to confirm the services already detailed within the claims.

Second, industry officials will point out that scarce audit and investigative resources would be better used on focused claims review than on random review. But focused reviews serve a different purpose and cannot offer the same protection that random reviews provide because fraud perpetrators watch to see where insurers are focusing and then deliberately play elsewhere.

Both of these objections can be mitigated somewhat by pointing out that the risk of random review does not need to be high; a base probability of 1 percent might be reasonable. Insurers who commit to systematic measurement will see double benefit to such sampling. Not only does it protect against multiclaim scams but it could also act as the foundation for ongoing systematic measurement.

Outside the context of measurement (which requires a uniform risk across every claim), it makes sense to devote additional resources to higher risk providers. Brand-new providers might enter the system with a higher risk of review, say 10 percent, and work their way down to the 1-percent floor only by establishing a record of accurate and trustworthy billing. In other words, providers would need to establish their trustworthiness. Similarly, the risk could be increased for providers whose randomly selected claims did not appear legitimate. As the claims examiners at Company X so clearly articulated, a provider caught cheating deserves to have the normal degree of trust withdrawn (i.e., a much higher rate of review imposed) until the insurer is satisfied the provider has reformed. Providers would no doubt explain false claims as isolated billing errors; the price for such errors, however, would be an increased risk of review until, over time, providers could once more demonstrate that their billing was reliable.

The fraud-control team would maintain and operate this selection system as an integral part of their prepayment operations; they would maintain a file of selection probabilities, one for each provider or billing entity, which would automatically control the random selection of claims for review. The team would be able to control the overall volume by adjusting selection probabilities, up or down, for different categories of claimant. The probability of review should *never* be zero—not for any provider, no matter how reputable; not for any claim, no matter how small.

Applicability to Managed Care

Admittedly this description of a model fraud-control strategy applies most directly to claims-payment systems. Nevertheless, some features of the general control philosophy apply equally well to capitated plans. The idea that fraud-control resources should be based on the size and seriousness of the problem also holds true. The erroneous belief that managed care provides a structural solution to the fraud problem threatens to strip away control resources even though the new forms of fraud pose significant threats to human health.

Clear designation of responsibility for fraud control and adoption of a problem-solving approach are both equally valid within the managed care domain. For payers to assume that managed care plans themselves will take care of fraud control is utter folly. After all, it is the plans themselves that have the greatest opportunities to commit fraud.

Proactive outreach and intelligence gathering under managed care becomes more critical than ever. The reactive workload will be minimal because almost nobody has the incentive to report fraud; there will be no claims-payment process within which detection and referral systems can be embedded. In the absence of such proactive outreach and intelligence gathering, fraud will remain completely invisible.

Under managed care, intelligence will come from different sources. The locus for fraud will shift to the corporate middle layers that separate the payers from the frontline service providers. The best informants (who will prefer to remain anonymous for professional reasons) will be physicians and other providers in a position to report on the policies and practices of the managed care organizations.

Even the sixth component of the model fraud-control strategy—the significance of a prepayment interception—is not irrelevant to managed care. A generalized version of that idea would be "Make sure you check things out before you pay the money"; such advice certainly applies to managed care. Capitated programs face the risk of paying capitated fees to plans in advance only to see the corporations evaporate or artfully slide into bankruptcy—leaving someone else to take care of the patients. A successful fraud-control operation would take responsibility for minimizing the risks associated with advance payments by conducting background inquiries before contracts are awarded; they would also spread payments out over time so that the sum at risk is never too great. Background inquiries should establish candidate plans as bona fide operations and flush out criminal affiliations.

The Prospects for Implementation

The seven features of a successful fraud-control strategy described here—systematic measurement, resource allocation based upon measurement, clear designation of responsibility for fraud control, adoption of a problem-solving approach, dedicated resources for proactive outreach and intelligence gathering, prepayment operation of fraud controls (including random verification), and ensuring that every claim faces some risk of review—will strike some officials within the industry as a useless and unrealistic wish list. In the real world of constrained resources, systems already creak under unmanageable operational loads. Some officials may accept the prescription in theory but write it off as a practical impossibility—of only academic interest.

The model fraud-control strategy described here is indeed, for the majority of insurers, a long way from reality. That is the point. The purpose of describing this model strategy is to show just how much it differs from current practice in the industry. Most insurers, public and private, do no systematic measurement of the fraud problem. They fly blind, oblivious to the magnitude of the problem. No insurers base resource-allocation decisions logically upon valid estimates of the size of the problem; thus the massive underinvestments in control. Most insurers fail to designate responsibility for control, and many equate control with investigation; they have no one responsible for playing the fraud-control game and little prospect of coordination between functional tools. Many fraud units remain bogged down in a reactive, case-making mode, unable to see the forest for the trees. At the other extreme, some proponents of electronic claims processing are in danger of proposing a strategy that focuses solely on prevention, threatening to decimate investigative and enforcement capacities. Insurers need problem solving as a rational, integrating, control-oriented framework. Most insurers, even if they believe in the value of proactive outreach and intelligence gathering, cannot find or protect resources for it; so they operate with a distorted and fragmentary picture of fraud, as revealed by ineffective detection and referral systems. And most payment systems remain vulnerable to multimillion-dollar quick-hit scams because they lack the necessary prepayment controls. So this model remains far from reality, at least for now.

Two things must happen before anything close to the model fraud-control strategy can ever become a reality. First, the complexity of the fraud-control challenge must be grasped and understood. Second, the health care industry and the public must learn the true extent of fraud in the U.S. health care system. (Without that knowledge, no one can justify the cost or inconvenience associated with operating such controls.) This book will, I hope, help reveal the complexity of the fraud-control challenge. Only a commitment to systematic measurement can produce an understanding of the extent of fraud in the health care system today.

Until these two things happen, fraud control will remain elusive, and health care fraud will continue to plague the United States.

10

Detection Systems

The last thing in the world I need right now is to detect more fraud.
—Senior Health Care Financing Administration (HCFA) official

Given the current state of affairs within the industry, many officials would prefer not to detect more fraud. They have far too many cases and far too few resources. They see too many investigations and prosecutions abandoned for lack of capacity in the court system and see little value in exacerbating the problem. Moreover, they suspect that a significant increase in the detection rate (which might result from improved detection systems) might be misinterpreted by many as yet more evidence of poor performance. As a matter of course, therefore, few within the industry show much eagerness to upgrade detection capabilities. For many practitioners, existing incentives push the opposite way: Their lives would be much easier if the level of detected frauds went down. Hopefully, a better understanding of the nature of the fraud-control business will eventually produce a greater enthusiasm for improved detection systems within the industry. The inadequacy of existing detection systems will become obvious when insurers start measuring the level of fraud systematically.

The IRS, in tackling tax-refund fraud, had no idea just how bad their detection systems were until they carried out their first random sampling in 1994 of claims based on the earned income tax credit (EITC). During the 1994 filing season, they detected 160 million dollars' worth of fraudulent refunds. The statistical measurement of the EITC fraud problem, through random sampling, indicated 3 billion dollars' worth of fraudulent refunds passing through the system. IRS detection systems were uncovering only a fraction (roughly 5 percent) of the total. Suddenly, the need for the IRS to upgrade its detection tools became obvious. Also, as the policy emphasis shifted from fraud investigation to fraud control, improving detection tools became more attractive. Officials want to see the fraud picture more clearly, and they feel less obligation to make a court case from every fraudulent claim they find.

This chapter is written for the sake of those within the industry who genuinely want to understand the limitations of existing detection tools and to grasp the opportunities for improvement. It has a slightly more technical flavor than the rest of the book, and some readers may therefore choose to skip it.

Earlier chapters have stressed the importance of relying upon humans, rather than systems, to play the fraud-control game. Some will undoubtedly interpret that emphasis as anti-technology. Some readers may interpret the account given of the small private insurer (in Chapter 8) as being an untimely and irrelevant glorification of outdated manual practices.

The issue is not whether to use technology but how to use it. The model of detection systems currently dominant in the industry—systems select; humans inspect—cannot offer protection. The basis upon which systems select seldom has much to do with fraud; the detection systems are static, easy for fraud perpetrators to learn and circumnavigate.

The advent of modern, flexible database access systems, coupled with an enormous number of potentially relevant analytic techniques, makes possible a new generation of fraud detection tools. But human beings must decide where these technologies should be used, and in what ways. Human beings must understand what these tools can do and what they cannot. And human beings must operate these tools day by day and evaluate their output. These tools can never be a substitute for human thought; they merely equip and support it. If the increased use of technology results in the displacement of human analysts and investigators, it will have done more harm than good. Thus this chapter's emphasis on equipping fraud-control teams with the very best technological tools as distinct from the dangerous notion that technological systems can actually do the work of fraud control for you.

The Multilevel Nature of Fraud Control

To analyze the strengths and weaknesses of existing detection tools, one has to understand the many levels at which fraud can be perpetrated. Frauds perpetrated at one level will not normally be detected by fraud controls operating at another level.

To illustrate the multilevel nature of fraud, let us turn for a moment to the world of credit card fraud. Because credit card fraud falls rather more neatly into distinct levels than many health care frauds, using credit card fraud as an example makes the underlying framework easier to grasp.

There are five distinct levels, summarized in the following table, at which credit card fraud can be perpetrated:

Level 1   Transactions
Level 2   Card (or "plastic")
Level 3   Account
Level 4   The cardholder (holding multiple products or accounts)
Level 5   Multiparty or "Ring" level

The first level of fraud control is the simplest. It involves monitoring for fraud at the transaction level. A transaction on a card is considered suspect only if the transaction itself, considered in isolation, is inherently suspicious. Examples of such suspicious transactions might include ATM (Automated Teller Machine) withdrawals at, or close to, the permitted maximum; mail-order bulk purchases of portable and valuable resaleable merchandise such as jewelry or electronics; or purchases of expensive domestic or personal items on a corporate card.

Because credit card issuers recognize these transaction-level threats, they design detection apparatus and controls to contain such activity. ATM withdrawals above some threshold will require confirmation of identity via telephone. Certain purchases will require additional authentication of the user.

In the face of such controls, fraud perpetrators move to the second level. Using stolen or found credit cards, they deliberately keep individual transactions small, but make their money by using the same card many times over. Fraudulent users of credit cards and cash cards have been known to stand at ATM machines for hours, repeatedly withdrawing $50 at a time, believing that monitoring systems will not pay attention to such small transactions, no matter how many in succession.

To defend against repeated use of stolen cards, the card issuers institute monitoring at the second level, which is the *card level.* These controls watch the overall behavior of the card—aggregating across multiple transactions—comparing the overall pattern with previous history and watching for "out-of-character" spending profiles or sudden accelerations in usage.

Now the game moves to the third level. Fraud perpetrators usurp the identities of account holders, or use fictitious identities to establish accounts. They obtain multiple cards on the same account, often by requesting the issuance of supplementary cards. Spreading their activity across several different cards defeats the card-level controls. The issuing banks then have to institute *account*-level controls to monitor the aggregate behavior across all the cards. The more sophisticated fraud perpetrators then learn that they can use the same cardholder identity to procure multiple accounts; they apply for, and obtain, multiple accounts from the same bank (using a fictitious or usurped identity). To frustrate efforts at detection, they also obtain accounts from many different banks. A bank that issues multiple products to the same individual now has to use controls at the *cardholder* level to watch for alarming trends in the bank's aggregate exposure to that individual.

Even this is not the end. The serious fraud perpetrators—for example, the major counterfeit credit card rings—move to the highest level: the multiparty or ring level. At this level, fraud perpetrators deliberately spread their fraudulent activities across hundreds or thousands of accounts to avoid all lower-level detection systems and controls. At this highest level, the credit card industry confronts organized criminal rings as opposed to the opportunistic petty thieves who deal in one or two stolen cards at a time. These criminal rings may involve collusive merchants, even bank employees, and may involve fifty or more conspiring individuals playing different roles. The most sophisticated schemes (and the most difficult to control) are global counterfeit card schemes, many of which have their roots in the Far East. These operations obtain credit card account information from members of staff at prestigious restaurants, hotels, or other high-volume service establishments. Those establishments are referred to within the business as "points of compromise." Once a week or so, the "source" at the point of compromise compiles a list of cards that have been used at that establishment, focusing mostly on gold or platinum or other prestige cards with higher credit limits. The source then transmits the list of account names, numbers, and expiration dates to the criminal counterfeiting organization, in exchange for a payoff of some kind. When the source is a senior staff member, they may also arrange placement of a magnetic stripe reader; this is hooked up to a personal computer so that the encoded magnetic stripe information can be read off the cards, stored in a database, and passed on with the rest of the account information.

Another piece of the operation involves "spending teams" that travel from city to city to use the counterfeit cards. Blank counterfeit card stock (much of which is manufactured in Hong Kong) is mailed to them as they travel and comes complete with counterfeit holograms and other security features. The teams carry with them card-embossing machines and magnetic stripe encoders, which, given the proliferation of card-based identification and security systems, anyone can buy. They receive lists of card numbers by telephone, passed on from the points of compromise, and spend their evenings in hotel rooms embossing the account details onto blank card stock and encoding the magnetic stripes to match. They then hold a more or less exact physical duplicate of the original card.

The spending teams then use these counterfeit cards vigorously, running them up to their credit limits within a day or two before discarding them. They buy expensive jewelry, designer clothing, consumer electronics, and other items that can be resold for cash. The spending teams seldom stay in the same city for more than two or three days. The legitimate cardholders have no idea that anything has happened to their accounts until they receive their statements a month later—by which time fraudulent use of their accounts has stopped and the teams that counterfeited their cards have long since moved on.

The credit card industry has developed reasonably good defenses at fraud levels 1, 2, and 3; but is generally much less well defended at levels 4 and 5. Some issuing banks have even tried to deny the existence of the counterfeit fraud problem and have held the account holders responsible for all charges unless they had reported their cards stolen. (Account holders are *not* responsible for such charges provided they report the unauthorized activity on their accounts reasonably quickly after receiving their statements.) To improve their detection capabilities, credit card issuers should focus on two things. First, they should pay special attention to those levels where they are least protected; second, to minimize losses, they should look for earlier detection opportunities at every level.

The health care industry has precisely the same needs. They have to understand at which levels they remain vulnerable and design tools to plug those holes; then, to minimize losses, they have to move detection tools forward to the earliest possible moment.

The Seven Levels of Health Care Fraud Control

Although the corresponding analysis of health care fraud is more complex, and what follows is an oversimplification of its richness and texture, this framework serves well enough to point out the narrowness of existing approaches. There are at least seven distinct levels of aggregation at which fraud-control monitoring is required. The lowest level (transaction level) and the highest level (multiparty criminal conspiracies) of health card fraud are analogous with credit card fraud, but there are more intervening layers. In order, they are:

Level 1 Claim, or Transaction level
Level 2 Patient/Provider relationship
Level 3 (a) Patient level
        (b) Provider level
Level 4 (a) Patient group/Provider
        (b) Patient/Practice (clinic)
Level 5 Policy/Practice relationship
Level 6 (a) Defined groups of patients
        (e.g., families or residents of one
        nursing home.)
        (b) Practice (or Clinic)
Level 7 Multiparty, criminal conspiracies

Level 1 concerns claims that are inherently suspicious, even without a broader context or history: men having hysterectomies; infants receiving psychotherapy; doctors treating their own families. These claims can be considered suspicious purely from information contained within the claim.

Level 2 concerns the relationship between one provider and one patient and examines the overall volume and nature of services delivered to that patient by that provider. Detection systems operating at level 2 would compare service frequency with reasonable norms for the provider's specialty and for the patient's diagnosis.

Level 3 requires a broader perspective, either looking at the patient's entire history (aggregating across all providers) or looking at the provider's overall practice patterns (across all patients).

Level 4(a) recognizes that several patients may be covered by the same insurance policy and that one practitioner may abuse the policy and distribute fraudulent or abusive activity across several patients.

Level 4(b) also deals with abuse of one patient's account by a *practice* (which may involve several practitioners), acknowledging that frauds may be perpetrated by clinic or hospital administrators who may deliberately distribute fraudulent activity across several practitioners.

Level 5 considers the overall use of a policy (which may cover several patients) by a practice (which may include several providers).

Level 6(a) considers misuse of a particular group of patients more broadly, perhaps by many different medical providers. The group of patients might be a family covered by one policy; they might be residents of an apartment complex, or residents of the same nursing home—any connection that enables perpetrators to manipulate the accounts for the group.

Level 6(b) concerns patterns of claims activity by groups of practitioners affiliated with one another through practices, clinics, or other cooperative business arrangements. Monitoring at this level would be suitable for detecting the activities of "Medicaid mills," where several providers set up under the same roof and continually refer patients to-and-fro among themselves for needless tests and services.

Finally, level 7 deals with the operations of criminal networks—such as prescription drug recycling schemes—where the pattern of fraudulent activity is broader than that of a restricted set of beneficiaries or providers. The art of detection at this (highest) level involves watching for broad patterns of coincidence or connection between hundreds or thousands of otherwise innocuous transactions.

Note that the higher levels of fraud monitoring are not necessarily better than the lower levels; they are just different. A fraud operated at level 5, where a clinic routinely makes claims on a policy but spreads the fraudulent activity between many different doctors and across several patients, will most likely not be detectable by monitoring at a lower level. Certainly each individual transaction (claim) will look perfectly normal.

Conversely, if insurers monitor at level 5 only, they would fail to catch opportunistic one-time frauds characterized by absurd claims at the transaction level (level 1). The individual fraudulent claims, manifestly unreasonable by themselves, would likely have insufficient impact on the overall use of a policy by a practice to trip level-5 alarms. The transaction-level frauds would get lost within a much larger set that comprises mostly legitimate claims.

The issue is not one of choice. No one should abandon level 1 controls and move to some other level. The issue is not simply one of monitoring at a high enough, or low enough, level. The issue is monitoring at the right level for the kind of scheme one intends to uncover, because most schemes will only be revealed at the *same* level at which the fraud perpetrators designed and operated them. Assuming that frauds will continue to be perpetrated at any and all of these levels, then fraud-monitoring capabilities will be required at all levels.

The characteristics of fraud schemes perpetrated at these various levels are substantially different from each other. The lower-level frauds are more numerous, often opportunistic, and net relatively low dollar amounts. By contrast, the higher-level frauds can run undetected for long periods, require significantly more technical and organizational sophistication to operate, and are therefore probably less common; but each scheme may net many millions of dollars.

The sensible next question to ask is at what levels are insurers most vulnerable and what might be done to remedy those vulnerabilities? Which levels are currently well defended? Which levels are undefended? Sometimes fraud schemes that run undetected for months or years show only too clearly which levels of control were missing.

NBC's *Dateline* ran a feature on Medicare fraud in November 1995.[1] Part of the program featured a patient in whose name a supplier of medical equipment had billed Medicare over $10,000 each month for several months, just for surgical dressings. In this case, the principal detection opportunity lies at level 2 (patient/provider relationship). Such flagrant billing could also be picked up at the patient level, or even at the provider level if the provider was abusing enough patients' accounts to distort their overall provider profiles.

Congressional testimony on fraud in the Medicare and Medicaid programs provided by the General Accounting Office (GAO) in 1995 cited several examples of schemes that, according to GAO, ought all to have been detected and stopped. However, they came to light only through tip-offs rather than through the operation of routine monitoring. In one case, a Medicare contractor processed and paid, without question, $1.2 million in claims from one supplier, all for body jackets supplied to various nursing home residents. The supplier's previous year total for the same item was just $8,500.[2]

Clearly, fairly rudimentary provider-level profiling ought to have spotted the anomaly—in particular, provider-level acceleration-rate monitoring, had it been present. In another example, a pharmacist from California had been billing Medicaid for improbably high volumes of prescription drugs and was being reimbursed without question, even though several recipients had each been receiving more than twenty prescriptions a day.[3] Had the overall volume of drugs been unusually high for a pharmacy, provider-level monitoring (level 3[b]) should have revealed the pharmacist as an outlier within the specialty, by total volume. If the real anomaly concerns a small number of individual patients who are receiving far too many prescriptions, the detection opportunity lies at level 2, where the unit of analysis is the aggregate transaction volume between a provider and a patient. Two more cases, where rudimentary monitoring at level 2 would have detected the scheme, came to light only through whistle-blowers or some other good fortune. Over a sixteen-month period, a van service billed Medicare $62,000 for ambulance trips to transport the same patient 240 times. Medicaid paid for more than 142 lab tests and eighty-five prescriptions for one patient within an eighteen-day period. The lab involved billed Medicaid for more than $80 million over two years. [4]

Another case described in the same testimony shows how some scams are organized around groups of patients, in this case, all residents of the same nursing home. More than $1 million in claims was paid over twelve months for therapy services within a small nursing home, which had previously had only nominal claims for therapy.[5] Conceivably, many therapy providers may have been involved; in this case, provider-level monitoring might not be expected to detect the pattern. Because the "therapy" was spread across multiple patients, beneficiary-level monitoring might not have caught it, either. Detection would depend on the capacity to monitor *groups* of patients (i.e., at level 6[a]), the patients being connected in this instance by residence in the same nursing home.

Medicare investigators monitoring durable medical equipment (DME) suppliers report a fairly new phenomenon that makes monitoring at level 6(a) particularly important. Fraud perpetrators describing themselves as salesmen walk into nursing homes and offer "to take care of everything"—the supplies, the billing, the works—at no cost to the patients or to the home. Once allowed in, they begin exploiting the residents' insurance policies, passing business to a range of providers. The nursing home gets showered with unnecessary services and products, and the insurers—principally Medicare—pay the bill. The salesmen themselves are not licensed; they make their money on a commission basis. Such schemes are organized by the salesmen and built around the nursing home population, so standard forms of provider profiling (level 3[b]) may not catch them. The detection opportunity lies in monitoring aggregate claims across the nursing home residents; at that level of scrutiny, the activities of such salesmen would stand out clearly.

Examples such as these demonstrate the critical need for detection tools at all levels. Fraud schemes designed and perpetrated at one level will normally be detected only by controls designed and operated at the same level.

The Current Emphasis

For the time being, most fraud detection tools used within the industry fall within certain narrow categories.

Prepayment Monitoring

At the prepayment stage, edits and audits within claims-processing systems perform monitoring at the transaction level (level 1) and at the patient level (level 3[a]).

Transaction-level monitoring (edits and audits) pick out those claims where the diagnosis does not match the procedure code; where the age or gender of the patient does not match the diagnosis; or where detectable forms of unbundling or price manipulation have occurred.

Patient-level monitoring examines each claim in the context of the patient's recent claims history. The most obvious question at this level is "Has this claim—or one similar enough to be considered a duplicate—already been paid?" Beyond the duplicate claim checks, patient-level monitoring examines the frequency of certain procedures: child-births less than nine months apart; more than one hysterectomy or appendectomy in a lifetime; too many visits to the chiropodist in a month. Patient-level monitoring also checks for incompatible treatments, for instance, the billing of outpatient or emergency services when the patient (according to hospital claims) was an inpatient.

Postpayment Monitoring

The vast majority of postpayment monitoring within the industry falls at level 3(b), taking the form of provider profiling. Profiling systems, used within the context of postpayment utilization review, calculate a set of variables or ratios for each provider descriptive of their overall treatment patterns. These indicators are then used, either one at a time or in various mathematical combinations, to select providers whose treatment patterns appear anomalous against the background of their peer group. Typically, provider profiling picks off 1 percent or 2 percent of the providers in each group examined.

Once a provider's billing patterns have been identified as suspicious, future claims from that provider can be suspended for review through the insertion of prepayment provider flags into the processing system. Some feedback occurs, therefore, between postpayment review and prepayment claims suspension.

The insertion of provider flags as a result of postpayment review should never be confused, though, with prepayment provider-level monitoring. The first offers no protection against rapid bust-out schemes because the prepayment flag appears only after postpayment analysis has been completed—several months after the fact. Provider flags may operate prepayment, but they result from postpayment claims analysis. By contrast, true provider-level monitoring on a prepayment basis would identify suspicious claims patterns on the basis of prepayment claims data and would trip alarms in real time to prevent the claims from being paid.

Postpayment utilization review teams vary in how they choose different medical specialties for attention. Some teams routinely work through each specialty in turn, looking for outliers worthy of more detailed scrutiny. Others first pick and choose the specialties by monitoring the aggregate behavior of the specialty as a whole. A specialty will receive attention if the aggregate dollar value consumed by that group accelerates rapidly from year to year or if the aggregate billing patterns for that specialty on a regional basis diverge from national norms.

HCFA's traditional emphasis on focused medical review seems to be exactly this: a way of selecting specialties, or procedures, as a preliminary step to provider profiling. A 1994 review of Medicare's post-payment utilization review procedures by GAO summarized the practice:

> In 1993, HCFA developed a new emphasis on data analysis. Calling its approach focused medical review, HCFA required carriers to better focus their profiling efforts and to begin identifying general spending patterns and trends that would allow them to determine the causes for unusually high spending. Carriers are now required to examine spending for specific services or procedures largely by comparing their own spending amounts for certain procedures with these procedures' spending averages across carriers.[6]

This approach provides a useful way to drill into the data from the top level to ascertain where program dollars are being spent and where further review or policy reevaluation might offer key opportunities for cost control. But its limitations as a fraud-control measure need to be understood. First, it is much better suited for identifying broad utilization problems (which is its purpose) than for detection of fraud. Second, if used as a preliminary filter for subsequent provider profiling, it substantially re-

TABLE 10.1   Detection Tools Broadly Available Within the Industry

		Prepayment	Postpayment
Level 1	Transaction	X	
Level 2	Patient/Provider		
Level 3(a)	Patient	X	
Level 3(b)	Provider		X
Level 4(a)	Patient group/Provider		
Level 4(b)	Patient/Practice (clinic)		
Level 5	Patient group/Practice		
Level 6(a)	Defined patient group		
Level 6(b)	Practice (or clinic)		
Level 7	Multiparty conspiracies		

duces the probability of fraudulent providers from being detected unless they happen to be in sufficient bad company or to be so prolific themselves that their fraudulent activities distort aggregate regional trends for their specialty.

Current Developments

For the time being, the bulk of the industry's detection toolkit is therefore focused at levels 1 and 3, with prepayment operation of transaction-level and patient-level monitoring, and postpayment provider-level monitoring. Table 10.1 (above) summarizes this situation and clearly illustrates the opportunities for development of additional detection tools.

The industry has plenty of scope for the development of new detection tools. Ideally, payment systems should be protected at all levels and at the earliest possible moment—that is, prepayment. Some interesting technologies that can help plug some of these holes are available. Unfortunately, the industry falls into the trap of using technology to enhance *existing* detection capabilities rather than to build new capabilities. Most recent new applications of technology support either prepayment transaction-level monitoring, or postpayment provider-profiling—two of the three areas best defended already.

This natural temptation afflicts many other fraud-control environments. It is much easier to throw fashionable new technologies (such as neural networks, artificial intelligence, or advanced statistical methods) at traditional forms of analysis than to understand the need for new forms of analysis. Organizations do the former because they generally do not see the need for the latter. Making hi-tech investments in existing forms of analysis has an easy appeal; it makes the organization look good (by acquiring the very latest technology). It also requires no fundamental change in the way the organization conceives of or conducts its fraud-control operations. These are the *natural* fraud-control enhancements.

The most promising prospects for enhanced fraud-detection tools are not necessarily the most natural. Providing state-of-the-art defenses at certain levels is not as important, or as urgent, as providing even the crudest of defenses at other levels, where there is nothing. The vulnerability of most health insurers' payment systems to bust-outs results directly from the absence of provider-level monitoring at the prepayment stage. Even the crudest of provider-level aggregate monitoring tools and acceleration-rate checks would substantially eliminate this threat. Nothing terribly sophisticated is required, just a broader understanding of the complete detection toolkit and the will to shore up the weakest points first.

Artificial intelligence, neural networks, and other sophisticated technologies do have an important role to play in fraud control, but they offer no panacea. Their acquisition will increase, not diminish, the need for dedicated fraud analysts and investigators. There are limits to the benefits they can bring.

First, and most obvious, applying highly sophisticated models at one level does nothing to help at another level. For example, having the very best provider-profiling system in the world still only helps with provider profiling.

Second, and a little less obvious, in "training" the new models, the model developers often use historical data sets that may contain many undetected frauds (partly because there was no previous capacity to detect them, and partly because many fraud types do not reveal themselves even retrospectively). Thus the new models may be trained to replicate past fraud-detection performance rather than to take a meaningful step forward.

Third, with the use of sophisticated modeling techniques, the users of the system (investigators, fraud analysts, claims reviewers) lose touch with the grounds upon which claims are being picked out. In such situations, tensions can arise between those who support the model and those who do not really understand how the model works and prefer to rely upon their own judgment and experience. The end result, too often, is that a rift appears between the people and the systems involved in fraud control. Use of more sophisticated tools ends up displacing human judgment and expertise rather than equipping it.

Fourth, the more expensive and intensive the model development effort the more likely the resulting model to remain unchanged for long periods. Investment in highly sophisticated filters can, on occasions, result in the production of static fraud controls that will quickly be outpaced by developments and mutations in fraud methods.

To provide broader protection, the industry needs to shift its technological emphasis. Instead of focusing upon state-of-the-art analytical methods, the industry should focus on providing its fraud-control teams a range of flexible, user-friendly claims analysis tools. These teams should be able to construct their own searches quickly and easily, slicing and dicing the claims data in many different ways, inserting and deleting different types of search as different fraud threats wax and wane. The people operating the systems should not have to be technical wizards to get what they want. The most important tools in the fraud-detection toolkit are timely and easy access to claims data (including prepayment data); friendly, easy-to-use nontechnical interfaces; and a broad range of analytical tools that can be easily sequenced to answer complex ad hoc inquiries.

Recently, the problem of fraud detection has attracted several major vendors of analytical systems to the health care industry. They see health insurers, concerned about fraud and abuse, as a ripe market for a new generation of analytical systems. These vendors, whose interest in fraud detection is most welcome, should think about the undefended levels and figure out what they can offer there rather than presenting sophisticated tools that are of marginal utility and focusing on areas (such as postpayment provider profiling) where systems are comparatively well defended. First things first!

Defense at the Higher Levels

One major opportunity to apply modern technology to great effect for fraud control lies in the development of detection tools aimed at the highest levels (levels 6 and 7). The health care insurance industry currently has almost no capacity to monitor at such levels, and it certainly has no warning systems that can detect the most sophisticated schemes early enough to prevent major losses. These schemes, involving extensive collusion, operate across multiple patients, multiple providers, and often across multiple insurers. The schemes are designed and operated to be undetectable by lower-level detection tools.

An example of such a scheme was revealed through analysis performed within Blue Cross/Blue Shield of Florida in 1993. An analyst working on

Medicare data held within the company's claims databases was curious to know whether there were large-scale patterns of fraud, linking lots of providers with lots of patients, that could be found within the data. He devised and implemented his own network analysis algorithm, using a modern database search engine supplied by HOPS International, of Miami Lakes, Florida.[7]

Taking twenty-one months of Medicare data, he explored the network of patient-provider relationships, treating a patient as *linked* to a provider if the patient had received services during the twenty-one-month period (regardless of the value or frequency of the services). The resulting patient-provider "network" had 188,403 links within it, representing that many patient-provider relationships. The analyst then set about looking for unnaturally dense cliques within that structure. His algorithm found one. A massive one. At its densest core, the cluster he found consisted of a specific set of 122 providers, linked to a specific set of 181 beneficiaries. The (symmetric) density criteria between these sets was as follows:

A. Any one of *these* 122 providers was linked with (i.e., had billed for services for) a minimum of 47 of *these* 181 patients.

B. Any one of *these* 181 patients was linked with (i.e., had been "serviced" by) a minimum of 47 of *these* providers.

The second condition represents a stunning anomaly. How many different providers does a patient need within a twenty-one-month period? Maybe 2 or 3 primary practitioners if they moved or switched doctors. Maybe 5 specialists if they were really sick. Plus labs, radiology, home health, etc. Most patients would struggle to get to 20. All these patients had a minimum of 47, and an average of about 80—and they all had them within this one group of 122 providers. Within this clique, almost all the providers were billing for almost all the patients. A little each time, but a lot overall.

None of the controls or detection systems in operation at the time had ever spotted this pattern. When the analyst went looking for patterns at level 7, however, this one jumped out immediately. Field investigations then confirmed a variety of illegal practices that helped explain the pattern. Some providers were indeed using lists of patients for billing purposes without seeing the patients. Other patients were being paid cash to ride a bus from clinic to clinic and receive unnecessary tests, all of which were then billed to Medicare.

How much had these providers billed within the twenty-one months? Between them, $326 million. After the operation of price controls and claims reviews, they had been paid roughly $120 million. There were not 122 of them, but around 70. They had been using multiple provider identification numbers to spread the activity out to avoid detection—at least, that is, until someone did a nontraditional form of analysis. They had made, on average, just under $2 million each during this twenty-one months—just from Medicare. Having established their conspiratorial network, they no doubt targeted other programs, too.

For many institutions facing fraud committed by organized criminal rings—both within and outside the health care context—transaction-level and other lower-level defenses are no longer enough. As the perpetrators shift their attention to multiaccount schemes, so the defending institutions have to develop multiaccount or ring-level detection systems—preferably systems that can spot major schemes early enough to cut them off and make them unprofitable.

New Opportunities for Fraud Detection

The advent of electronic claims processing actually provides substantial new opportunities for fraud control at the higher levels, and these opportunities have received less attention from the health care community to date than the corresponding fraud threats.

First, the electronic format for data makes it easier to separate the service functions (claims processing) from fraud monitoring. The two processes used to be coincident because both had to track the physical movement of paper. With the data in electronic format, background monitoring and review by fraud-control staff can be conducted without interference from, or reliance upon, the service side of the organization. (This is an opportunity that HCFA's use of Medicare Integrity Program (MIP) contractors, distinct from its claims processors, is in part designed to exploit.)

Second, with so much data in electronic format, it will be possible to run much more complex pattern-detection searches than could ever have been attempted manually. When it comes to higher-level monitoring, modern processing capabilities will make it possible to aggregate and manipulate massive volumes of claims data in ways inconceivable in a paper-based environment.

To take advantage of these new opportunities, and to provide the broadest possible range of detection opportunities, we should look for fraud and abuse detection technologies to provide all the following capabilities:

1. Flexible and easy access to claims data. Claims history databases should span at least two years, preferably more. They should include claims denied as well as claims paid, because claims denied provide a rich source of information about efforts by fraud perpetrators to test, and then game, a payment system. Simple logical queries, initiated and launched by users, should run almost real-time, producing results within minutes (maybe hours in some cases; but certainly not days or weeks as many officials report).

2. A broad range of detection algorithms, built on top of that underlying data access capability, generating periodic reports to reveal a range of fraudulent and abusive billing practices. Provider-profiling and beneficiary-profiling techniques alone are not enough. Attention needs to be paid to the detection of higher-level fraud scams where perpetrators spread their activities broadly across multiple provider numbers and hundreds or thousands of patients.

3. A broad range of different analytic techniques, all available through a common interface. Many analytic tools are relevant to fraud detection. These include simple statistical summaries and comparisons; anomaly detection; geometric ratios; trends over time; acceleration rates; cluster analysis; regression analysis; discriminant analysis; artificial intelligence, rule-based and expert systems; neural networks; similarity profiling; alias detection; network analysis; and geographic analysis (perhaps using Geographic Information Systems tools). Purchasers should avoid systems and vendors that seem to rely on a single underlying technology or analytic approach. Analysts should be able to pick the right tool for the job—which means having the broadest set of tools at hand and knowing how to use them.

4. Continuous and dynamic updating of detection tools, based on intelligence received from other agencies and sites, from analytic and investigative insights developed locally, and from news regarding emerging fraud schemes elsewhere in the country. Fraud control is a dynamic game played against intelligent opponents who adapt continuously. Effective fraud control relies upon early recognition

of emerging fraud problems, coupled with the technical capacity to design and implement new searches quickly and easily. Therefore insurers should look for an *adaptive fraud detection service, rather than a static fraud detection system.*

Multiaccount Detection Systems

One important key to early detection of sophisticated, multiaccount schemes involves spotting patterns of unnatural coordination between different accounts that might indicate they have all come under common control, even when the behavior of each account (or patient) shows nothing suspicious when viewed in isolation. The health care insurance industry has substantial motivation for investing in development of multiaccount fraud-detection systems that could exploit this possibility. That motivation arises from two kinds of promise:

First, that the ability to spot unnatural coordination in the transactional behavior of different policies may make it possible to detect some fraud schemes that were previously undetectable. Second, that the ability to spot unnatural coordination in the transactional behavior of different accounts may make it possible to detect some fraud schemes (which would have been detected eventually) much sooner than previously possible.

Which of these two kinds of benefit accrues depends on the fraud-control environment and the nature of the fraud threats. With fraud schemes of the non-self-revealing type, the ability to spot the criminal coordination or orchestration of activity across several accounts might be the only clue, even in retrospect, that can reveal massive scams.

With other types of fraud, the scheme might come to light eventually, but too late to prevent significant losses. For example, counterfeit credit card schemes reveal themselves ultimately as unauthorized activity spread across multiple cardholders' accounts. Depending on the billing cycle and speed of subsequent dispute resolution processes, two or three months may elapse before the transactions are confirmed as fraudulent. The ability to see that a group of accounts appears to have come under common control (control by one person or group) may provide an opportunity to detect the scheme much earlier, maximizing the potential for loss prevention or recovery.

The following three situations illustrate the potential for multiaccount detection systems in a variety of different fraud-control contexts, including health care fraud control.

Credit Card Fraud

Suppose that twenty separate credit card accounts belonging to twenty different people all used the same car rental agency in Boston during August, all had supplementary cards with ATM privileges issued during September, and all began using the same ATM machine for cash withdrawals in Seattle during October; suppose also that none of the basic account holders had ever used that particular ATM machine before. It sounds like an obvious case of "dumpster-diving" (the practice of retrieving carbon copies of credit card slips from trash bins to obtain account information) with subsequent fraudulent use of the appropriated account details.

This kind of pattern, or network, lends itself readily to detection through network analysis techniques. It is not a behavioral profile as such, because credit card companies would not be much concerned with use of car rentals in general, or use of new ATMs in general, or a sequential combination of the two. The profile is too common, and generally legitimate.

Rather, it is the linkage through a specific car rental, followed by linkage through a specific ATM location, coupled with common set-up operations (requesting issuance of supplementary cards), that make this pattern interesting. The specific linkages make the pattern detectable, too, even though each account's behavioral profile might not be particularly unusual.

Under most credit card companies' current arrangements, such a scheme would not show up until the cardholder saw some evidence of unauthorized account activity and disputed it. Even then, the different accounts might never be linked together as part of the same scheme, and many issuing banks would not be able to identify the merchant (the connecting link) where the account information had been compromised. If fraud analysts were able to piece the scheme together, they would be far too late to prevent the losses.

This fraud scheme creates a pattern that is detectable fairly early during the set-up stage, even before losses accrue. The relevant pattern to search for, in this case, would be a set of accounts that have as a common feature the use of one particular merchant in August and that, as a group, show an unusually high rate of supplementary applications during September. With that kind of monitoring, this scheme could be detected in September, and steps could be taken to protect all the accounts at risk. In this case, the key to the earliest possible detection of the scheme is to use the point of compromise itself as the key to revealing the scheme. The advantage of this approach is that it informs the credit card company of all accounts that might be similarly compromised, even if the perpetrators have not yet had time to begin manipulating many of them. It permits all the customers at risk to be warned and protected, even those whose accounts have not yet been touched—offering enormous benefits in terms of customer relations as well as loss avoidance.

Health Insurance Fraud

Criminal rings have developed many methods for obtaining insurance policy details, together with enough personal data to support the submission of fraudulent claims for medical treatment. The simplest method involves stealing or buying lists of patients' details from clinics or other providers.

Suppose that medical claims are received by an insurer for a group of seventy residents of Washington, D.C., all of whom purportedly received emergency treatment during October while traveling in Philadelphia. Suppose also that the patients received their Philadelphia treatments from a variety of physicians, all of whom happen to use the same billing service. Moreover, none of these patients has ever received treatment in Philadelphia before. Apart from these odd coincidences, the only link that connects all seventy patients is that each one of them used a particular pharmacy in Washington, D.C., at least once during the preceding April.

This pattern—if only one could spot it—is inherently suspicious. It suggests that the Washington, D.C., pharmacy is the point of compromise from which insurance policy information was leaked, and it suggests the Philadelphia billing agency to be the fraudulent user of that information.

Each transaction viewed in isolation is not suspicious. The insurer would not normally reject, or even question, a claim for emergency treatment just because it came from a provider in a city other than the city of residence. Thus transaction or patient-level monitoring could never reveal this scheme. To detect this type of pattern one would have to be monitoring for specific patterns that suggest improper distribution and use of lists, which would mean being able to link claims or policies together in ways that could reveal the extraordinary coincidences suggestive of organized multiaccount fraud schemes.

Automated Inquiry Systems

The provision of hi-tech services to customers, whether in government or private sector financial services, often involves provision of 24-hour automated telephone information systems. Using 800 numbers and touch-tone phones, customers navigate menu-driven information services to check their bank balances, their frequent-flier mileage balances, the status of their tax refunds, their available credit limits, or details of a variety of other personal service products. Access is often controlled through a pass-word system, but passwords often consist of readily available information such as social security numbers or mothers' maiden names. Fraud perpetrators make extensive use of such systems to gain information about target accounts without having to speak to a human being. They use these systems to avoid arousing anyone's suspicions.

In many instances, such automated telephone assistance systems have an ANI (automatic number identification) capability built in for billing and record keeping. Thus a record, which includes the source telephone number, is created for each call.

An account-level fraud-monitoring system might use such data to check whether the source number matched the telephone number on the account records. Assuming genuine customers are allowed to call from anywhere, their not being at home when they called is not particularly useful information. If the company keeps a "trouble list" (a database of names, addresses, or telephone numbers known to have been associated with fraud in the past), then call-source numbers could also be checked against that list.

Higher-level multiaccount fraud-detection systems would ask different questions. They would monitor any telephone number from which in-quiries about numerous accounts originated, maybe within the same day or the same week. That someone had systematically called ten times in succession from the same phone number, asking questions about ten apparently unrelated accounts, would be highly suspicious. Such an obser-vation might be an early indication that this group of accounts had been compromised in some way and that fraudulent redemption or other con-version to gain was being planned.

As with all multiaccount fraud-detection systems, it is the unnatural coordination itself, rather than anything about the behavior of the indi-vidual accounts, that acts as the first sign of trouble. Subsequent follow-up inquiries, triggered by such an alert, should continue to focus on the group of accounts as a whole rather than on each in isolation.

Follow-up inquiries would include such issues as which merchants were common to the recent transaction history of the accounts (if this is really a multiaccount fraud scheme in the early set-up stages, can we iden-tify the point of compromise?) or what information in the original applications for the accounts might support the notion that they are all under common control (for example, employer references supplied by the same individual, or the same address given for next of kin).

This example illustrates another feature of multiaccount-level controls: the cost efficiency and effectiveness of verification procedures. Callback procedures—inquiring of just one or two of the affected account holders whether *they* called the automated inquiry system—would give a strong indication as to whether the entire group of accounts was at risk or whether there was some other (legitimate) explanation for the series of calls from the same phone. Just one or two verification callbacks provide valuable information about the exposure of a large group of accounts. Depending on company policies and priorities, the exposure can then be protected or set up for arrest. If the pattern turns out to have a legitimate explanation, little human effort is wasted.

These examples should help clarify the distinction between the potential class of coordination-detection tools envisaged here and the more traditional and familiar kinds of fraud-monitoring systems. Those who grasp the fundamental conceptual differences will have no trouble generating their own ideas for application of these ideas. Nothing is inherently complicated about them; they are just different from traditional forms of fraud control and constitute a different way of looking at fraud-control situations.

Health care insurers—whether they be private companies, nonprofits, or government—know they are victimized by many different types of extensive and sophisticated fraud schemes. They acquire that knowledge through a variety of mechanisms. Sometimes they receive unsolicited tip-offs from disillusioned or marginalized conspirators. Sometimes an astute claims-processing clerk happens to notice some unusual and coincidental pattern of linkages between claims (which may be something as simple as common handwriting). Sometimes a tip-off reveals fraudulent activity but—through rigorous follow-up investigation—what appeared at the outset to have been a small case of abuse or fraud grows into something much larger and more sinister.

Insurers know from experience that they have, on occasion, been victimized by large, sophisticated, multiaccount schemes. Because few insurers have developed the capability for routine monitoring at the higher levels, it remains impossible to estimate the extent of such activity.

There are several pressing reasons for developing multiaccount fraud-detection systems in a wide variety of fraud-control environments. First, they address the most sophisticated and expensive forms of fraud threat (where individual schemes, if successful, typically net hundreds of thousands or millions of dollars). Second, fraud-control defenses have traditionally been weakest at the multiaccount level (due to the predominance of transaction-level and other lower-level approaches).[8] Third, a wide variety of U.S. institutions have witnessed rapid growth in the activities of organized fraud rings, particularly the targeting of major payment systems like Medicare and Medicaid, often by immigrant or foreign groups.

Applicability of Network Analytic Tools and Concepts

In developing fraud-detection tools, many ideas and concepts from the social science discipline of network analysis may turn out to be relevant, especially when monitoring at the higher levels, and at level 7 (organized and collusive multiaccount frauds) in particular. Simply put, multiaccount fraud schemes are *networks* of a kind, consisting of a number of entities (accounts, or transactions, or practitioners) linked together in curious and specific ways.

Network analysis is a small but fast-growing academic discipline emerging from social science.[9] It has only been recognized as a discipline in its own right for about eighteen years. Since 1978, network analysis has had its own international journal; there is now an international association for network analysts.[10]

Network analysis studies the effects of network structure (which is described as connections of various types between objects, or "nodes") on various processes. The networks might variously show family associations, friendships, professional contacts, membership of different entities, participation in different activities, or communication channels connecting different people or institutions. Network processes studied by social scientists include group behavior, coalition formation, innovation adoption, influence transmission, product awareness and preference transmission, and the emergence of leadership within groups.

Network analysis is now recognized as being of substantial interest not only to social scientists but also to organizational theorists, epidemiologists, anthropologists, psychologists, business strategists, and political scientists—to name but a few. Anyone dealing with organized crime or complex frauds has good reason to pay attention to this field. The key to detection of criminal conspiracies often lies in developing the capacity to spot the subtle patterns of linkages that connect myriad individual transactions. Under present arrangements, the necessary data sits within claims databases, but virtually no analytical techniques exist to facilitate extraction of the patterns. Often, the linkages may be subtle: the appearance of common or similar addresses, permutations of names, same telephone numbers being given for different patients, same or similar bank destination codes or account numbers for payments, or coincidental histories (such as common use of one Washington, D.C., pharmacy followed by unexpected emergency treatments in Philadelphia a few months later). Tools for extraction of such patterns of linkage from massive databases are seldom used within the health care industry. Many officials are too focused on doing what they already do (i.e., mostly provider profiling) just a little bit better.

Here are a few brief examples of some patterns, potentially indicative of major fraud schemes, which network analytic techniques could extract using available technology platforms. There are also many other potential applications.

- *Transfer of a pool of patients.* Identify when one provider or supplier takes over an entire pool of patients from another. Such patterns may reveal the same people doing business under a new business name when their old business has come under scrutiny or has been excluded from program participation.

- *Mills, and mill-like activity.* Identify clusters of providers/patients with unnaturally dense sets of interconnections (using clique-detection methodology), which may reveal so-called "ping-pong referral" schemes.

- *Use of patient/beneficiary lists in fraud schemes.* Identify when a particular group of clients/beneficiaries show up on the billings of multiple providers. Such patterns may reflect inappropriate referral practices or the use of lists circulated for billing services not rendered.

The health care field is perhaps the most pressing and promising application for such tools. Insurers have masses of existing claims data and will be collecting much more data in standardized electronic formats, and gaining better access to it, in future years. As far as complex fraud schemes exist in the industry, these databases contain the telltale structures—patterns of interconnection and coincidence—that would permit early detection if only the analytic methods for extracting those patterns could be developed.

For all such applications, however, the hard work yet to be done is to build effective bridges between investigators, analysts, and technologists and to design organizational policies, industry incentives, and legislative frameworks that support the design and operation of fraud-detection tools more appropriate to the electronic environment, and to the sophistication of organized criminal frauds.

———

Conclusion

The question this book set out to answer was why health care fraud has not been brought under control, despite the unprecedented degree of attention the subject has received over the last eight years.

The answer is clear enough. Health care fraud has not been brought under control because the health care industry has underestimated the complexity of the fraud-control business and has never developed reasonable defenses against fraud. The defenses currently in place may protect against incorrect billing and certain forms of overutilization, but they offer little protection against criminal fraud. Insurers have no way of knowing how much they lose to fraud and have little incentive to find out. Unable to see the magnitude of the problem, public and private programs massively underinvest in control resources. Insurers rely upon fraud-detection and referral mechanisms that barely work. The majority of them lack a coordinated fraud-control strategy, or the organizational infrastructure to carry it out.

The scale of the government's interventions, so far, does not match up to the potential scale of the problem. Many of the legislative provisions of the last few years—granting the right to conduct criminal background checks on would-be-providers, to make sure that excluded entities actually stop billing, to visit companies' premises to make sure they really exist—are remedial and twenty years overdue. According to the Health Care Financing Administration (HCFA), the agency "is now working to develop a substantive testing process to help determine not only whether claims are paid properly but also whether services are actually rendered and medically necessary."[1] That's good, although it's happening slowly. Like so many other initiatives, this one has been held up or put off because of HCFA's need to pay attention to its Y2K problem.

Meanwhile, fraud in the health care system has been, and remains, out of control. Electronic claims processing has introduced alarming new threats, to which the industry has paid insufficient attention. Managed care will not eliminate fraud as many believe; rather it will make fraud more dangerous for patients, and much more difficult to control.

The government has so far not found the courage to measure the fraud rate in its major programs. The health care industry's provider associations and lobbyists have worked hard to contain and soften the government's fledgling enforcement campaign; they no doubt fear the possibility of a serious and sustained examination of the broader business practices that pervade the industry.

My modest hope for this book is that it will provide a better understanding of the complexity and seriousness of the fraud-control challenge and help those within the industry see why and how existing control systems fail.

It would be naive to believe that understanding the situation will automatically lead to progress. Reflecting on the enormity of this challenge has led me on several occasions to question whether there really is any way out of the current predicament. Maybe, with respect to fraud and fraud control, this is just the way things have to be. Maybe this is just the pathology of fraud control; maybe, too, this pathology is inescapable.

Before abandoning hopes for radical improvement, however, we should weigh the consequences. The pressures for health care cost control persist, especially in major public programs. Costs *will* be controlled one way or another. If we learn the art of fraud control, the country will have learned a discriminating way to save money—by investing in the capacity to distinguish between legitimate and illegitimate claims. The alternative is to use less discriminating methods, such as across-the-board reductions in benefits, further restrictions on eligibility, or lower reimbursement rates for providers. All these, in theory, hit the honest and the dishonest alike.

In practice, these less discriminating methods hit the honest providers and the genuinely needy patients much harder than they hit the dishonest. Restricting eligibility or reducing benefits has a negligible effect on fraud because fraud perpetrators can easily adjust their billing patterns and patient lists to fit the new rules. When reimbursement rates drop, the honest providers take the pay cut, not the crooks. In the major public programs such as Medicare and Medicaid, cuts in reimbursement rates and changes in reimbursement structures drive away honest providers, who can no longer afford to participate. Dishonest providers compensate by increasing their billing volume and inventing new ways to cheat.

Across-the-board cuts and structural changes will therefore have a perverse effect: Genuinely needy patients will be denied services and honest providers will be driven out of the system. What will remain will become more rotten, more crooked, more wasteful. Ultimately, in a vicious cycle of decay, the crooks will dominate and important public programs will be destroyed.

By learning the art of fraud control, the health care industry could substantially cut costs without restricting eligibility, denying the needy, or squeezing honest providers out of business.

ACRONYMS AND ABBREVIATIONS

AARP	American Association of Retired Persons
AFDC	Aid to Families with Dependent Children
AHA	American Hospital Association
AMA	American Medical Association
ANI	Automatic Number Identification
ATM	Automated Teller Machine
ATPS	Automatic Transaction Processing System
BBA	Balanced Budget Act
BCBS	Blue Cross/Blue Shield
CMHC	Community Mental Health Centers
CMNs	Certificates of Medical Necessity
DME	Durable Medical Equipment
DMERC	Durable Medical Equipment Regional Contractor
DRG	Diagnosis Related Group
EDI	Electronic Data Interchange
EEG	Electroencephalogram
EITC	Earned Income Tax Credit
EOMB	Explanation Of Medical Benefits
EPO	Exclusive Provider Organizations
EROs	Electronic Return Originators
FBI	Federal Bureau of Investigation
FCA	False Claims Act
FFS	Fee-for-Service
FTEs	Full-Time Equivalents
FY	Fiscal Year
GAO	General Accounting Office
GDP	Gross Domestic Product
GME	Graduate Medical Education Program
HCFA	Health Care Financing Administration
HCFAC	Health Care Fraud and Abuse Control Program
HCSC	Health Care Service Corporation
HHA	Home Health Agency

HHS	Department of Health and Human Services
HHS IG	Inspector General of the U.S. Department of Health and Human Services
HIAA	Health Insurers of America Association
HIMR	Health Insurance Master Records
HIPAA	Health Insurance Portability and Accountability Act
HMO	Health Maintenance Organization
HOPS	Heuristic Optimized Processing System
IG	Inspector General
IME	Indirect Medical Education
JAMA	Journal of the American Medical Association
IPA	Individual Physician Associations Model HMO
MCO	Managed Care Organization
MFCU	Medicare Fraud-Control Unit
MIP	Medicare Integrity Program
NHCAA	National Health Care Anti-Fraud Association
NHL	National Health Labs
NIJ	National Institute of Justice
NME	National Medical Enterprises
NPIs	National Provider Identifiers
OCR	Optical Character Reader
OIG	Office of Inspector General
PATH	Physicians at Teaching Hospitals
PHP	Partial Hospitalization Program
PPO	Preferred Provider Organizations
PPS	Prospective Payment System
PRO	Peer Review Organization
QC	Quality Control
RAL	Refund Anticipation Loan
RHC	Rural Health Center
SIU	Special Investigative Unit
SMAC	Sequential Multiple Analysis Computer
SURS	Surveillance and Utilization Review Subsystem
TCMP	Taxpayer Compliance Monitoring Program
TENS	Transcutaneous Electrical Nerve Stimulation Unit
TRICARE	The Armed Forces Health Insurance Program (previously called CHAMPUS)
UPIN	Unique Physician Identification Number
UR	Utilization Review
WHO	World Health Organization

NOTES

Preface

1. Projections based upon the 1997 version of the "National Health Expenditures," released in November 1998 (i.e., last available). Source: Office of the Actuary, Health Care Financing Administration, Department of Health and Human Services, Washington, D.C.

2. Information available to the public via WHO's Web site at http://www.who.int.

3. "Swindles and Scams Rife in Health Insurance," Judith Randall. Book review of *License to Steal: Why Fraud Plagues America's Health Care System,* by Malcolm K. Sparrow. *Washington Post,* Health section, Tuesday, December 24, 1996, p. 1.

4. Foreword by Donna Shalala, Semiannual Report, Department of Health and Human Services, Office of Inspector General, Washington, D.C., October 1, 1998–March 31, 1999.

5. Press release, March 25, 1999, "Vice President Gore Announces New Efforts to Fight Health Care Fraud and Abuse," White House, Office of the Vice President, Washington, D.C.

6. "What Do Americans Know About Health Care Fraud?" Lee Norrgard (Lead Investigative Specialist, American Association of Retired Persons). In *Health Care Fraud Report,* National Association of Attorneys General, Washington, D.C., September/October 1997, pp. 8–10.

7. Monthly Treasury Statement of Receipts and Outlays of the United States Government. Financial Management Service, U.S. Department of the Treasury. 1999 Annual Reports of the Board of Trustees of the HI and SMI Trust Funds. Office of the Actuary, Health Care Financing Administration, Department of Health and Human Services, Washington, D.C., Table 3.

8. National Health Expenditures and Average Annual Percent Change, by Source of Funds: Selected Calendar Years 1970–2008. Projections based upon the 1997 version of the National Health Expenditures, released in November 1998. Source: Office of the Actuary, Health Care Financing Administration, Department of Health and Human Services, Washington, D.C.

9. "America Speaks Out on Health Care Fraud." A consumer survey conducted for the American Association of Retired Persons by International Communications Research Survey Research Group. American Association of Retired Persons, Washington, D.C., 1999.

10. State of the Union address by President Clinton. House of Representatives, January 25, 1994. Comments regarding the need for health care reform.

Introduction

1. Testimony of Edward J. Kuriansky, special prosecutor, Office of the New York State Special Prosecutor, before the U.S. House of Representatives Select Committee on Narcotics Abuse and Control, July 29, 1992, p. 2.

2. "Health Care Fraud Report: Fiscal Year 1998," Department of Justice, Washington, D.C., August 5, 1999, p.7.

3. "Phantom Firms Bleed Medicare: Cost of Fraud in Florida Is Estimated at $1 Billion," Tom Dubocq. *Miami Herald,* August 14, 1994, p. A1(3).

4. Ibid.

5. Ibid.

6. *Unloving Care: The Nursing Home Tragedy,* Bruce C. Vladeck. Basic Books, New York, 1980, p. 101.

7. "Medical Supply Company Guilty in Fraud Case," Jeff Testerman. *St. Petersburg Times,* Wednesday, May 12, 1999, p. B1, late Tampa edition.

8. "The Great Medicare Rip-Off," Randy Fitzgerald. *Reader's Digest,* April 1998, pp. 119–123.

9. "Health Care Fraud Report: Fiscal Year 1998," Department of Justice, Washington, D.C., August 5, 1999, p. 30.

10. "Health Care Fraud Report: Fiscal Year 1998," Department of Justice, Washington, D.C., August 5, 1999, p. 26.

11. *United States v. Finkel* (D MA No. 97–12806 RCL). Reported in *False Claims Act and Qui Tam Quarterly Report,* v. 17. Taxpayers Against Fraud, Washington, D.C., July 1999, p. 35.

12. Press release, July 22, 1999, "Director of Steubenville Clinic Convicted of Health Care Fraud," U.S. Attorney's Office, Columbus, Ohio.

13. *Millin's Health Fraud Monitor,* v. 1, n. 22, November 16, 1998, p. 3.

14. "New Allegations Raised in Dentist's Fraud Case," Mark Morris. *Kansas City Star,* June 12, 1999, p. A1.

15. Press release, June 29, 1999, "Federal Jury Convicts Dentist in Million Dollar Medicare Fraud Scheme," U.S. Attorney's Office, San Antonio, Texas.

16. "Kidney Dialysis Giant Guilty of Fraud." Reuters News Service, January 19, 2000; also, "Medicare Fraud." *USA Today,* Thursday, January 20, 2000, p. 3A; also, Office of Inspector General press release, January 19, 2000, "Settlement with Fresenius Medical Care." Statement of Inspector General June Gibbs Brown, U.S. Department of Health and Human Services, Office of Inspector General, Washington, D.C.

17. Semiannual Report, Department of Health and Human Services, Office of Inspector General, Washington, D.C., October 1, 1998–March 31, 1999, p. 33.

18. Testimony of Lewis Morris, Assistant Inspector General for Legal Affairs, Department of Health and Human Services, Office of Inspector General, before the Subcommittee on Immigration and Claims, Committee on the Judiciary, U.S. House of Representatives, April 28, 1998, p. 3.

19. "Week in Healthcare: A Home-Care Link? Charges in Texas Patient-Steering Suit May Overlap with Fed's Columbia Case," Charlotte Snow. *Modern Healthcare,* March 31, 1997, News section, p. 11.

20. "The Patient As Profit Center: Hospital Inc. Comes to Town," Carl Ginsburg. *The Nation,* November 18, 1996, p. 18.

21. "Office Buy Is Focus of Suit Against Columbia," Kris Hundley. *St. Petersburg Times,* June 3, 1998, Business section, p. E1, South Pinellas edition.

22. "Shareholders Sue Columbia: NY Law Firms Look for Investors to Join Class Action Suit," Bruce Japsen. *Modern Healthcare,* April 14, 1997, News section, p. 2.

23. "Justice Joining Lawsuit Alleging Insurance Fraud by Hospital Firms," Debbie Gebolys. *Columbus Dispatch,* October 6, 1998, Business section, p. E1.

24. "Board Games: Suit Accuses Columbia Directors, Execs of Insider Trading," Ron Shinkman. *Modern Healthcare,* August 4, 1997, News section, p. 3.

25. "Can Dr. Frist Cure This Patient?" Anthony Bianco, Nicole Harris, and Stephanie Anderson Forest. *Business Week,* November 17, 1997, People section, p. 74.

26. "Making It a Federal Case: Suit Alleges Widespread Fraud by Columbia, Quorum," Deanna Fellandi and Kristen Hallam. *Modern Healthcare,* October 12, 1998, cover story, p. 4.

27. See, for example, "Columbia's Code," Kris Hundley. *St. Petersburg Times,* February 22, 1998, p. H1.

28. "More Legal Woes at Columbia: Former Tenn. Hospital CEO Files Defamation Lawsuit," Karen Pallarito. *Modern Healthcare,* July 13, 1998, News section, p. 8.

29. "U.S. Charges Fraud by 2 Big Hospital Chains," Kurt Eichenwald. *New York Times,* October 6, 1998, p. A1.

30. "Hospital Chain Cheated U.S. on Expenses, Documents Show," Kurt Eichenwald. *New York Times,* December 18, 1997, p. D6. Medicare officials found that in 1995 alone, dozens of hospitals had obtained more than $150 million using this recapture technique.

31. "U.S. Joins Suit Targeting Columbia; Hospital Chain Faces New Fraud Charges," Josef Heber. *Boston Globe,* December 31, 1998, Economy section, p. D2.

32. "Cost Report Fraud Allegations Show Need for Employee Access to Compliance Staff." *Report on Medicare Compliance,* Atlantic Information Services, Inc., January 7, 1999, pp. 1–4.

33. "Medicare Cutoff of Drug Coverage Fueled Alleged Columbia/HCA Fraud." *Report on Medicare Compliance,* Atlantic Information Services, Inc., April 15, 1999, p. 6.

34. *U.S. ex rel. Ortega v. Columbia/HCA Healthcare Corporation et al.* (WD TX No. EP–95–CA–259H). Reported in "False Claims Act and *Qui Tam* Quarterly Review," v. 17. Taxpayers Against Fraud, Washington, D.C., July 1999, p. 28.

35. *U.S. ex rel. McLendon v. Columbia/HCA Healthcare Corp.* (No. 97-CV–0890 N.D. Ga.). Reported in "Olsten Corporation and a Subsidiary Agree to Pay $61 Million in Criminal Fines and Civil Damages," press release, Monday July 19, 1999, Department of Justice, Washington, D.C.

36. "Two Found Guilty of Hospital Fraud Charges," Kurt Eichenwald. *New York Times,* July 3, 1999.

37. "Columbia/HCA Hospital Settles Medicaid Case of Psych Care." *Report on Medicare Compliance,* Atlantic Information Services, Inc., August 12, 1999, p. 4.

38. *Millin's Health Fraud Monitor,* v. 2, n. 17, September 6, 1999, p. 5.

39. *Report on Medicare Compliance,* Atlantic Information Services, Inc., December 9, 1999, p. 8.

40. See, for instance, *Report on Medicare Compliance,* Atlantic Information Services, Inc., January 5, 1998, p. 2.

41. "Health Care Enforcement Update—Major Events in 1998," Harvey A. Yampolsky. Paper presented to the Second Annual National Congress on Healthcare Compliance, Washington, D.C., February 11, 1999.

42. "Dracula, Inc.: Bloodsucker of the Decade," Rick Hornung. *Voice,* December 26, 1989, p. 45; also in press release, June 29, 1989, State of New York, Deputy Attorney General for Medicaid Fraud Control, pp. 1–2.

43. Press release, June 29, 1989, "NYC Blood Trafficking Doctor Gets 5–10 Years in Jail for U.S.' Largest $3.6 Million Medical Lab Fraud," Office of the Special Prosecutor, New York State Medicaid fraud-control unit.

44. "Lab-Fraud Anemia," D. R. Stone, A. Duran, and K. C. Fine. *New England Journal of Medicine,* September 15, 1988, v. 319, n. 11, pp. 727–728.

45. "$111 Million Payment Set for Fraud in Health Claims; Large Testing Company Admits to False Billing" (National Health Laboratories, Inc.), Calvin Sims. *New York Times,* December 19, 1992, p. 1.

46. Ibid.

47. Statement of Louis J. Freeh, director, Federal Bureau of Investigation, before the Special Committee on Aging, U.S. Senate, Washington, D.C., March 21, 1995, p. 15.

48. False Claims Act (31 U.S. Code § 3730).

49. "Medicare Case Underlines Importance of Physician Compliance with All Rules When Claims Are Filed," Charles Marwick. *Journal of the American Medical Association,* February 3, 1993, v. 269, n. 5, p. 563.

50. "Corporate Compliance: Successful Strategies for Responding to the Medicare Fraud and Abuse Crackdown," *HealthcareBusiness* Roundtable (discussion). *HealthcareBusiness,* January/February 1999, special supplement, pp. CC5—CC19.

51. Press release, January 22, 1998, "Four Damon Lab Executives Indicted for Conspiracy to Defraud Medicare of Millions," U.S. Attorney's Office, Boston, Massachusetts.

52. Press release, February 26, 1997, "Clinical Laboratory Agrees to Pay $325 Million to Settle False Medicare Claims," Department of Health and Human Services, Office of Inspector General, Washington, D.C.

53. "Health Care Fraud Report: Fiscal Year 1998," Department of Justice, Washington, D.C., August 5, 1999, p. 22.

54. "Blood Money Snares 2 Lab Reps Hit in Fraud Case," Greg B. Smith. *Daily News* (New York), August 10, 1999, p. 6.

55. "U.S. Sues University of Chicago in Medicare Overbilling," Jeremy Manier. *Chicago Tribune,* March 14, 1999.

56. "Metzinger Case Ends in Exclusion: Other Billing Consultants Probed." Report in *Medicare Compliance,* v. 6, n. 17, May 19, 1997.

57. Press release, July 12, 1999, "Emergency Physician Billing Company to Pay $15 Million to Settle Health Care Billing Fraud Claims," U.S. Department of Justice, Washington, D.C.

58. Statement of Louis J. Freeh, director, Federal Bureau of Investigation, before the Special Committee on Aging, U.S. Senate, Washington, D.C., March 21, 1995, p. 2.

59. "Officials Say Mob Is Shifting Crimes to New Industries," Selwyn Raab. *New York Times,* Monday, February 1, 1997, pp. A1, B4.

60. Ibid., p. B4.

61. Testimony of Lewis Morris, Assistant Inspector General for Legal Affairs, Department of Health and Human services, Office of Inspector General, before the Subcommittee on Immigration and Claims, Committee on the Judiciary, U.S. House of Representatives, April 28, 1998, p. 2.

62. Semiannual Report, Department of Health and Human Services, Office of Inspector General, October 1, 1998–March 31, 1999, Washington, D.C., p. 16.

63. *Millin's Health Fraud Monitor*, v. 1, n. 15, August 3, 1998, p. 5.

64. "Man Convicted in Health Insurance Scam," Warren Richey. *Sun Sentinel*, Friday, July 12, 1996.

65. *Millin's Health Fraud Monitor*, v. 2, n. 17, September 6, 1999. p. 7.

66. Statement of Leslie G. Aronovitz, General Accounting Office, before the Special Committee on Aging, U.S. Senate, Monday, July 28, 1997, GAO/T-HEHS–97–180, p. 6.

67. "Health Care Fraud Report: Fiscal Year 1998," Department of Justice, Washington, D.C., August 5, 1999, p. 20.

68. *Fraud Focus*, Coalition Against Insurance Fraud, v. 5, n. 6, November-December 1998, p. 6.

69. *Health Care Fraud Report,* National Association of Attorneys General, Washington, D.C., June/July 1998, p. 5.

70. See *Florida v. Portas,* Florida Circuit Court, Orange County, #98–5388, April 22, 1998.

71. "Health Care Fraud and Abuse Control Program: Annual Report for FY 1998," Department of Health and Human Services and the Department of Justice, Washington, D.C., February 1999, p. 19.

72. ABC's *20/20,* November 6, 1998. Also reported in *Millin's Health Fraud Monitor,* v. 1, n. 22, November 16, 1998, p. 3.

73. "IN Doc Gets No Break, Loses Medical License for 100 Years." *Fraud Focus*, Coalition Against Insurance Fraud, v. 7, n. 1, January/February 2000, p. 6.

74. *Millin's Health Fraud Monitor*, v. 1, n. 14, July 20, 1998, p. 4.

75. "Arrest Made in $1.9 Million Medical Equipment Scheme," Carol Ostrom. *Seattle Times,* August 7, 1999, p. C4.

76. "Foot Docs Charged in $30 Million Medicare Scam," Greg B. Smith. *Daily News* (New York), September 9, 1999, p. 5.

77. "Fraud and Abuse: Providers Target Medicare Patients in Nursing Facilities," General Accounting Office, Washington, D.C., January 24, 1996, GAO/HEHS–96–18.

78. *United States ex rel. Figurski v. Forest Hospital System* (ND IL No. 96C4763). Reported in *False Claims Act and Qui Tam Quarterly Report,* v. 17, Taxpayers Against Fraud, Washington, D.C., July 1999, p. 31.

79. Statement of Leslie G. Aronovitz, General Accounting Office, before the Subcommittee on Human Resources, Committee on Government Reform and Oversight, House of Representatives, Wednesday, April 16, 1997, GAO/T-HEHS–97–114, p. 4.

80. United States v. Harris, Northern District of Ohio, January 20, 1999. Reported in *Millin's Health Fraud Monitor*, v. 2, n. 3, February 8, 1999, p. 4.

81. "Costly Fraud Was Built on Adult Diapers; Jury Indicts Metairie Man," Pamela Coyle. *Times-Picayune,* July 27, 1999, p. B1.

82. "Hospital Chain Sets Guilty Plea: Kickbacks, Bribes Paid for Referrals," Allen R. Myerson. *New York Times,* June 29, 1994, pp. C1(N) and D1(L).

83. "National Medical Resolves Last of Insurance Disputes," Milt Freudenheim. *New York Times,* December 14, 1993, pp. C5(N) and D5(L).

84. "Locked Wards Open Door to Booming Business," Dolores Kong and Gerard O'Neill. *Boston Sunday Globe,* Sunday, May 11, 1997, p. A1.

85. Ibid., pp. A1, A18–19.

86. Ibid., p. A18.

87. Press release, April 15, 1997, "Psychologist Convicted of Defrauding Medicare of $2.5 Million," Department of Health and Human Services, Office of Inspector General, Washington, D.C.

88. "Health Care Fraud Report: Fiscal Year 1998," Department of Justice, Washington, D.C., August 5, 1999, p. 30.

89. "Statement on Action Against Health Care Frauds," Weekly Compendium of Presidential Documents, June 30, 1992, pp. 1052–1053.

90. Statement of a supervisory special agent, Federal Bureau of Investigation, to the Special Committee on Aging, U.S. Senate, Washington, D.C., March 21, 1995.

91. Press release, November 18, 1998, "Individuals Charged with Defrauding Medicare," United States Attorney J. Rene Josey, Columbia, South Carolina.

92. Press release, December 6, 1988, State of New York, Deputy Attorney General for Medicaid Fraud Control, p. 1.

93. "Historical Background of New York State Medicaid Fraud Control Unit," Office of the New York State Special Prosecutor, November 1994, p. 4.

94. "Unwitting Doctors and Patients Exploited in a Vast Billing Fraud," Kurt Eichenwald. *New York Times,* Friday, February 6, 1998, pp. A1, C5.

95. "Worker Eyed in Medicaid Scam." Source: Associated Press, 13:40 EST, March 19, 1997.

96. "FL State Senator to Be Sentenced January 20." *Fraud Focus,* Coalition Against Insurance Fraud, v. 7, n. 1, January/February 2000, p. 6; also, "Gutman's Successor's Election Set." *St. Petersburg Times,* October 30, 1999, late Tampa edition, p. 5B; also, "Sen. Gutman's Wife Makes Plea Deal." *St. Petersburg Times,* September 23, 1999, South Pinellas edition, p. 5B.

97. Eichenwald, "Unwitting Doctors."

98. "Health Care Fraud Report: Fiscal Year 1998," Department of Justice, Washington, D.C., August 5, 1999, p. 29.

99. "Health Care: Fraud Schemes Committed by Career Criminals and Organized Criminal Groups and Impact on Consumers and Legitimate Health Care Providers." Letter to Senator Susan M. Collins, chairman, Permanent Subcommittee on Investigations, Committee on Government Affairs, United States Senate. Robert H. Hast, General Accounting Office, Office of Special Investigations, Washington, D.C., October 5, 1999, GAO/OSI–00–1R.

Chapter 1

1. "Medicare: Control Over Fraud and Abuse Remains Elusive." Testimony of Leslie G. Aronovitz, General Accounting Office, before the Permanent Subcommittee on Investigations, Committee on Governmental Affairs, U.S. Senate, Thursday, June 26, 1997, GAO/T-HEHS–97–165, p. 11.

2. Ibid.

3. For example, see "Data Sources on White-Collar Law-Breaking," Albert J. Reiss Jr., and Albert D. Biderman. September 1980, National Institute of Justice, U.S. Department of Justice, Washington, D.C., p. 91.

4. "A Partnership Approach: A Prescription for Enhanced Coordination of Medicaid Fraud Detection and Prevention in New York State." Unpublished report. Senator Donald M. Halperin. New York State Senate, Albany, New York, June 1993.

5. Testimony of Edward J. Kuriansky, special prosecutor, Office of the New York Special Prosecutor for Medicaid Fraud Control, before the U.S. House of Representatives, Committee on Energy and Commerce; Subcommittee on Health and the Environment, April 1, 1993, p. 6.

6. "Health Care Fraud: Prosecuting Lack of Medical Necessity," Andrew Grosso. *Federal Bureau of Investigation Law Enforcement Bulletin,* October 1992, v. 61, n. 10, pp. 8–12.

7. Testimony of Edward J. Kuriansky, special prosecutor, Office of the New York Special Prosecutor for Medicaid Fraud Control, before the U.S. House of Representatives, Committee on Energy and Commerce; Subcommittee on Health and the Environment, April 1, 1993, p. 6.

8. "Questionable Medicare Payments for Incontinence Supplies," Office of Inspector General, Department of Health and Human Services, OEI–03–94–00772, December 1994, pp. i, ii.

9. "Questionable Medicare Payments for Wound Care Supplies," Office of Inspector General, Department of Health and Human Services, OEI–03–94–00790, October 1995, p. i.

10. "Marketing of Wound Care Supplies," Office of Inspector General, Department of Health and Human Services, OEI–03–94–00791, October 1995, pp. i, ii.

11. "Medicare Part B Allowances for Wound Care Supplies," Office of Inspector General, Department of Health and Human Services, OEI–03–94–00793, June 1998, pp. i, ii.

12. Ibid., p. ii.

13. Semiannual Report, Department of Health and Human Services, Office of Inspector General, October 1, 1998–March 31, 1999, pp. i.

14. Ibid., p. 11.

15. Memorandum from Inspector General June Gibbs Brown, Department of Health and Human Services, to Nancy-Ann Min Deparle, administrator, Health Care Financing Administration. Transmittal letter for the report "Five-State Review of Partial Hospitalization Programs at Community Mental Health Centers," Office of Inspector General, Department of Health and Human Services, A–04–98–2145, October 1998.

16. "Medicare Home Health Agencies: Certification Process Is Ineffective in Excluding Problem Agencies." Statement of Leslie G. Aronovitz, General Accounting Office, before the Special Committee on Aging, U.S. Senate, Monday, July 28, 1997, GAO/T-HEHS–97–180, p. 1.

17. Ibid., pp. 1–2.

18. "Medicare: Need to Hold Home Health Agencies More Accountable for Inappropriate Billings," General Accounting Office, GAO/HEHS–97–108, June 1997, p. 2.

19. Ibid., p. 5.

20. Ibid., p. 4.

21. "Results of the Operation Restore Trust Audit of Medicare Home Health Services in California, Illinois, New York and Texas," Office of Inspector General, Department of Health and Human Services, A–04–96–02121, June 1997, pp. 2–3.

22. "Review of Medicare Home Health Services in California, Illinois, New York, and Texas," Office of Inspector General, Department of Health and Human Services, Washington, D.C., A–04–99–01194, October 1999.

23. "Usage and Documentation of Home Oxygen Therapy," Office of the Inspector General, Department of Health and Human Services, OEI–03–96–00090, August 1999.

24. "Medicare Part B Allowances for Wound Care Supplies," Office of Inspector General, Department of Health and Human Services, OEI–03–94–00793, June 1998, p. ii.

25. "Questionable Medicare Payments for Wound Care Supplies," Office of Inspector General, Department of Health and Human Services, OEI–03–94–00790, October 1995, p. ii.

26. Statement of Linda A. Ruiz, Director of Program Integrity, Health Care Financing Administration, before the House Ways and Means Committee, Subcommittee on Health, October 9, 1997, p. 13.

27. "Controlling Fraud and Abuse in Medicaid: Innovations and Obstacles." A Report from the Executive Seminars on Fraud and Abuse in Medicaid, sponsored by Health Care Financing Administration, December 1998—May 1999. Malcolm K. Sparrow, September 1999, p. 28.

Chapter 2

1. Public Law 104–191.

2. White House press release, December 7, 1998, "Remarks by the President on Medicare Fraud," Old Executive Office Building, Washington, D.C.

3. Public Law 105–33.

4. "Comprehensive Plan for Program Integrity," Health Care Financing Administration, Department of Health and Human Services, Washington, D.C., February 1999.

5. See, for example, "Medicare Beneficiary Access to Home health agencies," Office of Inspector General, Department of Health and Human Services, OE–02–99–00530, February 1999.

6. Projections based upon the 1997 version of the National Health Expenditures, released in November 1998 (i.e., last available). Source: Office of the Actuary, Health Care Financing Administration, Department of Health and Human Services, Washington, D.C., Table 6a.

7. For a summary of the current status of these projects, see Semiannual Report, Department of Health and Human Services, Office of Inspector General, October 1, 1998–March 31, 1999, pp. 3–6.

8. "Medicare Crooks," Marilyn Werber Serafini. *National Journal,* July 19, 1997, pp. 1458–1460.

9. "Fighting Fire with Fire." *HealthcareBusiness,* May/June 1999, p. 69.

10. *New Jersey Hospital Association v. United States, District of New Jersey,* March 3, 1998; and *Greater New York Hospital Assocation v. United States,* Southern District, New York, April 16, 1998.

11. HR 3523. Termed the "Health Care Claims Guidance Act."

12. "Health Care Fraud & Abuse and the False Claims Act." Testimony of Lewis Morris, Assistant Inspector General for Legal Affairs, before the Committee on the Judiciary, Subcommittee on Immigration and Claims, April 28, 1998.

13. Ibid., p. 8.

14. "Guidance on the Use of the False Claims Act in Civil Health Care Matters." Memorandum from Office of Deputy Attorney General Eric H. Holder, Jr., Department of Justice, Washington D.C., June 3, 1998.

15. Concerns over the Department of Justice's implementation of the new guidance prompted Congress to require the General Accounting Office to monitor and report on U.S. Attorneys' compliance with the guidelines. The requirement is imposed as a provision of the Omnibus Consolidated and Emergency Supplemental Appropriations Act of 1999. (Public Law 105–277). For GAO's first assessment, see "Medicare Fraud and Abuse: DOJ's Implementation of False Claims Act Guidance in National Initiatives Varies," General Accounting Office, GAO/HEHS–99–170, Washington, D.C., August 1999.

16. "Health Care Fraud Report: Fiscal Year 1998," Department of Justice, Washington, D.C., August 5, 1999, p. 15.

17. "Health Care Fraud Report: Fiscal Year 1998," Department of Justice, Washington, D.C., August 5, 1999, p. 2.

18. "Semiannual Report: April 1, 1999–September 30, 1999," Office of Inspector General, Department of Health and Human Services, Washington, D.C., p. i.

19. "Medicare: Program Safeguard Activities Expand, but Results Difficult to Measure," General Accounting Office, GAO/HEHS–99–165, August 1999, p. 6.

20. "Health Care Fraud Report: Fiscal Year 1998," Department of Justice, Washington, D.C., August 5, 1999, p. 2.

21. Information regarding agreements in 1998 was obtained from the Office of Inspector General under a Freedom of Information Act request filed by Foley, Hoag & Eliot, LLP. Published in "Health Care Fraud Update," Foley, Hoag & Eliot, Boston, Massachusetts, summer, 1999.

22. "Comprehensive Plan for Program Integrity," Health Care Financing Administration, Department of Health and Human Services, Washington, D.C., February 1999, p. 11.

23. National Health Expenditures, released November 1998 by the Office of the Actuary, Health Care Financing Administration, Department of Health and Human Services, Washington, D.C., Table 3(a).

24. Calculated as follows: Medicare projected costs for 2000 are $244.5 billion. Medicaid is projected at $193 billion, with roughly 57 percent of the cost borne by the federal government and the remainder by the states. Total federal outlays for these two programs are therefore projected at $354 billion. Assume 250 working days per year. Historical information on the federal/state split provided by the Division of Financial Management, Center for Medicaid State Operations, Health Care Financing Administration.

25. "Medicare: Control over Fraud and Abuse Remains Elusive." Testimony of Leslie G. Aronovitz, General Accounting Office, before the Permanent Subcommittee on Investigations, Committee on Governmental Affairs, U.S. Senate, Thursday, June, 26, 1997, GAO/T-HEHS–97–165, p. 20.

26. "Medicare: Control over Fraud and Abuse Remains Elusive." Testimony of Leslie G. Aronovitz, General Accounting Office, before the Permanent Subcommittee on Investigations, Committee on Governmental Affairs, U.S. Senate, Thursday, June, 26, 1997, GAO/T-HEHS–97–165, p. 15.

27. "Medicare: Program Safeguard Activities Expand, but Results Difficult to Measure," General Accounting Office, August 1999, GAO/HEHS–99–165, p. 8.

28. FY 1998 figures were obtained by the author from the Office of Inspector General, Department of Health and Human Services. The federal (actual) contribution was $85,793,887 and the states collectively contributed $28,413, 685.

29. Increases in the federal allocation are described in the testimony of John E. Hartwig, Deputy Inspector for Investigations, Office of Inspector General, Department of Health

and Human Services, before the House Committee on Commerce, Subcommittee on Oversight and Investigations, November 9, 1999. The take-up rate by the states, however, is determined by their own budget processes.

30. "Fiscal Intermediary Fraud Units," Office of Inspector General, Department of Health and Human Services, November 1998, OEI–03–97–00350.

31. Ibid. See table on p. 6.

32. The chronology of settlements was compiled and presented in "Fraud Fighters Gain Muscle," Kristen Hallam and Mark Taylor. *Modern Healthcare,* August 16, 1999. pp. 36–40.

33. "Medicare Improprieties by Contractors Compromised Medicare Program Integrity," General Accounting Office, GAO/OSI–99–7, July 14, 1999.

34. "Health Care Fraud and Abuse Control Program: Annual Report for FY 1998," Department of Health and Human Services and Department of Justice, Washington, D.C., February 1999, p. 20.

35. "Fraud in Medicare Increasingly Tied to Claims Payers," Robert Pear. *New York Times*, September 20, 1999, pp. A1, A3.

36. "Controlling Fraud and Abuse in Medicaid: Innovations and Obstacles." A report from the "Executive Seminars on Fraud and Abuse in Medicaid," sponsored by Health Care Financing Administration: December 1998—May 1999. Malcolm K. Sparrow. Published by Health Care Financing Administration, Washington, D.C., November 1999.

37. Ibid., p. 12. I am grateful to HCFA for their permission to reproduce material from that report in this book.

Chapter 3

1. "Medicare: Program Safeguard Activities Expand, but Results Difficult to Measure," General Accounting Office, August 1999, GAO/HEHS–99–165, pp. 12–13.

2. "America Speaks Out On Health Care Fraud," a Consumer Survey conducted for the American Association of Retired Persons by International Communications Research Survey Research Group. American Association of Retired Persons, Washington, D.C., September 1997, p. 14.

3. "Examples of Medicare Fraud, Waste and Abuse Found Through Calls to the Hotline or Medicare Insurance Companies," a component of a press kit compiled for a Medicare Fraud news conference on February 24, 1999, conducted jointly by the American Association of Retired Persons, Department of Health and Human Services, and Department of Justice. Provided to me by Lee Norrgard, Lead Investigative Specialist of the American Association of Retired Persons.

4. "Examples of Medicare Fraud, Waste and Abuse Found Through Calls to the Hotline or Medicare Insurance Companies," a component of a press kit compiled for a Medicare Fraud news conference on February 24, 1999, conducted jointly by the American Association of Retired Persons, Department of Health and Human Services, and Department of Justice.

5. Press release, "HHS Fact Sheet: A Comprehensive Strategy to Fight Health Care Waste, Fraud and Abuse," U.S. Department of Health and Human Services, February 10, 1999, p. 5.

6. Details of these programs are available at the Administration on Aging's Web site at http://www.aoa.dhhs.gov/ort. Also see "Administration on Aging's Health Care Fraud and Abuse Programs: 18-month Outcomes," Office of Inspector General, Department of Health and Human Services, August 1999, OEI–02–99–00110.

7. "America Speaks Out On Health Care Fraud," a Consumer Survey conducted for the American Association of Retired Persons by International Communications Research Survey Research Group. American Association of Retired Persons, Washington, D.C., 1999, p. 15.

8. "Health Insurance: Vulnerable Payers Lose Billions to Fraud and Abuse." Report to the chairman, Subcommittee on Human Resources and Intergovernmental Relations, Committee on Government Operations, House of Representatives, General Accounting Office, Washington, D.C., May 1992, GAO/HRD–92–69.

9. Ibid., p. 23.

10. "Comprehensive Plan for Program Integrity," Health Care Financing Administration, Department of Health and Human Services, Washington, D.C., February 1999, p. 11.

11. "Fighting Fire with Fire." *HealthcareBusiness*, May/June 1999, p. 69.

12. Foreword by Donna Shalala, Semiannual Report, Department of Health and Human Services, Office of Inspector General, October 1, 1998–March 31, 1999.

13. "Improper Fiscal Year 1998 Medicare Fee-for-Service Payments," Office of Inspector General, Department of Health and Human Services, February 1999, A–17–99–00099, pp. 3–4.

14. OIG officials have reported to me verbally that a small number of patients were interviewed in connection with some home health care claims that fell in the sample. However, patient contact was not specified as a part of the claims audit protocol, nor did it occur for the majority of the claims examined.

15. "The Great Medicare Rip-Off," Randy Fitzgerald. *Reader's Digest,* April 1998, pp. 119–123.

16. Author's emphasis, not Fitzgerald's.

17. "Historical Background of New York State Medicaid Fraud Control Unit," Office of the New York State Special Prosecutor, November 1994, p. 4.

18. Author acted as consultant to the study and helped design the sampling methodology and audit protocols.

19. "Report of the Board of Trustees of the AMA," American Medical Association, Chicago, 1997, 25 I–97, p. 1.

20. Ibid., p. 2.

21. Ibid., p. 2.

22. Ibid., pp. 2–3.

23. For an excellent history of the AMA's position on physician conflicts of interest, see *Medicine, Money & Morals: Physician Conflicts of Interest,* Marc A. Rodwin. Oxford University Press, New York and Oxford, 1993, pp. 21–45.

24. "Purse Strings and Heartstrings: The Home Health Dilemma," Sue Kirchhoff and Mary Agnes Carey. *Congressional Quarterly,* September 26, 1998, pp. 2556–2562.

25. "Corporate Compliance: Successful Strategies for Responding to the Medicare Fraud and Abuse Crackdown," *HealthcareBusiness* Roundtable (discussion). *HealthcareBusiness,* January/February 1999, Special Supplement, p. CC14.

Chapter 4

1. "National Summary of Medicaid Managed Care Programs and Enrollment: Managed Care Trends" June 30, 1998. (The figure for 1997 was 47.8 percent, and for 1998, 53.6 percent.)

2. Source: "Medicare Managed Care Plans: Many Factors Contribute to Recent Withdrawals," General Accounting Office, April 1999, GAO/HEHS–99–91.

3. For a more detailed (but still summary) listing of plan types, see "Fraud in Managed Health Care Delivery and Payment." Report of the National Health Care Anti-Fraud Association Task Force on Fraud in Managed Care, National Health Care Anti-Fraud Association, Washington, D.C., November 1994, pp. 5–20.

4. "Fraud in Managed Health Care Delivery and Payment." Report of the National Health Care Anti-Fraud Association Task Force on Fraud in Managed Care, National Health Care Anti-Fraud Association, Washington, D.C., November 1994, p. 1.

5. The emergence of underutilization as the predominant form of fraud under prospective payment systems was forecast in 1989 by Professor Pamela H. Bucy in "Fraud by Fright: White Collar Crime by Health Care Providers." *North Carolina Law Review,* v. 67, n. 4, April 1989, pp. 855–937. See p. 934.

6. "Health Care Provider Fraud: The State Medicaid Fraud Control Unit Experience." Report prepared for the President's Task Force on National Health Care Reform, May 1993, National Association of Medicaid Fraud Control Units, Washington, D.C., pp. 6–7.

7. "New York Acts to Curb Fraud in Managed Care for the Poor," Ian Fisher. *New York Times,* June 23, 1995, p. 1.

8. News release, June 13, 1995, Office of the Attorney General, Baltimore, Maryland, p. 1.

9. "New York Faults Medicaid H.M.O.s for Poor Service," Elisabeth Rosenthal. *New York Times,* November 17, 1995, pp. A1, B4.

10. A report summarizing the discussions at those seminars was published by HCFA in November, 1999. See "Controlling Fraud and Abuse in Medicaid: Innovations and Obstacles." A report from the Executive Seminars on Fraud and Abuse in Medicaid. Malcolm K. Sparrow. September, 1999. This section, regarding recent experience within the Medicaid program, draws heavily upon material first presented by the author in that report, particularly section 2.3, pp. 25–37.

11. "Medicaid Managed Care Fraud and Abuse," Department of Health and Human Services, Office of Inspector General, Washington, D.C., June 1999, OEI–07–96–00250.

12. That is, those that had the waivers in place when the study commenced in July 1996: Arizona, Delaware, Hawaii, Minnesota, Ohio, Oklahoma, Oregon, Rhode Island, Tennessee, and Vermont.

13. "Medicaid Managed Care Fraud and Abuse." Office of Inspector General, Department of Health and Human Services, June 1999, p. i.

14. Ibid. The "period studied" was calendar year 1996.

15. Ibid., p. 7. Note that in Arizona the requirement for the MCOs is to report instances of fraud and abuse to the Medicaid Agency rather than to the MFCU directly.

16. Ibid., p. 9.

17. Ibid., p. ii.

18. HCFA, and others, are clearly well aware of this abiding need. HCFA plans to release a report in the spring of 2000 titled "Guidelines for Addressing Fraud and Abuse in Medicaid Managed Care."

19. These measures, even within a fee-for-service environment, are output measures, not outcome measures; and therefore potentially problematic within the context of a fraud- and abuse-control strategy.

20. Most Medicaid Managed Care Contracts now explicitly state the requirements for submission of encounter data; many deem failure grounds for contract termination.

21. Disgruntled providers may be the most likely source of information (albeit many of them fear being blacklisted by the MCOs), and a few astute patients who recognize im-

proper policies being exercised. To date, investigators and prosecutors have relied heavily upon whistle-blowers within the managed care organizations to provide detailed accounts of company policies and how they operate.

22. The Internal Revenue Service, within the context of federal interagency cooperation on health care fraud, now offers the services of its revenue agents, special agents, and auditors to help in this area. These IRS officers have considerable experience in "following the money," unraveling complex corporate contractual arrangements, and uncovering improper or related-party subcontracts.

23. "While Congress Remains Silent, Health Care Transforms Itself," Erik Eckholm. *New York Times,* December 18, 1994, p. A1.

24. Ibid.

Chapter 5

1. *Management Accountant's Guide to Fraud Discovery and Control,* Howard R. Davia et al. Wiley, New York, 1992, pp. 60–61.

2. See, for example, the treatment given by *Fraud, Prevention and Detection,* I. K. Huntington. Butterworths, London, 1992.

3. "Fraud by Fright: White-Collar Crime by Health Care Providers," Pamela H. Bucy. *North Carolina Law Review,* v. 67, n. 4, April 1989, p. 857. See Note 11 for list of symposia on legal issues in health care where the subject was omitted.

4. Testimony of Paul M. Allen, "Medicare and Medicaid Frauds: Joint hearing before the Subcommittee on Long-Term Care and the Subcommittee on Health of the Elderly of the Senate Special Committee on Aging." Part I. 94th Congress, 1975. Cited in "Fraud by Fright: White-Collar Crime by Health Care Providers," Pamela H. Bucy. *North Carolina Law Review,* April 1989, v. 67, n. 4, p. 857.

5. "Data Sources on White-Collar Law-Breaking," Albert J. Reiss, Jr., and Albert D. Biderman. September 1980, National Institute of Justice, U.S. Department of Justice, Washington, D.C., p. 91.

6. Hearing before the Subcommittee on Health of the Committee on Ways and Means, House of Representatives, 103d Congress, 1st Session, March 8, 1993, Serial 103–3. Statement of Larry Morey, deputy inspector general for investigations, Office of Inspector General, Department of Health and Human Services, p. 35.

7. "Health Care Fraud: Actuarial Report," The Travelers, Hartford, Connecticut, February 1992.

8. The subset of the claims history consisted of all claims for Chicago area providers who had been paid more than $3,000 during the year.

9. For a discussion of techniques for studying the biases inherent in detection systems, so that inferences can then be drawn about the underlying patterns of noncompliance, see "Detection Controlled Estimation," Jonathan Feinstein. *Journal of Law and Economics,* v. 33, April 1990.

10. "Welfare Fingerprinting Finds Most People Are Telling the Truth," Kimberley McLarin. *New York Times,* September 29, 1995, pp. B1 and B4.

11. Ibid., p. B4.

12. Quoted in testimony of Edward J. Kuriansky, special prosecutor, Office of the New York Special Prosecutor for Medicaid Fraud Control, before the U.S. House of Representatives, Committee on Energy and Commerce, Subcommittee on Health and the Environment, April 1, 1993, p. 12.

13. "Viewpoints," James P. Pinkerton. *Newsday,* March 18, 1993, p. 118.

14. Edward Kuriansky, quoted in "Health Care Fraud," Gordon Witkin. *U.S. News & World Report,* February 24, 1992, v. 112, n. 7, p. 34(8).

15. For example, see last sentence of "Medicaid Fraud: It Can Be Costly." *New York Times,* July 15, 1991, p. B7(L).

16. "One Scheme Illustrates Vulnerabilities to Fraud." Report presented by the General Accounting Office to hearing on Medicare Fraud, Waste, and Abuse, Subcommittee on Health, Committee on Ways and Means, House of Representatives, 102d Congress, 2d session, September 10, 1992. Government Accounting Office, Washington, D.C., August 1992, GAO/HRD–92–76, p. 16.

17. "The Control of Insurance Fraud: A Comparative View," Michael Clarke. *British Journal of Criminology,* v. 30, n. 1, winter 1990, p. 2.

18. "Ghost Riders Are Target of an Insurance Sting," Peter Kerr. *New York Times,* August 18, 1993, p. 1.

19. "Public Attitude Monitor, 1993," Insurance Research Council, Oak Brook, Illinois, 1993, p. 3.

20. Ibid., p. 20.

21. Testimony of Dr. "A," before the Senate Special Committee on Aging, Washington, D.C., March 21, 1995.

22. Hearing before the Subcommittee on Health of the Committee on Ways and Means, House of Representatives, 103d Congress, 1st session, March 8, 1993, Serial 103–3. Testimony of William J. Mahon, executive director, National Health Care Anti-Fraud Association, p. 49.

23. Statement of Louis J. Freeh, director, Federal Bureau of Investigation, before the Special Committee on Aging, U.S. Senate, Washington, D.C., March 21, 1995, p. 4.

24. "Stopping Abusive and Inappropriate Medicare Billings." Opening statement of Senator Tom Harkin, Senate Appropriations Subcommittee on Labor, Health, and Human Services, May 5, 1995, p. 3.

25. Medicare Part B is funded from general tax revenues (roughly 75 percent) and from premiums paid by the elderly (roughly 25 percent).

26. *Prescription for Profit: How Doctors Defraud Medicaid,* Paul Jesilow, Henry N. Pontell, and Gilbert Geis. University of California Press, Berkeley, 1993, p. x.

27. "Doctor Involved in Blindings Is Given a 4-Year Term for Fraud," Robert Welkos. *Los Angeles Times,* April 27, 1984. Quoted in *Prescription for Profit,* p. 20.

28. *Prescription for Profit,* p. 11.

29. Book review by Helen L. Smits of *Licensed to Steal: Why Fraud Plagues America's Health Care System* by Malcolm K. Sparrow. *New England Journal of Medicine,* v. 336, n. 7, February 13, 1997, pp. 517–518.

30. "Licensed to Steal: Action and Inaction by State Medical Boards in Disciplining for Insurance Fraud," Coalition Against Insurance Fraud, Washington, D.C., October 1998, p. 3.

Chapter 6

1. Hearing before the Subcommittee on Health of the Committee on Ways and Means, House of Representatives, 103d Congress, 1st Session, March 8, 1993, Serial 103–3. Statement of Janet L. Shikles, director, Health Financing and Policy Issues, Human Resources Division, General Accounting Office, p. 17.

2. Medicare-Medicaid Anti-Fraud and Abuse Amendments, Public Law 95–142, 1977.

3. *Prescription for Profit: How Doctors Defraud Medicaid*, Paul Jesilow, Henry N. Pontell, and Gilbert Geis. University of California Press, Berkeley, 1993, p. 12.

4. *The Fraud Control Game: State Responses to Fraud and Abuse in AFDC and Medicaid Programs*, John A. Gardiner and Theodore R. Lyman. Indiana University Press, Bloomington, Indiana, 1984, p. 10.

5. "The Control of Insurance Fraud: A Comparative View," Michael Clarke. *British Journal of Criminology*, v. 30, n. 1, winter 1990, p. 2.

6. Ibid.

7. This paragraph and the following two draw from the author's testimony before the Committee on Ways and Means, Subcommittee on Oversight, in support of the IRS' TCMP program, July 18, 1995. Serial 104–30, pp. 75–80. U.S. Government Printing Office, Washington, D.C.,1996.

8. *Fraud Control Game*, p. 7.

9. "Control of Insurance Fraud," p. 1.

10. Of the $136.7 million fraudulent returns detected during the 1993 filing season, $102 million were found soon enough to prevent payment. The remainder was paid.

11. "EITC Compliance Study: Tax Year 1993," p. 5. The study was released publicly as an appendix to the statement of Margaret Milner Richardson, Commissioner of Internal Revenue, before the Subcommittee on Oversight, House Ways and Means Committee, U.S. House of Representatives, Washington, D.C., June 15, 1995.

12. A final sample size of 1,059 gave a 95 percent confidence interval around these proportions of plus or minus 3 percent.

13. "Federal Income Tax Credit." Statement of Margaret Milner Richardson, commissioner of Internal Revenue, before the Subcommittee on Oversight, Subcommittee on Human Resources, House Committee on Ways and Means, June 15, 1995, Washington, D.C., p. 8.

14. Ibid., p. 7.

15. "IRS Puts on the Brakes: Anti-Fraud Slowdown Angers Filers." *USA Today,* March 10, 1995, p. 1.

16. "Federal Income Tax Credit." Statement of Margaret Milner Richardson, commissioner of Internal Revenue, before the Subcommittee on Oversight, Subcommittee on Human Resources, House Committee on Ways and Means, June 15, 1995, Washington, D.C., p. 6.

17. "Budget Bulletin," July 17, 1995, Senate Budget Committee, p. 1.

18. Meeting of the IRS executive committee, augmented by the regional commissioners, at IRS Headquarters, Wednesday, November 10, 1993. Author was present as a consultant.

19. Texas Senate Bill 30, 1997.

20. Available through the Inspector General's Web site at http://www.state.il.us/agency/oig.

21. *Fraud Control Game*, p. 28.

Chapter 7

1. Testimony of Gregory Kaladjian, executive deputy commissioner, New York State Department of Social Services, before the Senate Standing Committee on Social Services, Albany, New York, March 7, 1991, pp. 2–4.

2. HIMR: Health Insurance Master Records. Beneficiary-based history file showing the status and eligibility of each Medicare beneficiary.

3. *The Fraud Control Game, State Responses to Fraud and Abuse in AFDC and Medicaid Programs,* John A. Gardiner and Theodore R. Lyman. Indiana University Press, Bloomington, Indiana, 1985, p. 85.

4. Personal communication with the author as part of a response by senior HCFA managers to drafts of some of the material contained in this book.

5. "Health Care Fraud: The Silent Bandit," Joseph L. Ford. *FBI Law Enforcement Bulletin,* October 1992, v. 61, n. 10, pp. 2–7. Joe Ford was special agent in charge of the FBI's Health Care Fraud Unit at the time.

6. "A Partnership Approach: A Prescription for Enhanced Coordination of Medicaid Fraud Detection and Prevention in New York State." Senator Donald M. Halperin. New York State Senate, Albany, New York, June 1993.

Chapter 8

1. The National Health Care Anti-Fraud Association (NHCAA), based in Washington, D.C., maintains an on-line provider database for its member organizations.

Chapter 9

1. These objections were voiced by Stephen Teichler in "Reinventing Health Care Fraud and Abuse." *Legal Times,* February 28, 1994, v. 16, n. 41, pp. 36–37.

2. The position was created in April 1993.

3. For an expanded version of this discussion regarding the potential conflict between reactive and preventive strategies and the ways in which the conflict should be resolved, see "Of Strategies Reactive, Preventive, and Proactive" (Chapter 13), in *The Regulatory Craft: Controlling Risks, Solving Problems, and Managing Compliance,* Malcolm K. Sparrow. Brookings Press, Washington, D.C., 2000.

4. The challenge of embracing such a philosophy as the basis for operations in regulatory and enforcement agencies is discussed at length in *The Regulatory Craft: Controlling Risks, Solving Problems, and Managing Compliance,* Malcolm K. Sparrow. Brookings Press, Washington, D.C., 2000. See chapters 7–15.

5. Herman Goldstein described the relevance of problem solving to the police profession and detailed the problem-solving methodology in *Problem-Oriented Policing,* McGraw-Hill, New York, 1990.

6. Ibid., p. 66.

7. For an explanation of these phases, see *The Regulatory Craft: Controlling Risks, Solving Problems, and Managing Compliance,* Malcolm K. Sparrow. Brookings Press, Washington, D.C, 2000. Chapter 10.

Chapter 10

1. *Dateline,* Tuesday November 7, 1995, NBC, 10:00 P.M. EST, Segment 1.

2. "Medicare and Medicaid: Opportunities to Save Program Dollars by Reducing Fraud and Abuse." Statement of Sarah F. Jagger, director, Health Financing and Policy Issues,

Health, Education, and Human Services Division, General Accounting Office. Testimony before the Subcommittee on Human Resources and Intergovernmental Relations, Committee on Government Reform and Oversight, House of Representatives. Washington, D.C., March 22, 1995, p. 8.

3. Ibid., p. 9.

4. Ibid., p. 5.

5. Ibid., p. 8.

6. "Medicare: Inadequate Review of Claims Payments Limits Ability to Control Spending." Report to the chairman, Subcommittee on Oversight and Investigations, Committee on Energy and Commerce, House of Representatives, General Accounting Office, Washington, D.C., April 1994, GAO/HEHS–94–42, p. 3.

7. The analyst, Gene D'Angelo, has since moved from BCBS Florida to work with HOPS International. HOPS, an acronym, means "Heuristic Optimized Processing System."

8. In part this results from the legacy of paper-based transaction-processing environments. Where claims processing, or acting upon redemption requests, or payment of tax refunds were essentially paper-based operations, fraud-control systems most naturally consisted of physical diversions (branch points) within physical process flows. Returns or claims would be kicked out for review based solely on the information content of that particular file. Casting around inside massive electronic databases for patterns of particular types was inconceivable.

9. This brief note regarding the relevance of network analytic tools to fraud detection is condensed from a previous paper, "Network Vulnerabilities and Strategic Intelligence in Law Enforcement," Malcolm K. Sparrow. *International Journal of Intelligence and Counter-Intelligence*, v. 5, n. 3, fall 1991, pp. 255–274. This paper describes potential applications of network analysis within the broader field of criminal intelligence analysis. Another paper covering similar ground, but written for the social science audience, is "The Application of Network Analysis to Criminal Intelligence: An Assessment of the Prospects," Malcolm K. Sparrow. *Social Networks*, v. 13, 1991, pp. 251–274.

10. The journal is *Social Networks*, published by Elsevier. The International Network of Social Network Analysts is supported by the newsletter *Connections*.

Conclusion

1. Press Release, February 10, 1999, "HHS Fact Sheet: A Comprehensive Strategy to Fight Health Care Waste, Fraud and Abuse," Department of Health and Human Services, February 10, 1999, p. 5.

INDEX

CPSIA information can be obtained at www.ICGtesting.com
230824LV00001B/66/A